SONS OF ANARCHY AND PHILOSOPHY

The Blackwell Philosophy and PopCulture Series
Series Editor: William Irwin

A spoonful of sugar helps the medicine go down, and a healthy helping of popular culture clears the cobwebs from Kant. Philosophy has had a public relations problem for a few centuries now. This series aims to change that, showing that philosophy is relevant to your life—and not just for answering the big questions like "To be or not to be?" but for answering the little questions: "To watch or not to watch *South Park*?" Thinking deeply about TV, movies, and music doesn't make you a "complete idiot." In fact it might make you a philosopher, someone who believes the unexamined life is not worth living and the unexamined cartoon is not worth watching.

Already published in the series:

SONS OF ANARCHY AND PHILOSOPHY

BRAINS BEFORE BULLETS

Edited by
George A. Dunn
and
Jason T. Eberl

WILEY Blackwell

This edition first published 2013
© 2013 John Wiley & Sons, Inc

Registered Office
John Wiley & Sons, Ltd, The Atrium, Southern Gate, Chichester, West Sussex, PO19 8SQ, UK

Editorial Offices
350 Main Street, Malden, MA 02148-5020, USA
9600 Garsington Road, Oxford, OX4 2DQ, UK
The Atrium, Southern Gate, Chichester, West Sussex, PO19 8SQ, UK

For details of our global editorial offices, for customer services, and for information about how
to apply for permission to reuse the copyright material in this book please see our website at
www.wiley.com/wiley-blackwell.

The right of George A. Dunn and Jason T. Eberl to be identified as the authors of the editorial material
in this work has been asserted in accordance with the UK Copyright, Designs and Patents Act 1988.

Library of Congress Cataloging-in-Publication Data

Sons of anarchy and philosophy: brains before bullets / George A. Dunn, Jason T. Eberl [editors].
    pages   cm
  Includes bibliographical references and index.
  ISBN 978-1-118-64157-6 (pbk. : alk. paper)
1. Sons of Anarchy (Television program)   I. Dunn, George A., 1957 – editor of compilation.
II. Eberl, Jason T. editor of compilation.
  PN1992.77.S63944S66 2013
  791.45′72–dc23
                                                    2013016776

A catalogue record for this book is available from the British Library.

Cover image: Main image © Pgiam/Getty Images; © Shanina Wain/iStockphoto; © Jerry Downs/
iStockphoto; © Jörg Röse-oberreich/Shutterstock
Cover design by www.simonlevy.co.uk

Set in 10.5/13pt Sabon by SPi Publisher Services, Pondicherry, India

3   2015

Contents
Lessons from J.T.'s Manuscript

Introduction
"Gotta Look This Life in the Eye"

Aristotle with an AK ... Heidegger on a Harley ... Men of Machiavellianism—FX's hit television series, *Sons of Anarchy*, has been described as "*Hamlet* on motorcycles," but any of these other descriptions would fit as well. Kurt Sutter's dramatic tale depicts a world in which violence, hedonism, and power plays—along with loyalty, self-sacrifice, and honor—are the social norm. The show leaves us wondering what it would be like for Jax and Tara's sons to grow up in this world and brings to mind a number of tough questions. For example, should the Sons always have one another's back no matter what bad shit a member might do? Does the club truly represent an *anarchic* ideal? Do the rankings of women in the MC as "crow eaters," "sweet butts," and "old ladies" keep them from asserting any real power over their men? These are questions that Jax Teller will have to face if he's to continue as SAMCRO's president and attempt to reform the club to his father's original vision of a "Harley commune." It's certainly not an easy life for the Sons, their families, and their friends. But is it really that different from the lives of the show's weekly viewers? All of us "gotta look this life in the eye" and make moral decisions every day that'll drive us down the open road to the unknown future—let's just hope that Clay hasn't sabotaged our bikes!

While our journey down life's highway doesn't always have a clear path or a definite destination, we've passed a number of road signs along the way: wisdom from various PCs—*philosophical* clubs—portraits of whose legendary members adorn the halls of academia like the mugshots in SAMCRO's clubhouse. Like the anarchists of

SOA who thumb their nose, and sometimes point an automatic weapon, at authority and societal conventions, philosophers from Socrates onward have often been *countercultural*—sometimes motivating society to great change and sometimes suffering for attempting to teach rationality to unreasonable people. Socrates was found guilty by his fellow Athenians and sentenced to death for calling widely held assumptions into question, for allegedly corrupting the Athenian youth with his questions, and for not adhering to the Greek religious traditions. By their extreme, yet entertaining and somewhat attractive, lifestyle, the Sons challenge us to re-examine the social norms by which we live, often unreflectively. Their violent, criminal, ultra-hedonistic, and—by many accounts—immoral ethos spurs us to ask, "Why not?" Of course, it doesn't take too much reflection to realize why it'd be bad to mule cocaine or deal in automatic weapons; but risking their lives together week after week also cements an enviable bond of brotherhood, exemplifying virtues such as loyalty to family and community.

Perhaps watching *SOA* hasn't (yet) inspired you to buy a Harley, join an outlaw motorcycle club, or become a "companionator." But maybe reading this volume will coax you into reading a leather-bound volume of Plato's dialogues instead of donning a leather cut. Becoming a prospect in a PC requires only an open-minded, yet critically analytical, attitude toward the various "truths" asserted by individuals and social institutions—the very ones against which anarchists like Emma Goldman influenced the young John Teller to rebel. So if you think you have what it takes, keep reading as we ride free toward philosophical discovery.

Acknowledgments
Thanks to the Reaper Crew

George and Jason are immensely grateful to all of our contributors for agreeing to be patched-in to this club of "philosophy enthusiasts" and for breaking several speed limits to get their chapters to us. Each one of their contributions has expanded our appreciation of the show's philosophical dimensions and we're sure they will do the same for you, our readers. This volume wouldn't have been possible without our club's officers, Jeff Dean and Bill Irwin, and "friends of the club" Lindsay Bourgeois, Jennifer Bray, Louise Spencely, and Paul Stringer, who worked to get this book out of the Teller-Morrow garage and out on the streets. George would like to extend a special thanks to his friend Allison, who first introduced him to the show and to sundry other forms of mayhem that will here go unmentioned. Jason similarly thanks his sister-in-law Jessica Vines for introducing him to the show. She and Jennifer Vines helped him to appreciate not only the show's dramatic depths, but also the aesthetic value of Jax Teller's hair.

Finally, we both wish to express our deepest gratitude to Kurt Sutter and the incredibly talented cast and crew of *Sons of Anarchy* for getting our hearts and minds racing with each new chapter in the unfolding drama of the lives of Jax, Opie, Gemma, Clay, Tara, Wayne … and, of course, Chuckie! As sufferers from what the world sometimes calls "compulsive *mental* masturbation syndrome"—we just call it philosophy—we can certainly relate to the scorn you've had to endure, Chuck.

Part I

"AN EQUAL MIX OF MIGHT AND RIGHT"

ETHICS AT 92 MPH

CHAPTER 1

Virtue and Vice in the SAMCROpolis
Aristotle Views *Sons of Anarchy*

Jason T. Eberl

At the end of Season 5 of *Sons of Anarchy*, just before she's arrested as an accessory to murder, Tara informs Jax that she and their boys are leaving Charming. She doesn't want her and Jax to "end up like the two people we hate the most"—Clay and Gemma Morrow—and their boys to be "destined to re-live all of our mistakes" ("J'ai Obtenu Cette"). Jax faces an ultimatum: either leave SAMCRO behind or lose his family. Less than two years earlier, after getting out of a three-month stint in Stockton prison, Jax had told Tara that he was done with SAMCRO and had made a deal with Clay to give him a way out. So Tara's ultimatum should be a no-brainer for Jax, yet he seems torn.

In the past several months, Jax has assumed the presidency of the MC and taken on more responsibility for the future direction of the club. But is his allegiance to the club and his sense of responsibility to its members—his brothers—the only thing holding him back from going to Oregon with his family? Could it be that he simply can't bring himself to leave SAMCRO? After all, it's the only life he's ever known: "Since I was five, Tara, all I ever wanted was a Harley and a cut" ("Potlatch"). He has also confessed that, without SAMCRO, he's just "an okay mechanic with a GED. The only thing I do well is outlaw" ("Out"). And when Bobby Munson discovers that Jax is planning to leave the MC, he exhorts, "Your solution to a problem will always be a club solution. It's the way you're wired" ("Kiss").

Sons of Anarchy and Philosophy: Brains Before Bullets, First Edition.
Edited by George A. Dunn and Jason T. Eberl.
© 2013 John Wiley & Sons, Inc. Published 2013 by John Wiley & Sons, Inc.

Has life in SAMCRO held Jax back from being all that he could've been or has it allowed him to develop his potential in a way no other lifestyle could? Jax has certainly grown as a leader—outmaneuvering not only the ruthless ATF Agent June Stahl but also the diabolical Damon Pope, while at the same time appeasing the Galindo Cartel. Even Clay comes to admit that Jax is a better leader of the MC than he ever was ("Darthy"). Indeed, leadership and cunning are examples of Jax's *virtues*. The term "virtue" is derived from the Latin word for "power" (*virtus*), which is also linked to the word for "man" (*vir*) and "manliness"—so "virtue" shares a root with "virile." Perhaps Jax could only have cultivated such virtues within the violent, anarchic world of SAMCRO, but he also missed out on cultivating other character traits—such as gentleness and moderation—that don't fit well in the world of unbridled violence and lust that is the Sons of Anarchy Motorcycle Club.

The Greek philosopher Aristotle (384–322 BCE) famously argues that human beings aren't born with inclinations toward either virtue or vice; rather, each person's moral character traits are cultivated through a combination of social influence and individual rational choice. The social environment—*polis* ("city") in Aristotle's original Greek—in which one is born and raised, or currently lives, is centrally important to one's initial and ongoing moral character development. It's clear that having been raised in the *polis* of SAMCRO had a tremendous influence on the young Jax and Opie Winston, fostering their development of certain key virtues that Aristotle would commend: courage, loyalty, deep friendship, and willingness to make sacrifices for the common good. But this band of outlaws is also home to many vices: Clay's greed, Tig Trager's uncontrolled lust, and Gemma's manipulative power games. Jax is clearly not immune to these malign influences, especially once he moves up to the head of the table as president. As he tells Bobby, "The gavel corrupts. You can't sit in this chair without being a savage" ("Darthy"). Far from being pure, the SAMCROpolis tends to nurture both virtues and vices in its "citizens."

"Balance Between Might and Right"

Sons of Anarchy relies on our fascination with "anti-heroes,"[1] morally ambiguous protagonists for whom we often cheer even if we can't justify all of their actions. Nobody wants to see SAMCRO go down under the RICO Act, even though the federal government's job is precisely to protect us from illegal activities such as gun-running, drug-muling, and criminal violence. Jax is forever trying to get the club out of such activities, but he can't avoid using violence, deception, and collaboration with other criminals to achieve his laudable goal—and that's just in one episode ("J'ai Obtenu Cette")! Clearly, Jax and his fellow Men of Mayhem aren't your typical "white hat" good guys. But neither are they just a gang of violent law-breakers, for otherwise we'd have no sympathy for them. Part of the show's appeal stems from recognizing the members of SAMCRO as kindred spirits who exemplify—albeit to dramatic extremes—the mixture of virtue and vice found in every human being's moral character. No one is perfectly good or perfectly bad: Clay loves Gemma deeply and is genuinely, compassionately heartbroken when he learns of her rape, but this same man is also capable of bouncing her face off of the floor ("Hands").

When Clay attacks Gemma, it's a shockingly brutal scene of spousal abuse, but it's not all that surprising given what we know about Clay's moral *character*. He's inclined toward violence, greed, self-protectiveness, and using people as means to get what he wants—just ask Elliot Oswald—or removing those who confront him as obstacles—such as the Nomads Clay initially hired to do his bidding. Gemma is the latest in a long line of people Clay has abused in various ways for his own self-centered purposes. So his treatment of her, despite his genuine love for her in other contexts, is consistent with the *type of man* Clay is. When Juice Ortiz asks Clay what he did to make Tara declare him "already dead" to her, he responds forlornly, "Same thing I always do"; and later, when Wayne Unser speculates that sentimentality caused Clay to spare his life, Clay responds, "Ain't my nature" ("Toad's Wild Ride").

Virtues and *vices* are Aristotle's terms for such *inclinations* toward acts that are either good or bad, respectively. For example, Gemma knows exactly what Opie is doing when he attacks Sherriff Roosevelt and is hauled off to prison with Jax, Tig, and Chibs Telford—he's "staying close" to Jax as he has since the two were little boys riding Huffys before trading up to Harleys. Opie's virtue of selfless devotion to Jax is just as integral to the type of man he is as Clay's greed is to his moral character. Of course, Opie isn't morally perfect. His character is also comprised of some questionable traits. His loyalty to the club, for example, overrides his fidelity to his first wife, Donna, eventually resulting in her death; and his jealousy over Lyla's chosen profession, while understandable, nevertheless leads to an unhealthy marital dynamic.

What distinguishes a virtue from a vice is that the former involves acting and feeling *in the right amount*—that is, performing the right action, or feeling the right emotion, at the right time and for the right reason. Vice, on the other hand, involves either an *excess* or a *deficiency* of action or feeling:

> Some vices miss what is right because they are deficient, others because they are excessive, in feelings or in actions, whereas virtue finds and chooses what is intermediate.[2]

Take the virtue of loyalty, for example.[3] Bobby and Tig are both loyal to Clay, but they don't just blindly follow him. Both have challenged Clay when they judge him to be going down an unwise or unjustifiable path. Bobby constantly badgers Clay about the drug-muling deal with the Galindo Cartel in Season 4; yet, he goes behind Jax's back to broker a deal to save Clay's life in Season 5. Contrast this with Chuckie Marstein's obsequiousness—pathetically "accepting" whatever the club members bid him to do, which is often simply to get lost—or with Stahl's easy betrayal of her partner and lover, killing her to serve Stahl's own ambitions. Courage is another virtue exemplified by our collective protagonists, acting with boldness at the right time and for the right reason. Being bold, even risking one's life, is virtuous if it's for the right reason; but Juice acts rashly when he charges into a minefield. By the same token, being cautious can be virtuous too, but not if your caution involves putting innocent children at risk, as when cowardly Ethan Zobelle hides from SAMCRO in a convenience store full of children.

"What Kind of Nasty Shit Did Your Momma Do to You?"

Virtues and vices are not things a person is born with, nor can they be merely bestowed upon you by another person.[4] Rather, they are *cultivated* through habituation, practicing the behaviors modeled by others whom one looks up to as moral *exemplars*:

Virtues ... we acquire, just as we acquire crafts, by having first activated them. For we learn a craft by producing the same product that we must produce when we have learned it; we become builders, for instance, by building, and we become harpists by playing the harp. Similarly, then, we become just by doing just actions, temperate by doing temperate actions, brave by doing brave actions.[5]

Lowell Harland Jr. probably apprenticed as a mechanic at Teller-Morrow under the guidance of experienced mechanics such as his father and Clay. Likewise, one develops moral virtues by apprenticing under those who already possess such virtues, practicing the moral trade until it becomes *second nature*. The only problem is that vice may be cultivated in the same way as virtue—Lowell Jr. could just as easily have learned from his dad how to sabotage a motorcycle and get its rider killed.

And once a particular virtue or vice has become ingrained as part of one's character, it's as difficult to break as any habit—again, consider the drug-addicted Lowell Jr. Aristotle notes that "the reason why habit is also difficult to change is that it is like nature ... 'Habit, I say, is longtime training ... and in the end training is nature for human beings.'"[6] Tara observes how mired in habit Jax is when she admonishes him, "You keep saying you want to change things, but you keep repeating old behavior. You can't have it both ways" ("Potlatch").

Aristotle stresses the importance of the right environment for becoming virtuous, especially when it comes to children. Our tendency to become habituated is the reason why

we must perform the right activities, since differences in these imply corresponding differences in the states [of moral character]. It is not unimportant, then, to acquire one sort of habit or another, right from our youth. On the contrary, it is very important, indeed all-important.[7]

This view is well captured by the precept, "Children learn what they live."

We see this most clearly played out in the politically unstable and violent world of Belfast, as depicted in Season 3. Consider the contrasting aims of the two IRA leaders, Jimmy O'Phelan and Fr. Kellan Ashby. Jimmy O has been working behind the scenes, recruiting day and night, to set up his own revolutionary campaign separate from the control of the "Irish Kings" who govern the Real IRA. Jimmy O's army of choice? Teenage boys he can easily entice with dreams of "glorious revolution" and "fighting the good fight" for the cause of a free Northern Ireland.

Though he is a leader in the Real IRA's violent struggle and long-standing arms-dealing relationship with SAMCRO, Fr. Ashby objects to Jimmy O's plans and recruitment methods. He complains about how Jimmy has been "recruiting off the streets. Broken kids, some as young as ten, eleven. Promising there'll be a united Ireland, all the cash and prizes that go with it. This isn't a child's war ... Jimmy's lost sight of who we are, why we struggle. He's not a soldier anymore, just a gangster" ("Home").[8]

Importantly, Fr. Ashby was also a close friend and confidant of John Teller. He's thus well aware of J.T.'s "resolute desire" to sever the MC's ties to the IRA and to raise his boys, Thomas and Jax, in a more serene "biker commune." We all know how *that* story ended. But Fr. Ashby sees a second chance at redemption when Abel, kidnapped by Cameron Hayes, is brought to Belfast and put in the care of Maureen Ashby: "I couldn't do anything to help save the son, but I can do something to save the grandson ... from the life of his father" ("Firinne"). Fr. Ashby sees Jax as a willing participant in the same cycle of violence from which J.T. had failed to free him. Is being in Jax's care truly what would be best for Abel? Won't he, just like his father, want nothing but a Harley and a cut by age five? Wouldn't Abel be likely to succeed his father at the head of the table in "church" and perpetuate the violence (and porn and prostitution, too) into the next generation?

Fr. Ashby is determined not to allow Jax's vices to negatively impact Abel's moral development. He succeeds in convincing Jax that a better life awaits Abel "with a father who didn't torture and murder a man yesterday," as we witness in the powerfully moving scene when Jax follows Abel and his adoptive parents around not long after seeing his mother pull a gun on some nuns—NUNS!—and threaten to kill a baby if they didn't give up Abel's location ("Bainne"). As we know, Gemma's eligibility for "Mother/Grandmother of the Year" award slips away even further in Season 5. She and Clay certainly didn't model the best behavior for Jax. Would he and Tara—who's already helped Gemma kill and dispose of an innocent woman—do any better?

"A Unique Little Town"

SAMCRO is embedded within the small town of Charming, California. As Clay affirms, "If it happens in Charming, it's SAMCRO's problem" ("Smite"). Jax and Opie, along with their generational cohorts Tara and David Hale, all grew up together in this community; yet they took different paths. Jax and Opie's path we know well. Hale, proud son of one of Charming's founding families, went in a different direction. And Tara had to get completely out of this "backwards, incestuous, and small-minded" town in an attempt to carve out her own identity and find her vocation as a healer, noting, "I didn't hate Charming, just me in it at the time" ("Seeds").

Charming is just as vital to *Sons of Anarchy* as any of its colorful residents. Charming has its own characteristics (though not virtues and vices in a literal sense) that have been formed by those who've invested their lives in the community—such as SAMCRO and the Hale and Oswald families—and is resistant to outside influences. As Unser quietly warns Zobelle when he's setting up shop on Main Street, "Charming's a special town. Not many folks take to it. I like to think the town chooses its occupants. Right ones stay, wrong ones disappear" ("Eureka"). We also witness Clay's concern over the gentrifying effect of Mayor Hale's Charming Heights suburban development initiative—just what sort of new people will be moving into town? Of course, this may reflect more Clay's self-centered worry that the town's expansion will shine a greater light on it and bring more intensive law-enforcement scrutiny—as if there isn't enough already! He explains the situation to Jax after leveraging Oswald over the killing of his daughter's rapist: "If Oswald's land goes commercial, that means housing developments. Population rises, brings more cops, more state and federal involvement. Charming goes Disney, and SAMCRO gets squeezed out by the most dangerous gang of all: old white money" ("Fun Town"). President Jax, on the other hand, isn't afraid to deal with Hale to help Charming Heights go through and bring some lucrative—and legitimate—business opportunities for Teller-Morrow Automotive.

The community of Charming and its leadership is indeed of central importance as the ironic, Mayberry-turned-upside-down setting in which SAMCRO operates. But it's also an influential force in the moral formation of its long-time residents. Claiming something directly opposed to the individualistic and anarchic worldview of Clay and company, Aristotle affirms a *communitarian* ethic in which political leaders do more than protect the innocent and make sure the town's traffic lights are working. For Aristotle, "the legislator makes the citizens good by habituating them, and this is the wish of every legislator; if he fails to do it well he misses his goal. Correct habituation distinguishes a good political system from a bad one."[9]

This level of moral leadership isn't at all evident in the case of Mayor Jacob Hale, Jr., whose goals for Charming are more focused on business opportunities that'll benefit his pocketbook—to the point of partnering with members of the League of American Nationalists ("Albification") and the largest purveyor of deviant sex products in Asia ("To Be, Act 2"). His conflict with SAMCRO is more about how Clay's values impact *him* and not the town. As outsider Lincoln Potter wonders, "Does it bother anyone in this town that their mayor is also their biggest developer? No one smells that stench?" ("Booster"). Later, Sherriff Eli Roosevelt, another transplant to Charming, challenges Hale, asking "And where are those lines, mayor? You know, the ones that separate public service from self service? ... You can wrap it in any type of 'I love Charming' package that you want. But it still funnels back to your pocket" ("Family Recipe"). Hale thus doesn't fit Aristotle's definition of a virtuous legislator whose primary interest should be the moral development of those who are governed. He's a far cry from Aristotle's "true politician," who "seems to have put more effort into virtue than into anything else, since he wants to make the citizens good and law-abiding."[10]

The mayor's deceased brother, on the other hand, aspired to succeed Unser as chief of police so that he could serve as an example of law-abiding leadership that doesn't mix itself up with "outlaw justice." According to Unser, Deputy Chief Hale "thinks Charming's stuck in 1969, wants to bring it into the twenty-first century." The deputy chief is also concerned about the fact that SAMCRO's members function as moral exemplars to the people of Charming, "You guys cruise around here like heroes, but you and I know the truth ... You're white trash thugs holding on to a dying dream ... You can't stop progress. It won't be long before SAMCRO is just an ugly memory in the history of Charming" ("Seeds").

Aristotle would endorse David Hale's desire to bring law and virtue into conformity:

For most lawful actions, we might say, are those produced by virtue as a whole; for the law prescribes living in accord with each virtue, and forbids living in accord with each vice. Moreover, the actions producing the whole of virtue are the lawful actions that the laws prescribe for education promoting the common good.[11]

Aristotle isn't proposing a *tyrannical* political system, however. In fact, he finds such an overbearing system to be the worst form of government.[12] Nevertheless, as we've already seen, it's the job of legislators to pass laws that will help cultivate virtue in the community's youth:

It is difficult, however, for someone to be trained correctly for virtue from his youth if he has not been brought up under correct laws; for the many, especially the young, do not find it pleasant to live in a temperate and resistant way. That is why laws must prescribe their upbringing and practices; for they will not find these things painful when they get used to them.[13]

Aristotle would be fine with the virtuous members of the community being more and more self-governing upon reaching maturity. But a truly *anarchic* state isn't possible because there'll always be "bestial" members of the community, whose vices can be controlled only through punitive measures:

That is why legislators must, in some people's view, urge people toward virtue and exhort them to aim at what is fine—on the assumption that anyone whose good habits have prepared him decently will listen to them—but must impose corrective treatments and penalties on anyone who disobeys or lacks the right nature, and must completely expel the incurable [Otto Delaney? Lenny "the Pimp" Janowitz?]. For the decent person, it is assumed, will attend to reason because his life aims at what is fine, whereas the base person, since he desires pleasure, has to receive corrective treatments by pain, like a beast of burden ... As we have said, then, someone who is good must be finely brought up and habituated, and then must live in decent practices, doing base actions neither willingly nor unwillingly. And this will be true if his life follows some sort of understanding and correct order that prevails on him.[14]

As his older brother is aware, though, Hale's "sense of self-righteousness can sometimes get the best of him" ("Albification") and it even leads him to temporarily buy into Zobelle's sermon about the erosion of "faith, values, morals, and decency" ("Fix") until he learns of Gemma's rape. Hale's sudden death at Half-Sack's funeral may be symbolic of the death of his form of noble, righteous chivalry on behalf of the people of Charming. Can Charming, or SAMCRO for that matter, be saved to serve as incubators for moral virtue?

"I'm Not Sure Which Cancer's Worse: the One in Me or the One in Charming"

When Clay gives Juice his "Men of Mayhem" patch, he tells him, "You know, most days this life is just riding around, getting shit done. Some days it's more than that. Some days we ask our guys to do shit very few men could do. That's what this means" ("Fruit for the Crows"). As we noted at the outset, the MC can be fertile ground for the cultivation of virtues, like courage, of which Aristotle would approve. But such courage is often put at the service of the second type of "shit" to which Clay refers, SAMCRO's lawless activities, which outsiders like Deputy Chief Hale view as fostering far more vice than virtue within the community of Charming. As Jax's ex-wife, Wendy, not necessarily a paragon of virtue herself, warns Tara, "The MC, this town, it kills all the shit you love" ("J'ai Obtenu Cette"). So, are there any virtues that SAMCRO could not only cultivate within its own membership, but also model for the good people of Charming and for us viewers of *Sons of Anarchy*?

Yes, SAMCRO models *loyalty* founded upon the deep friendship within the community of members, old ladies, prospects, crow eaters, and other "friends of the club" like Chuckie and Wayne Unser. When the club is preparing to face off against the League of American Nationalists, everyone and their families are brought under the protective umbrella of Teller-Morrow. Clay even gives a heartfelt speech in which he expresses his sincere love for everyone there ("The Culling"). Aristotle notes that "fellow voyagers and fellow soldiers [the brothers of the MC are both] are called friends ... And the extent of their community is the extent of their friendships [other charters, families] ... The proverb 'What friends have is common' is correct, since friendship involves community."[15] Aristotle is referring here to the function of *justice* within a community of friends and the fact that friends in such communities don't necessarily need "laws" of justice between them since they share what they have in common. It's only among members of the wider political community in which these more close-knit communities are embedded that laws of justice are necessary, since the bonds of friendship are weaker and the virtue of loyalty is not as prevalent.

We see this form of justice-without-law in play when Opie's first wife, Donna, who harbors no love for the MC that led her husband into prison for five years, can't pay for her groceries and Gemma steps in to help out, telling a skeptical Donna, "SAMCRO is not the enemy, it's the glue that'll pull you through the ugly shit" ("Seeds"). After Opie's death, Jax shows his widow Lyla *her* "family"—SAMCRO won't let her and her children go without ("Stolen Huffy"). How many other communities exemplify this degree of love and support for their members? And the club's generosity doesn't stop at the gates of T-M, as we see the club model other forms of community service activities for the people of Charming and surrounding towns: organizing a fundraiser for a local school ("Giving Back"), running a blood drive to support a children's hospital ("Eureka"), and working to save an urban garden from being paved over ("Family Recipe").

"It's in You. It's Who You Are"

SAMCRO may not be the best exemplar of moral virtues beyond loyalty and courage, but Jax is trying his damnedest to change the worst aspects of the MC's character. In line with Aristotle's advice about seeking out moral exemplars, Jax is following the lead of his father, John Teller, though he also recognizes that J.T. isn't to be admired in all respects. When Jax starts to lose hope that his father could really offer him further guidance, Piney exhorts, "Your father was the best man I ever knew. And before you let him die, you should find him and know that for yourself" ("Family Recipe").

While flawed, J.T. fits Aristotle's picture of a virtuous human being insofar as he exemplifies both *intellectual* and *moral* qualities worth emulating. As Piney describes him to Tara, "He's a complicated guy. He was angry and impulsive. Just righteous as hell. Hated being wrong. Not much of an education. Book smart, though. He used to devour three and four of them at a time. He was loyal. Too loyal" ("Una Venta"). J.T. was by no means a saint, but he remains a suitably inspirational figure for Jax. We even see Jax following his father's intellectual lead by writing reflections to pass on to his own sons ("Sovereign"). J.T.'s weaknesses, though, didn't allow him to reform the club without getting himself killed.

Jax knows he needs to be smarter, stronger, and more ruthless than his father in order to succeed where J.T. had failed. The environment of SAMCRO, under Clay's leadership, and Gemma's maternal influence have cultivated within Jax just the right strengths to accomplish this task and we see him having largely succeeded at the end of Season 5—that is, until Sheriff Roosevelt knocks on his door. But there's a moral cost to his success. Much blood had to be shed and perhaps Jax is right when he confesses to Bobby that only a "savage" could effectively lead the MC and bring about the reform J.T. sought. The particular mix of virtue and vice that comprises Jax's moral character may, in the end, be exactly what SAMCRO needs at this moment in its history. We can only hope that, if Abel or Thomas eventually succeeds their father at the head of the table, the environment in which they've been raised will have evolved closer to the "biker commune" that cultivates virtues such as loyalty, courage, and communal brotherhood and away from the vices passed on from the elder generation who founded the MC.

Notes

1. Other examples include the serial-killer *Dexter*, the tortured soul of *The Dark Knight*, and the morally gray world of the re-imagined *Battlestar Galactica* series.
2. Aristotle, *Nicomachean Ethics [NE]*, 2nd ed., trans. Terence Irwin (Indianapolis: Hackett, 1999), Book II, Ch. 6, 1107a4–6.
3. For further discussion of the virtue of loyalty, see Chapter 3 by James Mahon.
4. The thirteenth-century Aristotelian philosopher and Christian theologian Thomas Aquinas (c. 1225–1274) claimed that God could directly "infuse" certain virtues—faith, hope, and charity—in a person by grace, but we'll limit the discussion here to Aristotle's original theory.
5. *NE* Book II, Ch. 1, 11033a32–b2.
6. *NE* Book VII, Ch. 10, 1152a32–34.
7. *NE* Book II, Ch. 1, 1103b22–25.

8. For further discussion of Jimmy O's and Fr. Ashby's distinct visions of the how best to carry out "the cause" of the Real IRA, see Chapter 8 by Philip Smolenski.
9. *NE* Book II, Ch. 1, 1103b4–7.
10. *NE* Book I, Ch. 13, 1102a7–10.
11. *NE* Book V, Ch. 2, 1130b23–26.
12. *NE* Book VIII, Ch. 10, 1160b1–9.
13. *NE* Book X, Ch. 9, 1179b32–36.
14. *NE* Book X, Ch. 9, 1180a6–18.
15. *NE* Book VIII, Ch. 9, 1159b28–3.

CHAPTER 2

A Prospect's Guide to Nietzsche

Tim Jung and Minerva Ahumada

Watching *Sons of Anarchy*, it's easy to get caught up cheering for career criminals. It's hard not to root for SAMCRO's hijinks, to become endeared to Tig Trager's perversions and Happy Lowman's brutality, and to admire Jax Teller's cleverness and Opie Winston's loyalty. It isn't clear why we should like these hardened outlaws, but philosopher Friedrich Nietzsche (1844–1900) has some helpful things to say on the subject.

Nietzsche is known not only for his radical ideas but also for his distinctive literary style and his memorable aphorisms, such as, "Whatever does not kill me makes me stronger."[1] Even Jax knows that aphorism—he quotes it in the episode "Sovereign," though he identifies it as "an old saying," presumably unaware of where it's from, and says that he disagrees with it. "No victor believes in chance" is another one of Nietzsche's aphorisms, one Jax would probably have an easier time endorsing, considering how ingeniously he's able to maneuver SAMCRO out of sticky situations.[2] Nietzsche calls himself an "immoralist" and sometimes an "antichrist," so clearly he considers himself to be a bit of an outlaw. Nietzsche also has a penchant for questioning authority. If he rode a Harley, the Sons might even consider patching him in.

But Nietzsche doesn't simply thumb his nose at conventional morality. He's interested in tracing our contemporary morality back

Sons of Anarchy and Philosophy: Brains Before Bullets, First Edition.
Edited by George A. Dunn and Jason T. Eberl.
© 2013 John Wiley & Sons, Inc. Published 2013 by John Wiley & Sons, Inc.

to its origins in the distant past in order to understand how it came to be the way it is today, not unlike how John Teller—and later Jax—explore the history of SAMCRO in order to understand how the club "lost its way."[3] Nietzsche believes most philosophers have overlooked "where our good and evil really *originated*"[4] and he thinks we need to investigate this origin before we can assess the *value* of our reigning moral ideals, like sympathy and equality. As we'll see, not just Nietzsche, but also our admiration for the Sons of Anarchy calls into question these reigning moral ideals.

SAMCRO's Master Morality

In the town of Charming, there are numerous contending forces: SAMCRO, competing gangs like the Nords, the influential Hale and Oswald families, and the constant parade of law enforcement agencies—including the local PD, the San Joaquin Sherriff's Department, and the ATF. These forces constantly shift from being allies to antagonists and back again. Jacob Hale associates himself with Ethan Zobelle's League of American Nationalists; Deputy Chief David Hale assists—in more ways than one—ruthless ATF Agent June Stahl; and SAMCRO is constantly redefining its relationship with the Mayans, the One-Niners, the Galindo Cartel, and others. But as far as SAMCRO is concerned, Charming is its town, which it protects from noxious outside forces like meth, heroin, and pedophile rapists, while at the same time SAMCRO flouts the law—or at least conventional morality—by running guns, muling drugs, and producing porn.

So who's good and who's evil in Charming? Nietzsche would say that we're asking the wrong question. Instead of labeling people and their actions as "good" or "evil," Nietzsche uses *philology*—the study of the historical development of language—to figure out how we came to use these terms. We might assume that the word "good" origin-inated as a term of praise bestowed on those who perform kind or selfless actions. On this view, favored by some of Nietzsche's philosophical predecessors, the word "good" derives its positive con-notation from the pleasure or relief that the beneficiary of a good deed feels in being helped. Tara sewing up Cameron Hayes or offering to operate on Abel would be "good" actions in this sense. Nietzsche, however, after tracing the history of the word "good" (and its equivalents) in various languages, concludes that this widely held view is wrong: "the judgment 'good' did *not* originate with those to whom 'goodness' was shown!"[5] On the contrary, noble, high-minded, aristocratic warriors were the first to call *themselves* "good," *not* because they were kind and helpful, but rather because they were fierce and menacing. It's not the selfless or meek person, but the strong individual and the community that fosters and honors his strength (Vikings, Homeric heroes) that provides the basis for what Nietzsche calls *master morality*.

In the master morality of the ancient world, a "good" action didn't need to demonstrate kindness to others. Rather, an action was deemed "good" if it embodied the virtues associated with the ruling class of warriors, such as strength, bravery, cunning, wit, and leadership:

> The knightly-aristocratic value judgments presupposed a powerful phys-
> icality, a flourishing, abundant, even overflowing health, together with
> that which serves to preserve it: war, adventure, hunting, dancing, war
> games, and in general all that involves vigorous, free, joyful activity.[6]

Master morality defined "good" not only by referring to powerful individuals, but also by referring to those activities that were performed in order to maintain a powerful status and robust health. Master morality emphasizes the *activity* through which one gives expression to one's strength. Those who embody this active spirit may be carefree and playful, but they also have the capacity to endure hardship. Their strength is also on display in their loyalty and in their swaggering self-confidence.

Members of SAMCRO possess many of the traits Nietzsche associates with master morality. When we meet Jax in the pilot episode, he's buying a package of condoms. When the flirtatious cashier asks him why he doesn't just buy them in bulk, Jax jokes that he likes to keep himself humble. His confidence makes him attractive and is a sign of his virility. But the life of the master is not simply about sexual conquests. Nietzsche also mentions hunting and dancing as activities through which masters display their superabundant vitality. Think of a "patch-over party." When SAMCRO patches over The Devil's Tribe, we witness a raucous party—it's no wonder Tig wanted to be there so badly! But, since the main business of the masters is warfare, it's only fitting that the party be followed by a shoot-out with the Mayans the next day.

SAMCRO may not be a *real* aristocracy in the old fashioned sense of holding official titles, but it certainly acts just like one in many ways. How many times do we hear people refer to Gemma Morrow as the "queen" and Jax as the "prince"? More importantly, like the warrior class of the ancient world, SAMCRO members have their own moral code that doesn't reflect the morality of the rest of Charming or, presumably, most viewers of the show. After all, most of us don't typically treat our disloyal friends or family members to a meeting with Mr. Mayhem.

Yet despite the club's criminal activities and contempt for conventional morality, we can't help but admire their loyalty, friendship, endurance, and sense of honor. They clearly have moral ideals, even if they aren't the ones shared by most of us. Though their actions may seem "evil" in many respects, Nietzsche claims that our condemnation of them is really rooted in hidden envy and resentment. Don't we all secretly wish we could be like the Sons, who are clearly outstanding in so many respects?

"A Student's Prank"

The Sons of Anarchy exhibit master morality in ways that challenge our understanding of morality. Their *goodness* is so different from what we customarily deem to be *good* that we might be tempted to call it by an entirely different name—such as barbaric violence! Indeed, Nietzsche associates the ancient master with "Beasts of prey, the splendid *blond beast*."[7] The blond in question is the mighty predatory lion, but Nietzsche could just as easily have been referring to the splendidly blond Jax. Like the aristocratic masters of the ancient world, the Sons "go *back* to the innocent conscience of the beast of prey, as triumphant monsters," murdering government agents, castrating a rapist carnie, or blowing up a Mayan stash of guns and drugs "as if it were no more than a student's prank." The ancient master perpetrated similar acts of mayhem, "convinced they [had] provided the poets with a lot more material for song and praise."[8]

For the well-being of the club and the people of Charming, the members of SAMCRO are willing to kill, extort, and torture. Nietzsche, however, would suspect that such "hijinks" aren't merely a means to an end for the Sons, but rather are the exuberant outbursts of untamed men seeking an outlet for a superabundant vitality that cannot be constrained by civilized society. Remarkably, when all is said and done, they go back to living their lives as if not much had happened, untroubled by the carnage. We may feel envious that we can't destroy our enemies with the same remorseless nonchalance as the Sons dispatch the slimy Georgie Caruso. Nietzsche would discern in the actions and attitudes of SAMCRO "that enthusiastic impulsiveness in anger, love, reverence, gratitude, and revenge by which noble souls have at all times recognized one another."[9]

At times, the Sons' actions do have the feel of "a student's prank"— and not just because Piney Winston is driving a school bus with Opie and Chibs Telford at the end of Season 3. Throughout the season, we're led to believe that Jax has ratted out the club to Stahl. But it's all been part of a ploy that now comes to fruition, as Wayne Unser stops Stahl and tells her that he heard that the IRA is waiting for her to take Jimmy O'Phelan. Two agents are sent to scout the terrain while Opie, Piney, and Chibs—is he drinking a Jameson *juice box?*— arrive where Stahl, Unser, and Jimmy O are waiting. Chibs kills Jimmy, delivering both the IRA's and his own personal justice. At the same time, Opie delivers a dose of SAMCRO and personal justice to Stahl, and rips up Jax's signed statement. The prospects ride up next to the police vehicle in which Jax, Tig, Bobby Munson, Juice Ortiz, and Clay Morrow are being taken to prison and send a signal—there's laughter: Jax isn't a rat. Everything went according to plan!

Jax has made life better for the Sons: short-time in prison, a stronger alliance with the IRA, and two troublesome antagonists put down. Like the ancient masters, Jax demonstrates "bold recklessness whether in the face of danger or of the enemy."[10] Jax has a lot of these bold plans, such as using Tig as bait to exact revenge on Damon Pope, while framing Clay for the murder and guaranteeing that the club ends up on top again. Everything about the Sons reminds us of Nietzsche's description of the ancient ruling classes:

> This "boldness" of noble races, mad, absurd, and sudden in its expression, the incalculability, even incredulity of their undertakings, their indifference to and contempt for security, body, life, comfort, their hair-raising cheerfulness and profound joy in all destruction, in the voluptuousness of victory and cruelty.[11]

The Sons live to ride another day because of their audacious, bold, reckless decisions, which only *masters* have the will to risk.

Like Happy after he's nicked by a bullet, the Sons often feel "rapturous" when engaging in dangerous play. When Tig is captured by bounty hunters (for public nudity and something involving a chicken), Piney decides to back a truck into the hotel room where he's being held. This reckless and impulsive action elicits laughter and frivolity. Or remember the *other* time Tig needed to be rescued? Shortly after Tig tried to kill Laroy, SAMCRO found itself in the middle of a car chase and shoot-out, seeming more than happy to be dancing with bullets to the tune of AWOLNATION's "Burn It Down."

The strong nature that Nietzsche attributes to master morality can also be seen in the Sons' ability to make peace and even form alliances with former enemies. "To be incapable of taking one's enemies, one's accidents, even one's misdeeds seriously for a very long time," is, according to Nietzsche, "the sign of strong, full natures in whom there is an excess of the power to form, to mold, to recuperate and to forget."[12] The Sons and the Mayans have a history of mutual hostility, devolving into open warfare on occasion. The Mayans even protected Ethan Zobelle, the head of the League of American Nationalists, who ordered Gemma's gang rape. Yet when the Sons ambush the Mayans to get to Zobelle, Clay spares the life of his enemy Marcus Álvarez and relations between the two MCs improve as time goes on.

"How much reverence has a noble man for his enemies!" writes Nietzsche.[13] While master morality doesn't extol the Christian virtue of universal love—after all, not everyone is lovable!—it does make a virtue out of reverence and respect for others who exhibit exceptional degrees of strength and courage, even when they happen to be one's enemies. Thus, while the Sons may regularly go to war against rival MCs and other criminal organizations, they don't normally judge their enemies to be "evil," since these fellow outlaws possess many of the same superior qualities that the Sons respect in each other. Unprovoked acts of perfidy and betrayal, on the other hand, are not easily forgiven, as Stahl learns the hard way.

"I'm Going to Bury These Assholes"

As much as we may admire and even envy the virtues exhibited by the Sons and their free-spirited lifestyle, we also may sometimes feel uneasy with their actions and even judge them to be morally wrong.

Elliott Oswald doesn't have the balls to castrate the man who raped his daughter, but Clay doesn't hesitate to do the job for him ("Fun Town"). Oswald's decision reflects how we'd expect most normal people to react. However much that despicable rapist needed to be taught a lesson, we might just feel that Clay went too far. Or consider how Jax shrugs off as "collateral damage" Tig's cold-blooded murder of the wife of the prison guard who was responsible for Opie's death ("Small World"). The murder of an unarmed woman would probably strike most of us as a much more morally serious matter than it evidently is for Jax.

Nietzsche would say that our squeamishness reflects our modern morality, which he variously calls "slave morality" or "the morality of the herd." This morality entails a very different set of values than those upheld by ancient aristocratic warriors or, for that matter, by modern outlaw bikers. The rallying cries of our modern moral sensibility, according to Nietzsche, are "equality of rights" and "sympathy for all that suffers."[14] What may trouble us about the Sons is that they don't seem to share these values. To the contrary, like society's ancient noble masters, they see themselves as occupying the pinnacle of an order of rank, where their interests, both individually and as a club, invariably take precedence over those of lesser individuals—even over a terrified woman who merely wants to stay alive. Like Nietzsche's masters, the Sons sometimes seem to believe that the rest of society exists simply to be plundered by them so that they can enjoy their "outlaw" freedom and privileges. It's not surprising that their conduct provokes resentment from some quarters.

Nietzsche believes that resentment against the nobles—or *ressentiment*, as he prefers to call it, using the French word—is the original wellspring of the morality of equality and sympathy that has come to dominate our civilization. Among the first to give organized expression to this *ressentiment* were members of the priestly class, who felt victimized and bullied by the masters. Emboldened by *ressentiment*, the priestly class exacted its revenge, not as SAMCRO would likely do, by routing their enemies in a hail of bullets, but by enacting a *fantasy* of revenge that involves inverting the masters' values and declaring everything about them to be *evil*. Since this point of view also coincides with the attitude of the lower classes, the peasants and workers who likewise feel victimized by the masters, Nietzsche calls it "slave morality." Master morality can involve the kind of hell-raising typical of the Sons. Proponents of slave morality term such behavior "evil" and raise themselves up as the "good" ones:

> The wretched alone are the good; the poor, impotent, lowly alone are good; the suffering, deprived, sick, ugly alone are pious, alone are blessed by God, blessedness is for them alone ...[15]

By introducing the love of God and appealing to a higher law that should apply to everyone, the priests and their followers are able to claim that *they* alone are the good ones and that those who are most unlike them—namely, the masters—are evil.

For insight into the workings of *ressentiment*, we need look no further than the dangerous but brilliant Agent Stahl. After Otto Delaney leads Stahl to believe that he's going to rat on the club, he attacks her in the interrogation room, prompting Stahl, wild-eyed and bleeding, to vow, "I'm gonna bury these assholes" ("Better Half"). Virtually everything that she does subsequently is driven by her desire for revenge, though she dissembles her real motivations by claiming to be simply pursuing justice. According to Nietzsche, the slave morality fashioned by *ressentiment* requires "a hostile external world."[16] And while noble individuals like the Sons are able to respect their enemies (as long as they can discern in them the same noble qualities they see in themselves), someone in the throes of *ressentiment* like Stahl can only conceive of her enemies as different and evil. She can acknowledge none of their merits—their courage, loyalty, audacity, and strength. She sees only "assholes" who commit evil acts.

Conversely, though the Mayans and Sons have been enemies, neither considers the other to be evil. They fight over turf, but when it comes to moving business along, these two "noble" clubs know very well how to respect each other. When a brick of cocaine goes missing from a shipment jointly guarded by the two MCs, both clubs interrogate their men on the scene. When Álvarez concludes that his man didn't steal the brick, the Sons respect his word and his authority. Stahl, on the other hand, respects and trusts no one, pitting anyone against anyone to achieve her goals. Even Donna Winston, who has little love for SAMCRO, would rather stand with her husband and the club than trust Stahl ("Capybara"). Stahl doesn't respect her enemies. She only uses them, because she knows she's on the "right" or "good" side of things.

There's about as much love between Nietzsche and the "man of *ressentiment*" as there is between Jax and his ex-wife, Wendy. Nietzsche claims that noble men live in "trust and openness" with themselves, in addition to being "upright and naive."[17] Men and women of *ressentiment*, on the other hand, are "neither upright, nor naive nor honest and straightforward" with themselves.[18] Stahl uses SAMCRO to get to the IRA and push her career forward— even killing her own partner and lover to advance her own ends ("June Wedding"). According to Nietzsche, this sort of contradiction and dishonesty with oneself is what we should expect from a person afflicted by *ressentiment*. Stahl also isn't self-aware enough to recognize her *envy* of the club. As Clay tells her, "It kills you, doesn't it? To see me and my guys living good lives. Families, friends, nice homes. You hate the fact that we get the same rights and freedoms as you do" ("The Sleep of Babies"). If the Sons are "evil," they don't deserve the good lives they enjoy and Stahl is right to try to oppose them.

On being released from prison, Bobby asks Stahl, "That's it, huh? Your pretty face gets smashed in, you spend months—how many thousands of dollars—trying to crush us? What for, bitch? What do you get?" Stahl's response is telling: "Peace of mind" ("Albification"). Like those Nietzsche claims are full of *ressentiment*, Stahl gets her sense of worth from whether she can take others down a few notches. Contrast that with the spontaneous self-affirmation and robust self-esteem that we find in healthy human specimens like the Sons of Anarchy.

"The Good Guys Need a Win"

The slave morality that arose from *ressentiment* rejects the masters' belief in a rank order among human beings. While master morality insists that those who embody the sort of warrior virtues displayed by the Sons are entitled to greater privileges, slave morality will have nothing to do with the idea that some human beings are intrinsically superior to others. Of course, there is some measure of equality *within* SAMCRO, since everyone who rides has a vote at "church." Still, it's not an equality based on some intangible "intrinsic worth" that everyone has in equal measure, but rather on the rough equality of battle-ready prowess in their ranks. Those who lack the traits that make the masters superior have considerably diminished worth in the eyes of master morality. Notice how even a good friend of the club like Chuckie Marstein is regarded by members with a mixture of pity and contempt.

For Nietzsche, to require superior individuals like Jax and Happy to play by the same rules as the rest of us is like asking an animal to act contrary to its nature. Nietzsche draws an analogy to lambs and birds of prey:

> That lambs dislike great birds of prey does not seem strange: only it gives no ground for reproaching these birds of prey for bearing off little lambs. And if the lambs say among themselves: "these birds of prey are evil; and whoever is least like a bird of prey, but rather its opposite, a lamb—would he not be good?" there is no reason to find fault with this institution of an ideal, except perhaps that the birds of prey might view it a little ironically and say: "*we* don't dislike them at all, these good little lambs; we even love them: nothing is more tasty than a tender lamb."[19]

Of course, the resentful Stahl really isn't very lamb-like. She doesn't represent the virtues of meekness, humility, and peacefulness that slave morality promotes. In fact, she's awfully damn predatory in her own right. But there are others who pass through Charming who seem to be more clearly on the side of the "lambs" and who, unlike Stahl, aren't using morality as a cover to hide their unscrupulous pursuit of a private agenda. The real "good guys," according to slave morality, are those who oppose the masters by affirming the fundamental equality of all human beings and by defending the weak against "evil" predators who respect only might.

Assistant US Attorney Lincoln Potter is far more principled than Stahl—we can't imagine him killing his partner to fulfill a career-advancing deal with the Sons. He clearly identifies himself as one of the good guys. After his crusade against SAMCRO and the Irish Kings is derailed by the CIA, he interrupts a city council meeting to expose Mayor Jacob Hale's "moral bankruptcy," disclosing that a Japanese sex toy manufacturer backed Hale's financing of Charming Heights. Having failed to take down one set of "predators," Potter goes after another, explaining that "the good guys need a win" ("To Be, Act 2"). Yet even this "good guy" is not above using dirty tricks to plant doubts in the minds of Juice and Otto—leaving them feeling weak, abandoned, and exposed—in order to turn them against their own club.

When it comes to "good guys" in Charming, we can find nobody who better embodies the ideals of slave morality than Deputy Chief David Hale—or, as Unser called him once, "Captain America." Unlike other law enforcement personnel, Hale doesn't come across as particularly resentful or envious of the Sons of Anarchy. In fact, in a conversation that takes place after the murder of Donna, Hale acknowledges that he and the Sons may share some common ground. "We ended up on opposing teams, you and me," he tells Jax. "Don't like each other all that much. But seeing an innocent woman gunned down, two little kids with no mom. Man, I think that falls on the wrong side of the fence for both of us" ("The Revelator"). (Of course, Hale says that not knowing that a few seasons later Jax will dismiss Tig's murder of another unarmed woman as "collateral damage.") All in all, Hale seems to be a morally upright guy who's simply trying to enforce the law to protect the citizens of Charming.

But even if Hale doesn't draw his fire from *ressentiment* to the extent that someone like Stahl does, and even if he possess virtues like courage that are intrinsically admirable, Nietzsche would still fault him for having internalized a morality that has its historical roots in resentment against the powerful. And ultimately the problem with this morality is that if it's allowed to have its way, the world will be deprived of mighty and noble specimens of humanity, like Jax Teller and the other Sons of Anarchy. That, for Nietzsche, would be a tragedy beyond measure. Nietzsche's not one to petition heaven often, but, when he does, here is his heartfelt prayer:

> But grant me from time to time—if there are divine goddesses in the realm beyond good and evil—grant me the sight, but *one* glance of something perfect, wholly achieved, happy, mighty, triumphant, something still capable of arousing fear! Of a man who justifies *man*, of a complementary and redeeming lucky hit on the part of man for the sake of which one may still *believe in man*![20]

We can't be sure what Nietzsche's reaction to *Sons of Anarchy* would have been, but it's possible that at certain moments he would have regarded it as an answer to his prayers.

Why Do We Love These Criminals?

Reading Nietzsche and watching *Sons of Anarchy* might make us wonder why in the world we ever wanted to be cops when playing "cops and robbers" as children. The club may have its problems, but for the most part the Sons don't let their exuberant joy in living get poisoned by *ressentiment*. This doesn't necessarily mean that we should buy into all the values of master morality, but our admiration for the Sons makes it clear that we, like Nietzsche, find much to affirm in such a lifestyle. Despite being a violent criminal organization, the MC provides us with a sense of dangerous adventure, loyal companionship, and letting our inner "blond beasts" run wild.

On the other hand, there may be some good reasons why, over the course of history, slave morality came to prevail. Think for a minute about Jax and David Hale. Jax exhibits a "strong, full nature" that is able to "mold, recuperate, and forget," but Hale is upright, decent, and, in general, highly conscientious about doing what he perceives to be his duty. If you're a fan of *Sons of Anarchy*, you might want to have a beer and ride the open road with Jax, but in the back of your mind—molded by centuries of the slave morality that has dominated the Western world's collective conscience—you might already hear the explosions coming your way and secretly wish Hale were still around to protect you.

Notes

1. Friedrich Nietzsche, *Twilight of the Idols: or How to Philosophize with a Hammer*, trans. Duncan Large (New York: Oxford University Press, 2009), 1.
2. Friedrich Nietzsche, *Gay Science*, trans. Walter Kaufmann (New York: Vintage Books, 1974), 258.
3. For another take on SAMCRO's relationship to its history, see Chapters 17 and 18 by Peter Fosl.
4. Friedrich Nietzsche, *The Genealogy of Morals*, in *The Basic Writings of Nietzsche*, trans. Walter Kaufmann (New York: Modern Library, 2000), 452; Preface, section 3.
5. Ibid., 462; essay I, section 2.
6. Ibid., 469; essay I, section 7.

7. Ibid.
8. Ibid., 476; essay I, section 11.
9. Ibid., 475; essay I, section 10.
10. Ibid.
11. Ibid.
12. Ibid.
13. Ibid.
14. Friedrich Nietzsche, *Beyond Good and Evil*, in *Basic Writings*, 244; essay II, section 44.
15. Nietzsche, *Genealogy*, 470; essay I, section 7.
16. Ibid., 474; essay I, section 10.
17. Ibid.
18. Ibid.
19. Ibid., 480–481; essay I, section 12.
20. Ibid., 480; essay I, section 12.

CHAPTER 3

Tig Needs an Escort Home
Is Loyalty a Virtue?

James Edwin Mahon

For the Sons of Anarchy Motorcycle Club, Redwood Original (SAMCRO), loyalty is the most important quality in a member—not loyalty to a cause, but loyalty to the club's other members. To be loyal is to support one's brothers, to have their back and stick up for them, even to the point of risking one's life.

In "To Be, Act 1," Tig Trager, the former sergeant-at-arms of SAMCRO, is distraught, believing it's his fault that Clay Morrow, the club's president, has been shot and wounded—allegedly by black assailants. "This is on me," he says. "Clay wanted me to stay. He had a feeling something was going down ... Brother asked for help. I turned my back." Tig decides to hunt down Laroy Wayne—head of the One-Niners—whom he believes has ordered the hit. Tig tries to run down Laroy as he eats at a restaurant, but ends up killing Laroy's girlfriend, Veronica Pope. With Laroy and the rest of the Niners on his tail, Tig calls the rest of the club for assistance. When Chibs gets the message, he tells Jax: "Tig's in trouble, brother. Needs an escort home." Without a word, the rest of the club climb on their bikes and ride to Highway 580 where Tig's being pursued by the Niners. They form a convoy to protect him as Jax hangs back to shoot at the Niners, killing the driver of the lead SUV. They manage to get away.

This incident reveals what loyalty means to SAMCRO, because everything about Tig's action is rotten. First, Clay wasn't shot by black assailants. He was shot by Opie, because Clay murdered his

Sons of Anarchy and Philosophy: Brains Before Bullets, First Edition.
Edited by George A. Dunn and Jason T. Eberl.
© 2013 John Wiley & Sons, Inc. Published 2013 by John Wiley & Sons, Inc.

father. Laroy and the Niners are entirely innocent of the killing. Second, the only reason Tig believes that the Niners are responsible is because Jax lied to the rest of the club in order to protect Opie against reprisal. Tig's attempt on Laroy's life is thus a case of completely misplaced loyalty, in aid of a murderer and inspired by a lie. Finally, Tig going after Laroy on his own is an utterly irresponsible action, not sanctioned by the rest of the club. It endangers the lives of all of the club's members and leads to several deaths. In retaliation for his daughter's death, the gangster Damon Pope murders Tig's daughter, Dawn, by burning her alive before her father's eyes. Later, Opie is brutally murdered in prison on Pope's orders.

Tig's call for help, then, is a call that by rights should be ignored. And yet it's clear that none of the facts listed above, even the disastrous consequences of coming to Tig's aid, would make any difference to the club's decision to help him. Jax, for example, knows the truth about the attempted killing of Clay, but still comes to Tig's aid. The bottom line is that, if another crew is chasing Tig, the members of SAMCRO will protect him. That's just what they do.

"What We *Are*"

Some philosophers are highly suspicious of loyalty, because they see it as focused on something higher than another person or group, such as a cause, an ideology, or a principle. That's how the American philosopher Josiah Royce (1855–1916) thinks of loyalty: "The willing and practical and thoroughgoing devotion of a person to a cause."[1] Understood this way, one could be loyal to the cause of restoring old Harleys to their former glory. Much more frighteningly, one could be loyal to a cause that's positively harmful, such as white supremacy— just think of the burning zeal in A.J. Weston's eyes. Such loyalty can be admirable, since it involves devotion to something other than oneself and hence goes beyond mere self-interest, but it doesn't seem to elicit the same kind of instant and powerful admiration as loyalty to another person or group, which is the sort of loyalty valued by members of SAMCRO.

Loyalty to another person or group could be based on any number of things, including friendship, family relationship, marital relationship, university affiliation, team fandom, or national citizenship. One could even be loyal to an entire species (if the elephants ever decide to take us on). According to philosopher Andrew Oldenquist, this sort of loyalty must be distinguished from mere devotion to an ideal:

> If I say that I ought to defend my country, I have a putative loyalty. But if I am willing to replace "my country" with, e.g., "a democratic country" or "a Christian country," I have not a loyalty but an ideal; in this case what I am committed to is a kind of thing, not some particular thing.[2]

In short, the members of SAMCRO aren't loyal just to the ideals embodied by their MC—a certain conception of masculinity or the outlaw biker lifestyle—but are loyal instead to SAMCRO itself.

Likewise, they aren't loyal to Tig just because he has certain qualities they admire—say, his skill as a mechanic or an assassin—but rather because they have a certain connection or relationship to him. Otherwise, they'd have no reason for preferring Tig to another person with the same or better qualities. To be loyal is to favor my friend or my club over another *equally good* person or club—or even a *better* person or club—just because they're *my* friend or club. Why should Jax and the rest be loyal to Tig? Because he's a "brother." By the same token, SAMCRO expects the Niners to be loyal to each other and not to members of SAMCRO.

In "Eureka," Tig checks into a hospital to get his leg stitched up after running off the road. Bobby Munson's old "Fat Boy" Harley had spewed smoke in his face while the club was on a gun run. When a nurse at the hospital tips off bail bond recovery agents about Tig, the bounty hunters kidnap him at gunpoint. Hearing what has happened, Chibs immediately declares, "We gotta go after him." Clay demurs: "We got a delivery to make." It's clear that the other members look upon Clay's decision to make the delivery before attempting a rescue as an act of disloyalty; any delay will make it harder to recover Tig from the bounty hunters. Jax, seething with contempt for Clay, calls for a vote, but Clay replies, "Vote all you want. I'm delivering the guns."

After Clay's arthritic hands fail him and his bike falls to the ground, he walks away dejectedly. Opie goes over to talk to him. "We gotta go get Tig," Opie tells him, adding that the power struggle between Clay and Jax is "pulling the focus from what we are." By "what we are" Opie clearly means a group that sticks together and looks out for its members before everything else. In the end, Opie tells Clay, "I'm with you either way," an expression of loyalty that seems to give Clay the opening he needs to do the right thing. Opie tells Jax that Clay "just needs to know we've got his back." When Clay eventually walks back and climbs on his bike, he says simply, "Let's go get Tig."

Opie is correct that Clay can see his way clear to doing what's right only when he's assured that the other members aren't abandoning him. When Clay believes that others are loyal to him, he can be loyal to them. More importantly, Opie's correct that this is what the club *is*. Without the brothers sticking up for each other, having each other's back, and coming to each other's aid, there is no SAMCRO. Running guns as a business is what the club *does*, but loyalty to fellow members is what the club *is*.

"Rats Deserve to Die"

If loyalty is the most important quality in a club member—more so than intelligence, skill in riding a Harley, or any other trait—and if loyalty is what makes the club a *club*, then disloyalty to fellow members is the most serious threat to its existence. To be disloyal is to turn one's back on fellow members or, worse, to turn against them. The very worst disloyalty is to side with law enforcement against the MC. Squealing to the authorities about the club's illegal activities makes you a "rat." The penalty for this kind of disloyalty is death.

In "Capybara," Bobby is picked up by ATF Agent June Stahl for the murder of Brenan Hefner, an Oakland Port Commissioner who became greedy and demanded extra money from the Real IRA to allow their gun shipments through the ports. Bobby had in fact killed Hefner; however, Opie was supposed to be the shooter. He froze up at the last second. When Opie misses the meeting to discuss Bobby's arrest, the other club members suspect that Opie was also picked up by Stahl and may even be in protective custody, working with the feds as an eye-witness against Bobby. After all, Opie recently spent five years in jail for arson, which almost destroyed his marriage, and he doesn't want to go back. It's common knowledge that Donna, his wife, wants him to leave SAMCRO. But Jax, refusing to believe that Opie has turned, correctly suspects that Stahl is just trying to make it look like he ratted them out. But incriminating information keeps coming to light. What is the club to make of the fact that Opie left voluntarily with the police in the middle of the night and was brought to a witness protection facility in Stockton? Or that a large amount of Opie's considerable debt has been paid off by a federal wire transfer? Jax continues to believe it's a set-up by Stahl, but when Clay pushes Jax, he replies that if it turns out that his lifelong friend really is a rat, "Then I'll kill him myself."

Of course, Opie is completely innocent and Stahl had indeed set him up. But after finding bugs that Stahl had put in Opie's phone and car, Tig reports that "Opie has turned on us." He later affirms, "Rats deserve to die. End of story" ("The Sleep of Babies"). It makes no difference that, earlier that day, Opie had actually saved Tig's life in a shoot-out with the Niners, a shoot-out Clay had deliberately organized to give Tig an opportunity to kill Opie without suspicion. Rats deserve to die. End of story.

Tig holds that it's completely justified to kill a disloyal member of the club who has become an informant to the authorities, even after this same member saves his life. Jax admits that he'd kill Opie in cold blood if he believed that Opie was disloyal to the club and had become a rat, despite Opie being his best friend. The bottom line is that the loyalty that makes the club what it is must be enforced, and only the most severe penalty will fit the crime of ratting. Ostracism from the club isn't enough. The only suitable punishment for informing against the club is death and, in the case of Opie, even the mere suspicion of disloyalty is enough to warrant an attempted execution—tragically resulting in the death of Opie's wife, Donna. This is the very dark part of the bond of loyalty that keeps SAMCRO together.

While SAMCRO's punishment for disloyalty is severe, some kind of sanction for disloyalty is required for any club or group to survive. Keep in mind that we're talking about disloyalty that actively harms other members, potentially sending them to prison and maybe even bringing an end to the club itself. This is much worse than merely failing to come to the aid of the group. Those who are disloyal in this way may also have to face the music, but, as long as they're not rats or don't join another club, the price of their disloyalty may only be the permanent blackening out of all their club tattoos and the loss of the club's leather cut. Such excommunication is the usual fate of disloyal individuals, whether a cheating husband or a fan cheering for the opposing team.

Can Loyalty Make Jax Do Bad Things?

If loyalty is understood as sticking up for and supporting fellow members of one's group *because* they are fellow members, then it may involve making sacrifices for them. That seems admirable. Nevertheless, some philosophers have worries about the ethical status of loyalty, since it seems that loyalty might also lead someone to do things that are immoral. There are three ways to address this problem.

First, there are philosophers who defend loyalty, but deny that there can be such a thing as bad or misplaced loyalty that leads to wrongdoing. If it's bad or misplaced, they say, it's not really loyalty. Let's see how they reach this conclusion.

The Greek philosopher Aristotle (384–322 BCE) argues that only someone who's virtuous—generous, just, brave, self-controlled, and so on—can truly be a friend. "Complete friendship," he writes, "is that of good people, those who are alike in their virtue."[3] Without virtue, you can't really be friends with anyone, since, he says, "Bad people do not enjoy each other's company unless there is some benefit in it for them."[4] If loyalty is a characteristic of friendship and friendship requires virtue, it seems to follow that only virtuous people can be genuinely loyal. Philosopher John Ladd explicitly defends this claim when he says, "A loyal Nazi is a contradiction in terms."[5] A "Nazi," according to Ladd, is thoroughly evil, insofar as he's devoted to killing off entire groups of innocent people. A morally bad but loyal person is a contradiction in terms.

If this view is right, then Tig's attempt to kill Laroy to avenge the attempt on Clay's life can't be an act of loyalty if Tig isn't a virtuous person. It's possible for him to perform a loyal act only if he's a good person. Now, some might argue that attempting to kill another person, even in retaliation, and recklessly killing an innocent person in the process are vicious acts in themselves. If so, it'll be difficult to make a case for this being an act of loyalty. Even Jax's act of coming to Tig's rescue may fail to be an act of loyalty. While defending someone from an attack isn't normally considered bad, Jax knows that Laroy and the Niners were innocent of Clay's shooting and that Tig's attack on them was unprovoked. Hence, Jax is coming to the aid of an aggressor, a guilty person, not someone who's innocent. It's hard to see that as virtuous. And, if loyalty requires virtue, it's equally hard to see it as an act of loyalty.

Given the behavior in which members of SAMCRO typically engage—gun-running, drug-muling, pornography, prostitution, and killing people who've betrayed them—it seems that, on this account, "a loyal SAMCRO club member" is as much of a contradiction in terms as "a loyal Nazi." Members of SAMCRO just aren't virtuous enough for any of the things they do for each other to count as acts of loyalty.

The second way to address the problem of the ethical status of loyalty is to argue that loyalty, far from being tied to virtue, is actually bad in itself. But given the high esteem in which loyalty is normally held, why would anyone think that?

The answer is that, to many philosophers, showing any sort of favoritism is the complete opposite of acting morally. As Marcia Baron says, "Moral reasoning and moral conduct demand that one be impartial, that one not play favorites."[6] However, to be loyal is to discriminate in favor of fellow members of one's group and against outsiders. Jax helps to rescue Tig and shoots a Niner simply because Tig is a member of his club and the Niner isn't. If Jax had been a Niner, he'd have been trying to kill Tig instead. It's as though Tig and Jax were members of the Hatfields and the Niners were the McCoys, fighting each other simply because they're bearers of their respective identities. This sort of skirmish is presumably why philosopher David Hume (1711–1776) thought that loyalty was a matter of "bigotry and superstition."[7] In his view, loyalty is bad in itself, because it's biased.

The third way to address the problem of loyalty's ethical status is to argue that loyalty often seems blind to the wrongdoing of those to whom one is loyal, at least when it's outsiders who are being wronged. Jax knows that Laroy and the Niners were innocent of Clay's shooting and that Tig's attack on them was unprovoked. Jax also knows that he's coming to the aid of an aggressor. But he doesn't care. Loyalty to a fellow member of the club means having his back and sticking up for him even when he's in the wrong.

The German philosopher Immanuel Kant (1724–1804) insists that the only quality that's unconditionally good—good no matter what—is acting from a "good will" or the commitment always to respect other people.[8] Every other quality is only conditionally good, since someone could have the good quality and still do wrong. Loyalty to a friend or group, for instance, could require you to lie, cheat, or even murder, all actions SAMCRO members are willing to perform for each other, even though they're morally wrong. Coming to Tig's aid and shooting one of the Niners might be just such a wrongful act motivated by loyalty. On this view, then, loyalty supports any kind of wrongdoing.

A Virtuous Escort?

Joseph Surface, a character in Richard Brinsley Sheridan's play *The School for Scandal*, complains about another character, "That fellow hasn't virtue enough to be faithful even to his own villainy."[9] The implication is that a person who remains loyal to something, no matter what, is better than a person who isn't loyal to anything at all. Truly evil people, it seems, lack loyalty. But this would make loyalty something good in itself and disloyalty something that's always bad. As philosopher R.E. Ewin claims, arguing against Ladd, "The question to consider is this: is a disloyal Nazi better than a loyal Nazi? There are problems in the Nazism, but is there anything wrong with the loyalty? A disloyal Nazi, after all, still has all the vices of Nazism and has added disloyalty to them ... it is yet another thing to be held against him and yet another reason for us not to trust him."[10] The point is that loyalty is something good in itself and disloyalty is something bad in itself, contrary to the accounts of loyalty sketched above.

With respect to the first account, there may indeed be misplaced or mistaken loyalty, but this may not make the loyalty itself bad. There's nothing bad about Tig's feeling guilty for having let down a brother, nor his wanting to help a brother. Such a motivation is a good one— an unselfish, other-directed, beneficent desire to help a fellow member of the club when he's in need. Tig's mistake is to believe that Clay is innocent of wrongdoing and that the Niners are guilty of an attack. Moreover, some might think that he acts wrongly in seeking retaliation. But his false beliefs and his seeking retaliation are distinct from his loyalty, since it's possible for Tig to remain loyal and have different beliefs and do things other than seek retaliation. So it's not necessary to say that only good people can be loyal. Instead, we should say that loyalty, which is always good, will always issue in rightful actions only if the loyal person is virtuous.

In reply to the second account of loyalty, it seems that there's nothing wrong with being partial to others because they're members of the same group as oneself. Indeed, it seems wrong *not* to be partial to one's friend, sister, husband, university, team, country, or even one's species. Problems arise only when partiality conflicts with something else that's ethically relevant. But there's nothing in itself wrong with partiality to members of one's own group. Jax *should* be loyal to Tig, rather than to a member of another club. But what if loyalty motivates someone to do something wrong? Once again, this isn't a problem with loyalty as such. There's nothing wrong with Jax's loyalty to Tig and there's nothing wrong with his coming to Tig's aid, so long as Jax doesn't do anything morally wrong in the process. Since loyalty itself doesn't require any particular act, it doesn't require an act of wrongdoing.

Does this make loyalty a virtue? No, because loyalty is only a motive or reason, and not a way of acting. But we can be fairly certain that Tig would agree that loyal brothers are good to have if you ever need an escort home.

Notes

1. Josiah Royce, *The Possibility of Loyalty* (New York: The MacMillan Company, 1908), 16–17.
2. Andrew Oldenquist, "Loyalties," *Journal of Philosophy* 79 (1982): 175.
3. Aristotle, *Nicomachean Ethics*, trans. Roger Crisp (Cambridge: Cambridge University Press, 2000), 147.
4. Ibid., 148.
5. John Ladd, "Loyalty," in *The Encyclopedia of Philosophy*, 2nd ed., ed. Donald M. Borchert (New York: Macmillan, 2006), 596.
6. Marcia Baron, *The Moral Status of Loyalty* (Dubuque, IA: Kendall/Hunt Publishing, 1984), 5.
7. David Hume, *A Treatise of Human Nature*, ed. David Fate Norton and Mary J. Norton (Oxford: Oxford University Press, 2000), 359.
8. Immanuel Kant, *Groundwork for the Metaphysics of Morals*, trans. Mary Gregor (Cambridge: Cambridge University Press, 1997), 7.
9. Richard Brinsley Sheridan, *The School for Scandal, in Sheridan's Comedies: The Rivals and The School for Scandal*, ed. Brander Matthews (Boston: Osgood, 1885), 217.
10. R.E. Ewin, "Loyalty and Virtues," *Philosophical Quarterly* 42 (1992): 418.

CHAPTER 4

A Saint among the Sons
Aquinas on Murder and the Men of Mayhem

Randall M. Jensen

He's sometimes called "the Dumb Ox" because of his size and his silence. His quite respectable family has arranged for him to move into an acceptable career, but he wants to wander the open roads instead, free from society's expectations. He encounters a somewhat disreputable organization of like-minded men and becomes a member of their group. Predictably, his horrified family isn't ready to let him go. Less predictably, they kidnap him and hold him captive for two years in an attempt to change his ways. He's stubborn, though, like an ox. He fights them off when they try to strip him of the uniform that defines his identity as a member, and he resists all their efforts to bend him to their will, including a botched attempt to seduce him with a prostitute that finally provokes him into a violent response.

Does this sound like a promising new prospect who'll impress the motorcycle club more by his bulk and determination than his brains? In fact, the Dumb Ox is Saint Thomas Aquinas (c. 1225–1274) and the "club" he joins against his family's protests is the Dominican Order of Friars.[1] Aquinas is one of the most important figures in the history of Western philosophy, as well as one of the chief architects of medieval Christian theology.[2] He's the author of the shelf-bending series of volumes entitled the *Summa Theologica*, which in its scope and structure makes John Teller's *The Life and Death of Sam Crow: How the Sons of Anarchy Lost Their Way* look like a mere pamphlet. Aquinas talks about nearly everything under the sun—and above

Sons of Anarchy and Philosophy: Brains Before Bullets, First Edition.
Edited by George A. Dunn and Jason T. Eberl.
© 2013 John Wiley & Sons, Inc. Published 2013 by John Wiley & Sons, Inc.

it, too—including a topic with which fans of *Sons of Anarchy* are all too familiar: homicide and murder.[3] So what would this robe-wearing medieval saint make of Charming's crew of patch-wearing Men of Mayhem?

Murder in Charming

Homicide and murder—these terms don't mean the same thing. Homicide is simply the killing of one human being by another human being. There are a couple of points we should bear in mind. First, not every death of a human being is a homicide. For instance, John Teller's death was a homicide only if another human being caused it, either Lowell Harlan Sr. through sabotage under Clay Morrow's orders or the driver of the semi that ran him off the road. Second, "homicide" is a morally neutral term. To call something a homicide doesn't necessarily imply that it's wrong or unjustified. If Wayne Unser, in the line of duty and as a last resort, kills an armed criminal threatening innocent lives, it would be a morally justified homicide.

"Murder," however, is *not* a morally neutral term. A first step toward a definition is simply to say that a murder is an unjustified homicide, though a homicide can be morally wrong without it being a murder, as with the legal category of "manslaughter." For example, if Abel had been killed when Gemma Morrow went off the road while driving high ("Toad's Wild Ride"), we might not accuse her of outright murder, though we'd readily condemn her for causing Abel's death. Her action was negligent and would be the cause of Abel's death, but it was not undertaken with the deliberate *intention* of causing Abel's death. Another example of a homicide that many, though not all, people wouldn't regard as murder is capital punishment. When Otto Delaney is finally executed for the murder of the Aryan Brotherhood member who attacked him in prison, Otto's death will be an intentional homicide, but most people wouldn't consider it a murder since the agent of his death is the state.

For Aquinas, murder is the private, intentional homicide of an innocent human being. Defined this way, murder is always wrong. We'll call this the Murder Principle. Aquinas believes it to be an objective moral principle, part of the natural law—a set of ethical principles rooted in human nature—that he sees as the required basis for any government's criminal law. An actual murder law legislated by a society is truly just only to the extent that it reflects this deeper moral principle. For example, if the League of American Nationalists were to gain political power and pass a law authorizing the lynching of innocent non-white persons, such a law would be a "perversion" of the natural law, since it violates the Murder Principle. Aquinas believes that the Murder Principle is given a divine mandate in the sixth commandment ("Thou shalt not commit murder"), but he insists that we can reason our way to its truth as well.

Aquinas begins this reasoning by arguing that it's usually fine for us to kill plants and nonhuman animals because they're meant to be food for us and "there is no sin in using a thing for the purpose for which it is."[4] That doesn't mean that cruelty to nonhuman animals is okay. The Dumb Ox wouldn't be any happier about the cruel treatment and casual disposal of dogs used for sport than Tig is, though Aquinas's objections are more concerned with the bad effect such a "sport" has on the moral character of the human beings involved than with the welfare of the victims. In any case, since none of the Sons are "vegan pussies" and the vegetarian prospect Half-Sack Epps is no longer with us, SAMCRO is good with Aquinas so far. For there to be a murder, both the perpetrator and victim must be human beings, because Aquinas believes that we can only murder members of a species of *rational* animals, whose capacity for intellectual thought and autonomous volition makes them members of the moral community.

To the class of those whom it's permissible to kill, Aquinas adds *sinners*, provided it's the proper authorities who kill them following proper legal procedures. Murder is the killing of an *innocent*. Before Tig Trager (undoubtedly the MC's most disturbingly experienced sinner) gets too nervous, what Aquinas means by a "sinner" in this context is someone who's committed a capital crime (such as murder or heresy). Just as sometimes we have to amputate a limb to save the whole body, so Aquinas reasons that we sometimes have to "cut off" a sinner to protect the whole community. Sinners are to be killed for the sake of the common good. Later, he adds, "by sinning man departs from the order of reason, and consequently falls away from the dignity of his manhood ... he falls into the slavish state of the beasts, by being disposed of according as he is useful to others."[5] In other words, an unrepentant sinner who commits a capital crime has removed himself from the moral community. This smoothes the way for the common good defense of capital punishment: for Aquinas, executing a murderer is not all that different from disposing of any other dangerous animal.

Up to this point the Sons might be nodding their heads. They often take life for the good of Charming or the MC. And they are certainly prone to seeing their enemies—whether external or internal to the club—as threats to be eliminated and sometimes as having lost whatever value or rights human beings normally possess.[6] Think of how they deal with a member who rats on the club. If you rat, you *become* a rat and thus a matter for the exterminator.

The Cop and the Outlaw

But *who* is entitled to take a life in defense of the common good? Aquinas firmly prohibits private individuals—even clerics!—taking justice into their own hands.[7] Only agents of the government may kill, so one way to commit homicide and escape a murder charge is through government work. Although the notion of a cleric with a license to kill reminds us more of *The Boondock Saints* than clergy in contemporary society—Fr. Kellen Ashby perhaps being a notable exception[8]— numerous familiar stories raise the issue of execution outside the law. Why does Aquinas rule it out? He returns to the amputation analogy. Just as it's fitting for a doctor to amputate a diseased limb, since he has the requisite expertise and authority, so it ought to be a public official, the presumed authoritative expert on such matters, who takes the life of a sinner. This seems to leave the Sons—a private organization rather than an arm of the state—without the legitimate authority to take a life.[9]

But let's look more closely at this analogy. Obviously, we'd prefer that a doctor amputate a limb that's got to go. We really hope Tara is around. But if she isn't available or if her hand is still busted, then surely we'll settle for Chibs or Gemma or whoever is handy—as long as it isn't Chuckie! What we have here is a reason to prefer the relevant authoritative expert if one is available, not a reason to prohibit any others from helping in the absence of such an expert. Why doesn't the same hold in the case of killing in defense of the common good? It'd be preferable, certainly, if the killing were done by some organized and knowledgeable body of folks with the public's trust. But what if that isn't going to happen? Wouldn't it be better for somebody else to step up than for these sinners—the diseased parts—to continue to threaten the health of the whole? And who better than SAMCRO, Charming's ever-vigilant benefactors?

Clay often presents the club as Charming's protectors, concerned to keep it from being overrun by outside gang members or by greedy developers. In "Fun Town," the club hunts for the man who raped Elliot Oswald's daughter and helps to serve up some justice. As Clay puts it, "People get jammed up in this town, they don't go to the cops. They come to us. And that means something to me." The ongoing deal Clay has struck with Unser is that the chief will help keep the club's illegal dealings on the down low as long as Clay makes sure that drugs and violence stay out of Charming. Isn't the common good more effectively protected by the club and the Charming PD working together? Can't the club sometimes find some justice when the cops aren't able or willing to do the job? We might reach this conclusion if we were a bit naive and had stopped watching *Sons of Anarchy* after the first few episodes. For as the show progresses it becomes ever clearer that Clay is no Robin Hood. Whatever concern Clay has for the good people of Charming is outweighed by his desire to make sure the town remains under his control and off the Feds' radar screen, so that the club's business (and Clay's bank accounts) can prosper. He even turns the hunt for the rapist into a ploy to gain leverage against Oswald. Like Clay's then-VP Jax Teller, we're skeptical of Clay's claim that "the leverage was just a fortunate by-product of my community spirit."

So we can't really defend the Sons from Aquinas's disapproval by appealing to the incompetence or corruption of law enforcement and depicting the club as defenders of Charming. But we can still question the distinction between governmental officials and private individuals that underlies Aquinas's argument. As the narrative of *Sons of Anarchy* develops, this distinction becomes more and more difficult to draw. At first, the basic conflict is between the Sons, the Mayans, and the Charming PD—two outlaw clubs and a local police force. Even here in the beginning, it's a bit murky who the good guys and the bad guys are. As fans of the show, should we root for Jax or Deputy Chief Hale, a true-blue "boy scout" cop? As the show takes off, though, the number of organized outlaw groups proliferates. SAMCRO turns out to be part of a much larger international SOA organization. Other outlaw and criminal organizations appear: the One-Niners, the Grim

Bastards, the Calaveras, the Wahewa tribe, the Nords, the League of American Nationalists, the Real IRA, the Galindo Cartel, the Lobos Sonora Cartel, the Lin Triad, and the Russian Mafia, not to mention the once shadowy figure of drug kingpin Damon Pope and his henchmen. The government agencies SAMCRO must contend with also multiply: the San Joaquin County Sheriff's Department, the ATF, the FBI, the DEA, a joint agency Task Force headed up by the very strange Lincoln Potter, and the CIA. The tiny town of Charming is the intersection of numerous hierarchically structured and rule-governed organizations. Some are run by the state, others are not. Can this difference bear the weight Aquinas needs to place on it? The show wants us to think it cannot.

While it's true that it becomes harder and harder to see the members of SAMCRO as the proverbial "white hats" in this tale, the same can be said of the law enforcement agencies in play. Early on, the two main federal players are Josh Kohn and June Stahl. Kohn is stalking Tara, who left Chicago to get away from him, and he's creating problems for SAMCRO largely because he resents Tara reviving her romance with Jax. Kohn eventually breaks into Tara's apartment, assaults her, and tries to rape her. Stahl is so ambitious and driven that she makes a play against the club that leads to the death of Opie Winston's wife, Donna, and in the end she frames and murders her own partner (and lover!) to save herself from being investigated for a bad shooting. Are we to take these individuals seriously as "doctors" of justice, empowered to judge who needs to be taken out for the good of the community? The show tempts us to see government agencies as just larger and more powerful bands of thugs. In this moral universe, it is difficult to agree that any significant moral authority comes with the badge.

In at least one instance, the distinction between state and non-state actors is impossible to draw. At the end of Season 4, we learn that the Galindo Cartel's leader Romeo Parada and his right-hand Luis Torres work for the CIA. We've watched these men supervise and get personally involved in some extremely violent operations, and we know they're moving large quantities of heroin into the US. They are the baddest of the bad. Their hands are dripping with blood and stained by ruined lives. Yet they function as part of the US government and are able to use the threat of a federal RICO prosecution to force Jax to do their bidding. So, are they members of a criminal cartel working for their own private interest or contractors working on behalf of the government for the public good?

In the world of *Sons of Anarchy*, the line between the wicked and the righteous—and between murder and the justified use of lethal force—is not the line between private citizen and agent of the state. We come to think of Unser and Jax as having a level of moral credibility and authority that Stahl and Clay don't, even though one is a cop and the other an outlaw. Unser and Jax don't abide by the state's rules any more than Stahl and Clay, but at least they have some level of concern for the well-being and rights of innocent people. We might even say they have a sense of justice, and that's more important in their world than having a badge. Tragically, though, even admirable characters like Jax and Unser end up compromised by the nearly impossible predicaments in which they find themselves.

God and "Mister Mayhem"

Watching *Sons of Anarchy* makes us increasingly suspicious of the moral authority of the state and its agents, who hardly seem like the competent "doctors" of Aquinas's amputation analogy. The word "anarchy" isn't in the show's title for nothing. But the fact that one argument for a view fails doesn't entail that the view is mistaken. Aquinas's deeper objection to private killing is *theological*. We can approach this objection by thinking about one of the problems that besets both public and private execution: the possibility of killing an innocent person by mistake. We don't want to be like Clay, who hastily orders a hit on Opie because he rushes to the conclusion that Opie's a rat. Part of why the amputation analogy has force is because a vigilante seems more likely to make this kind of mistake. Indeed, one of the most familiar current objections to capital punishment is that we might execute an innocent person in error, even if "due process" is faithfully and fairly carried out.

Aquinas believes that "God is the Lord of life and death, for by His decree both the sinful and the righteous die."[10] Because God gave us life, our lives are his to preserve or to take as he wishes. This means that God can't murder anyone, for he's entitled to take anyone's life under any circumstances. God is the Reaper, the genuine article. The idea that God could commit a murder is as nonsensical as the idea that I could steal my own wallet. God may even choose to wipe out most of humanity in a flood; that is his prerogative.

God may also use human beings as his agents and appoint them to carry out his orders. Since "the person by whose authority a thing is done really does the thing,"[11] if you are obeying God's orders to kill someone, the responsibility for the death doesn't rest on your shoulders but on God's. Thus, when God commands the Israelites to kill all the inhabitants of Canaan, the Israelites are morally in the clear because they do not do the killing. Rather God does the killing, acting through them.[12] By the same token, since Aquinas also regards the state as an instrument of God's will, the execution of Otto Delaney will really be an act of God rather than human beings. In a sense, anyone who takes it upon himself to kill without divine permission is committing murder. Only when acting under divine authority—as God's "Sergeant-at-Arms," so to speak—is a human being licensed to kill.

This theological justification of capital punishment means that Aquinas doesn't really need the amputation analogy. On his view, God is justified in killing anyone, even the innocent, and the same goes for God's executioners. Of course, Aquinas also has a stake in convincing us that the state acting under God's authority aims to kill only sinners and is best equipped—like the analogous physician—to determine who needs to be cut-off from the rest of the body politic. While God has the right to take the lives of innocent people, it would seem out of character for a good God to do so without some good reason, albeit perhaps one that is beyond our ken.

Most folks will balk at Aquinas's view of the divinely appointed state, some because they do not believe in God at all and others because they do not accept the idea that any human institution enjoys that kind of transcendent authority. Indeed, some of us may sympathize with the aspiration of Emma Goldman (1869–1940), as quoted in John Teller's journal in "Patch Over," to achieve "liberation from shackles and restraint of government" and deny that governments have any legitimate authority at all or at least no more than any other organized group of folks. But even if we accept the necessity of government, most of us are far too familiar with tales of governmental corruption throughout history and around the world to assume that every state acts with God's approval and authority. Watching a few seasons of *Sons of Anarchy* should disabuse us of that naive notion.

But then where does a state get its moral authority if it's not given from on high? Probably the most promising such story will involve the familiar idea of a *social contract*: the state's authority depends in some way on an agreement among its citizens.[13]

To Kill or To Be Killed: That Is the Question!

Suppose Jax's life is threatened. This does happen on occasion! Since he's not a cop or a soldier, is Jax entitled to kill in self-defense? Aquinas's answer is yes and no. In order to explain why, we need to talk about the last important element in the Murder Principle: *intention*. The short version of Aquinas's ambiguous answer is this: even though Jax is a private individual, he's morally permitted to kill in self-defense, but only as long as his *intention* is to save his own life, rather than to kill. Only agents of the state may *intend* to kill in defense of self or others. Aquinas explains this important distinction in a crucial passage:

> Nothing hinders one act from having two effects, only one of which is intended, while the other is beside the intention. Now moral acts take their species according to what is intended, and not according to what is beside the intention, since this is accidental as explained above. Accordingly the act of self-defense may have two effects, one is the saving of one's life, the other is the slaying of the aggressor.[14]

Jax sees an enemy about to fire at him but Jax shoots first. Is this morally acceptable? Yes, says Aquinas, if Jax's intent is to save his own life. No, if his intent is to kill his attacker. Let's figure out how this works.

I suspect the Sons and most of us are inclined to think that an enemy who launches an unjust attack *forfeits* his own right to life and is thus a legitimate target for *intentional* defensive violence. On this view, Jax would be able to point and shoot with no questions asked about his intentions. But Aquinas rejects this plausible forfeiture rationale for self-defense in the case of private individuals. On the other hand, when Aquinas says that the killing must not be *intended*, he isn't talking about a killing that's "pure accident," where the attacker's death is wholly unforeseen,[15] as might happen if Jax were cleaning his gun and it just happened to go off as a disgruntled banger stepped into the doorway to take out the Sons' VP. That also wouldn't count as a murder, but that's not what Aquinas is after here. The crucial idea is that Jax is allowed to defend himself even though he foresees that his attacker may die, as long as killing his attacker is just an unavoidable byproduct of his defensive action and not his intended objective.

Contemporary philosophers have articulated this idea as the Doctrine of Double Effect (DDE), the gist of which states that *it is sometimes morally permissible to bring about as a foreseen but unintended side-effect what one would not be permitted to bring about intentionally.*[16] Some philosophers call this side-effect an "indirect" intention, since it may seem strange to say that Jax doesn't in any way intend to kill his attacker when pulling the trigger on a gun aimed at his head. Others prefer to speak in terms of mere foreseeability without intention. Roughly, the idea is that you might know that something is going to happen (or is likely to happen) as a result of your action, but not *intend* for that thing to happen. Puzzling out the difference between what's *intended* and what's merely *foreseen* can be a tricky business, and whether it really matters is often controversial. After all, either way somebody is dead and it's no surprise to the killer.

One way to begin is to distinguish various elements in a person's action: her *end* (what she hopes to achieve), her *means* (how she plans to achieve it), and the *side effects* of her action (the various other things that may result that are neither her end nor her means). Some of these side-effects may be *unforeseen* while others are *foreseen*. The DDE then says that a homicide might be morally permissible if it's a foreseen side-effect of someone's action but neither the end nor the means—because, according to the DDE, an agent directly intends both her end and the means of achieving it. So if Jax's *end* is to save his own life by effectively stopping his attacker and the only effective *means* available to him is to fire his gun at the attacker, then Jax may be in the clear, since the attacker's death, while foreseen, is unintended.[17] But how do we know that? One way to determine whether Jax intended his attacker's death is to consider what he'd do if his first shot disabled his attacker non-fatally. As his assailant lies moaning in pain on the ground, does Jax call for an ambulance or put three more rounds in the guy's chest? If the former, then we can assume that killing his assailant was not his intention. If the latter, then Aquinas would definitely consider Jax a murderer.

This doctrine can be applied in various moral contexts. Aquinas believes that one of the human beings you may not kill is yourself. So is Juice Ortiz guilty of attempted murder because he tries to hang himself? As always, the answer depends on his intent. Juice's *end* is to avoid betraying his beloved club and his chosen *means* is to kill himself. So it looks like his attempted suicide is intentional and he's guilty of attempted self-murder. Could we see his death as a foreseen but unintended side-effect of his plan to avoid the pressure to inform and testify? That seems like a stretch. But imagine if Juice were to throw himself on a land mine to save his brothers in the episode "Call of Duty." We could ask the same question about that heroic act: would his death be a means of saving others or just a foreseen consequence of his action of throwing his body on the mine? In this case, his death really does appear to be only a side-effect. First, it's not Juice's death per se that saves his comrades, but rather his shielding them from the explosion. If, miraculously, Juice survived, his goal would still have been accomplished. Second, while the only way for Juice to save lives in the land mine case is to throw himself on top of it, there are other ways he could have avoided being a tool of the Feds.

Toward the end of Season 4, Opie discovers that Clay was not only responsible for the murder of Opie's wife, Donna, but has now also killed his father in cold blood. Unsurprisingly, Opie retaliates by shooting Clay, failing to kill him but landing him in the hospital on life-support. Meanwhile, Jax learns some things that supply him with reasons of his own to kill Clay—Clay also killed Jax's father and was responsible for an unsuccessful attempt on Tara's life. Tara gives Jax a syringe that'll do the job, but Jax doesn't follow through because it turns out that he needs Clay alive. Had he pushed that lethal dose into Clay's IV, however, Jax would have killed Clay intentionally. Jax's end would have been to kill and his means would have been the syringe.

But what if we change the example? Imagine now that it's Wayne Unser in the hospital, suffering terribly through the last stage of his cancer. Tara, as a virtuous physician, is compelled to do everything she can to ameliorate Unser's suffering, short of intentionally killing him. She administers the minimally effective amount of morphine to ease his suffering, but she knows that his death will be hastened because drugs like morphine depress the respiratory system. Unser's death is neither Tara's end nor her means, but simply a side-effect. The DDE explains why Tara's act of mercy might be morally permissible while Jax's act would definitely be murder, even though both are administering drugs that will contribute to a patient's death.

Murder Redux

Aquinas's Murder Principle condemns much of what the Sons do. They have no public authority, theologically sanctioned or otherwise, giving them a license to intentionally kill and very little of the killing they do is likely to be only foreseen but not intended. Nobody should be surprised that a traditional religious moralist like Aquinas and a band of outlaws aren't on the same page. However, Aquinas's *Summa* confronts us with many of the same questions as watching *Sons of Anarchy*. Who, if anyone, has the authority to sanction a killing? Is it always wrong to kill an innocent person? How far can we go to protect the common good or to save our own lives? All of these questions belong to the project of deciding to what extent SAMCRO's Men of Mayhem are emissaries of murder.[18]

Notes

1. G.K. Chesterton's *Saint Thomas Aquinas: The Dumb Ox* (New York: Doubleday, 1956), 19–65, is a very readable sketch of the saint's early life. I have taken certain liberties in creating a parallel here. The differences between the Dominicans and the Sons, and between Aquinas and a typical wearer of the Reaper, are numerous and obvious.
2. For readers interested in finding out more about Aquinas's thought, a good place to start is *The Cambridge Companion to Aquinas*, ed. Norman Kretzmann and Eleonore Stump (New York: Cambridge University Press, 1993).
3. St. Thomas Aquinas, *Summa Theologica* [*ST*], Second Part of the Second Part [IIa–IIae], Question 64. Most of the references that follow are to the several Articles that fall under this Question. The entirety of Question 64 is approximately a dozen pages long.
4. Ibid., Article 1.
5. Ibid., Article 2.
6. For more discussion of how to think about the Sons' relation to their enemies, see Chapter 9 by Alex Leveringhaus.
7. *ST* IIa–IIae, Question 64, Articles 3 and 4.

8. Although we don't witness Fr. Ashby killing someone by his own hand, he certainly condones the killing of Cameron Hayes right in front of him, and in a church no less!
9. For discussion of whether a private organization such as SAMCRO or only states may justifiably declare "war," see again Chapter 9 by Alex Leveringhaus.
10. *ST* IIa–IIae, Question 64, Article 6.
11. Ibid., Article 3.
12. See, for example, Deuteronomy 7:1–5 and 20:16–17.
13. For more on social contract theory, see Chapter 5 by George Dunn.
14. *ST* IIa–IIae, Question 64, Article 7.
15. Aquinas discusses accidental killings in Article 8 of Question 64.
16. One classic essay on the DDE is Philippa Foot's "The Problem of Abortion and the Doctrine of the Double Effect," *Oxford Review 5* (1967): 5–15. For a more recent, thorough analysis of DDE, see T.A. Cavanaugh, *Double-Effect Reasoning: Doing Good and Avoiding Evil* (New York: Oxford University Press, 2006).
17. I say "may be" because the DDE comes with a list of further conditions that must be met if one's action is to be morally justified. For example, the end must be sufficiently important and the means must not be inherently immoral. Jax can't casually run somebody off the road while in a hurry and get off the hook because he didn't plan to do it, nor can he torture someone under any circumstances, no matter what he does or doesn't intend.
18. I would like to thank George Dunn, Jason Eberl, and Bill Irwin for their very helpful comments on this chapter.

Part II

"OFF THE SOCIAL GRID"
THE POLITICS OF MAYHEM

CHAPTER 5

SAMCRO versus the Leviathan
Laying Down the (Motor)Cycle of Violence

George A. Dunn

What went wrong?

That's the question that John Teller weighs as he composes his memoir *The Life and Death of Sam Crow: How the Sons of Anarchy Lost Their Way*. It's the question Jax Teller broods over as he reads his father's manuscript, imbibes J.T.'s original vision, and then, looking to what his father's club has become, judges, "It's just fear and greed now" ("Out"). It's a question that most thoughtful viewers of *Sons of Anarchy* have probably pondered as well. And it's a question that we can perhaps answer—with a little help from some great philosophers.

"Off the Social Grid"

J.T.'s anarchist ideal of "living off the social grid" is based on the optimistic assumption that human beings can live together peacefully without any coercive external authority keeping us in line. That would be a reasonable expectation if it were true that human nature is basically good and we were all naturally inclined to cooperate with each other. What does philosophy have to say about this question? Is human nature basically naughty or nice? Unfortunately, philosophers find it about as easy to reach an agreement about human nature as Jax and his father-in-law Clay Morrow find it to reach an agreement

Sons of Anarchy and Philosophy: Brains Before Bullets, First Edition.
Edited by George A. Dunn and Jason T. Eberl.
© 2013 John Wiley & Sons, Inc. Published 2013 by John Wiley & Sons, Inc.

about, well, anything. One reason why the debate is still going strong after thousands of years is that the evidence on either side is so ambiguous and inconclusive.

Proponents of the essential goodness of human nature like to highlight our capacity to be moved by sympathy for the plight of others, a capacity that is said to be present within virtually all human beings to some degree. Even a remorseless killer like Tig Trager is deeply disturbed by the animal cruelty he witnesses at Dante's hellish dogfight ("J'ai Obtenu Cette"). If sympathy for the suffering of others is present even in someone like Tig, who's hardly a model of moral rectitude, then there's good reason to expect to find it in every human heart, even if it's wedged in alongside some other less wholesome attributes. The ancient Chinese philosopher Mengzi (c. 372–289 BCE)—often referred to in the West by the Latinized form of his name, Mencius—believed that our natural sympathy was the seed from which full-fledged moral goodness invariably sprouts, as long as nothing prevents it from maturing in the right way. "Human nature's being good is like water flowing downward," he waxed optimistically. "There is no human who does not tend toward goodness."[1] When this natural tendency to goodness doesn't blossom in a virtuous adult personality, Mengzi believes that a poor upbringing is the most likely culprit. "What kind of nasty shit did your momma do to you?" Clay Morrow asks in dismay at the depths of Tig's cold-bloodedness ("Pilot"). Mengzi, whom legend says was raised by a perfect jewel of a mother, would probably share Clay's suspicions that something must have been seriously amiss in the Trager household for someone with as much natural sympathy as Tig to have turned out so twisted.

Mengzi's optimistic view of human nature was echoed in the modern world by a couple of the most influential Western philosophers, the Scotsman David Hume (1711–1776) and the Swiss Jean-Jacques Rousseau (1712–1778). Like Mengzi, Hume believed that our natural sympathy was the ultimate source of human morality and, since sympathy is present to some degree in everyone, so too are the seeds of moral goodness. Rousseau, who sought asylum at Hume's home in England while on the run from persecutors who had driven him out of France for his unorthodox views, was in substantial agreement with the Scotsman on this and many other matters, though curiously the two them got along about as well as Tig and Herman Kozik. As with the bad blood between Tig and Kozik, there appears to have been a dog involved.[2]

Rousseau is an extraordinary figure in the history of philosophy—and not just because of his remarkable knack for antagonizing even the legendarily good-natured Hume, in addition to just about everyone who had the misfortune of spending much time in his company. The *enfant terrible* of the Enlightenment, Rousseau was in many ways a forerunner of the hippie/anarchist movement that captured the imagination of young John Teller after his return from Vietnam. Whatever Rousseau's personal failings may have been, he had a flair for composing stirring aphorisms such as: "Man is born free, and everywhere he is in chains. He who believes himself the master of others does not escape being more of a slave than they."[3] We can't know if J.T. ever came across these famous words from the opening paragraph of Rousseau's book *On the Social Contract*, but we can be sure that they would have resonated deeply in his rebellious soul if he'd found them scrawled on a rock wall in the Nevada desert.

According to Rousseau, human beings are naturally free, but find themselves in chains forged by the oppressive institutions of society. Moreover, human beings have no natural incentives to vices like greed, envy, or spite. We pick up these moral pathogens from being raised in a society that twists our naturally healthy inclinations toward freedom and happiness into a toxic desire to dominate and outshine others. Rousseau was much more articulate at diagnosing the problem than he was at prescribing a workable remedy. But there's a direct line that runs from his writings to the aspirations of the hippie movement of the 1960s that apparently shaped John Teller's original vision of the Sons of Anarchy: drop out, "move off the social grid," and get back to nature—not just the wild nature of the majestic redwood forests through which the First 9 cruised as they rode their bikes along Pacific Coastal Highway 101, but also the original innocence of a human nature that had been damaged by the values of a corrupt society.

"Not Violent by Nature"

Other philosophers haven't been nearly as sanguine about human nature. The Englishman John Stuart Mill (1806–1873), for instance, was highly suspicious of the rosy picture of natural human goodness painted by Rousseau and his many acolytes in the Romantic movement.

Mill accused these proto-hippie philosophers of "exalt[ing] instinct at the expense of reason," so that "almost every variety of unreflecting and uncalculating impulse receives a kind of consecration," with the sole exception of those few orderly inclinations that are the result of good habits acquired from living in society.[4] Reading Mill on the dangers of following our natural instincts conjures up visions of life as one long and extremely debauched patch-over party, interrupted every so often for some random gunplay and an occasional gratuitous act of homicide. Given his view that our natural impulses would feel most at home in an MC clubhouse on a Saturday night, Mill concludes that "nearly every respectable attribute of humanity is the result not of instinct, but of a victory over instinct."[5] The ancient Chinese philosopher Xunzi (312–230 BCE) held a similar view, comparing the cultivation of virtue to the forced bending of a plank of wood into a wheel. Goodness isn't a spontaneous natural result of "letting go," but a product of human civilization and artifice.

When young J.T. founded the Sons of Anarchy, he was stepping into the middle of this ancient debate and declaring himself on the side of Rousseau's hippie progeny. In fact, if Gemma Teller's characterization of him is at all accurate, J.T. was a committed, freak-flag-waving member of the Rousseauist cult, with his vision of the club as a "hippie-biker commune." But, as he poignantly records in his memoir, chucking aside society's rules and regulations in order to enjoy a life of freedom didn't result in a blossoming of their suppressed natural goodness. To the contrary, with each passing year the club found itself more deeply embroiled in violence against its external enemies, while experiencing within its own ranks a steady erosion of the trust necessary to sustain it as a community. Writing in his memoirs, J.T. ponders what went wrong:

> Most of us were not violent by nature. We all had our problems with authority, but none of us were sociopaths. We came to realize that when you move your life off the social grid, you give up the safety that society provides. On the fringe, blood and bullets are the rule of law and, if you're a man with convictions, violence is inevitable. ("Seeds")

The problem, as J.T. considers it in retrospect, wasn't what John Stuart Mill might diagnose it as—it wasn't as though the club members had naturally violent and sociopathic tendencies that started rising to the surface once the iron fist of civilization was no longer there to smack them down. Rather, there was something about the circumstances in which they found themselves—operating "off the social grid" and outside the protection of society—that required them to act that way.

In other words, J.T. discovered that, contrary to Mill, the causes of human violence and destructiveness might have nothing to do with some innate "badness" of human nature, such as a natural tendency to sociopathy that requires the intervention of society to stanch. On the other hand, J.T. came to recognize that, contrary to Rousseau, there isn't some cherubic natural goodness waiting to surge up from nature's primal depths once we've broken free of all of society's "unnatural" institutions and customs. The truth is that we have a variety of natural impulses, some of which can foster conflict, while others incline us to cooperate in peace. Along theses lines, the English philosopher Thomas Hobbes (1588–1679) believed that the causes of violence should be sought not in human natural impulses per se, but rather in a certain insidious social logic that can turn even those who are "not violent by nature" into killers.

Although Rousseau and his successors may have supplied J.T. with his vision for SAMCRO as a community dedicated to freedom from stultifying social conventions and institutions, it may be Hobbes who can best explain how the Sons of Anarchy lost their way and why their fall into violence was, as J.T. describes it, "inevitable."

"Nasty, Brutish, and Short"

Philosophers typically distinguish what happens according to nature from what results from arbitrary and changeable human conventions or customs. That teenage Jax was attracted to teenage Tara Knowles (and vice versa) was the result of a natural upsurge of adolescent hormones, but that these lovebirds later acquire marital status after exchanging rings and vows in Nero Padilla's brothel is conventional—despite the decidedly unconventional wedding venue! When Jax tells Tara that he intends to "make an honest woman out of you," his language is a bit misleading, since their natural feelings toward each other are already as honest or genuine as can be. What he sets out to change is Tara's legal status, which requires complying with certain conventional procedures, such as obtaining a marriage certificate and finding someone with the legal authority to perform the ceremony—and, lucky for them, Nero's regular clientele includes a local judge ("Authority Vested").

There's long been a tendency to elevate the natural above the conventional, on the assumption that there's a tacit wisdom in the natural ordering of things that we'd all do well to heed. Of course, respect for nature doesn't require disdain for convention. Even conventional institutions like marriage have often been justified by claiming that they somehow fulfill nature's intentions. But there's a more radical view according to which the relationship between nature and convention is more like the asymmetrical conflict between SAMCRO and the US Attorney's Office, with tight-assed social convention seeking to suppress wild nature, while nature aspires only to be free. John Teller adopted this view from the anarchist Emma Goldman (1869–1940). In a passage that J.T. first encountered painted in red on a wall near the Nevada border, she writes:

> Anarchism stands for liberation of the human mind from the dominion of religion; the liberation of the human body from the dominion of property; liberation from shackles and restraint of government. It stands for social order based on the free grouping of individuals.[6]

Religion, property, and government—all conventional institutions that impose hierarchies and enforce inequality. Both Teller and Goldman oppose them in the name of our natural state of freedom.

But what would human life be like if we really did toss off all these social hierarchies in order to confront each other as free and equal in the state of nature? What if Mayor Jacob Hale had no more political clout than the lowliest fluffer at Cara Cara and Elliot Oswald had no more legal claim to his ranch than the mysterious homeless woman who's always crossing paths with Jax and Gemma? Far from sharing the optimistic expectations of Goldman and the young J.T., Hobbes believes that in such a world human beings wouldn't naturally congregate in happy-go-lucky hippie communes, living side-by-side peacefully. To the contrary, open warfare would be the norm and our lives would become—much like Piney Winston's ex-wife—"solitary, poor, nasty, brutish, and short."[7] This isn't because human beings are naturally bellicose or bloodthirsty, but rather because we're rational and in the state of nature there are powerful incentives to violence that no rational person can afford to ignore.

Hobbes arrives at his conclusion by way of some fairly minimal assumptions about human nature. To start with, we're all interested in protecting our own lives and the lives of those dear to us. Much of the violence the members of SAMCRO commit is motivated by nothing more than this primal instinct to protect oneself and one's "family" from harm. When Clay dispatches Happy Lowman and Tig to kill the teenage girl who witnessed Bobby Munson's murder of Brenan Hefner ("The Revelator") or when Juice Ortiz kills Eric Miles, after he caught Juice with a stolen brick of cocaine ("With an X"), their motives fall into this category. Hobbes also notes that by nature we tend to be covetous of other people's "stuff," another potent cause of conflict. Georgie Caruso wants to steal Luanne Delaney's performers, the Mayans want a cut of SAMCRO's gun business and would like to elbow their way into One-Niner and Lin Triad turf, and Ima wants to take Tara's man. Finally, Hobbes observes that we're concerned about the opinion others hold of us—maybe sometimes a bit *too* concerned for our own good. SAMCRO realizes what a liability it is to appear weak to its rivals and, when some poor slob has the temerity to sit on Jax's bike, Jax can't permit such an egregious show of disrespect to go unpunished ("Patch Over").

From these minimal but universal facts about human nature, Hobbes deduces what he calls the "three principle causes of quarrel," which at least in some circumstances provide us with powerful incentives to commit acts of violence. These causes are:

> first, competition; secondly, diffidence [fear]; thirdly, glory. The first maketh men invade for gain; the second, for safety; and the third, reputation. The first use violence to make themselves masters of other men's persons, wives, children, and cattle; the second, to defend them; the third, for trifles, as a word, a smile, a different opinion, and any other sign of undervalue, either direct in their persons, or by reflection in their kindred, their friends, their nation, their profession, or their name.[8]

Or, we might add, in their MC. However, Hobbes never claims that these facets of human nature automatically spur us to violence in all circumstances. In fact, he notes that an overriding concern for self-preservation may also serve as a powerful incentive to seek *peace*. Jax's eagerness to extricate SAMCRO from its perilous involvement with the Galindo Cartel and the Real IRA is motivated by his desire to preserve himself, his club, and his family. Hobbes is aware that human nature provides us with as many incentives to make peace as it does to make war, but which incentives come to dominate depends on the social environment in which we operate. Our nature is neither inherently good nor inherently bad, but there are certain situations that tend to bring out the worst in us, as J.T. learned from his experiences with SAMCRO.

"We All Want the Same Thing Here"

What sort of situation brings out the worst in us, according to Hobbes? Ironically, it's precisely the sort of situation on which the young anarchist J.T. pinned his greatest hopes: one in which we have broken the chains of all those procrustean institutions and conventions—governments, laws, property, and hierarchies of every sort—that force naturally free and equal human beings into the unnatural shape of obedient citizens of the state. For Hobbes, it's precisely when we are enjoying our natural condition of freedom and equality that violent conflict becomes practically inevitable, while the imposition of unnatural hierarchies and restraints makes it possible for us to live in peace.

Let's consider *competition*, the first of Hobbes's three causes of quarrel. According to Hobbes, the real culprit here isn't so much our natural covetousness that inevitably causes us to desire many of the same things that other people want or even already have, but rather the explosive cocktail—worthy of a master arsonist like Opie Winston—that results from the combination of our natural covetousness with our natural equality. To understand why, we need to appreciate precisely what our natural equality means to Hobbes. It's not just that we're naturally endowed with equal rights, though that's something he strongly affirms. Indeed, he even goes so far as to say that we all enjoy the same natural right to do whatever we see fit. It's not hard to see how taking equality to such an extreme might cause problems, but even that's not the most worrisome aspect of our natural equality, according to Hobbes.

The big problem is that we are all more or less equally *deadly*. That may seem counter-intuitive, since a veteran assassin like Happy seems much more lethal than a tiny wisp of a girl like Cherry (née Rita Zambell). But try telling that to Cherry's abusive husband, who might have ended up as a pile of cinders had he been in his condo when his furious firecracker of a wife burned it to the ground. If even a wee thing like Cherry can cause that much destruction, then it's never possible to predict with certainty who will emerge as the victor when any two individuals find themselves in competition with each other. With an unflinching bluntness, Hobbes lays out the fatal consequences of this predicament arising from our natural equality:

> From this equality of ability ariseth equality of hope in the attaining of our ends. And therefore if any two men desire the same thing, which nevertheless they cannot both enjoy, they become enemies; and in the way to their end (which is principally their own conservation, and sometimes their delectation only) endeavour to destroy or subdue one another. And from hence it comes to pass that where an invader hath no more to fear than another man's single power, if one plant, sow, build, or possess a convenient seat, others may probably be expected to come prepared with forces united to dispossess and deprive him, not only of the fruit of his labour, but also of his life or liberty.[9]

This is a lesson that SAMCRO has learned the hard way on several occasions, such as when the Mayans blow up their warehouse and steal their guns ("Pilot"), when the Mayans later ambush them during a meet with the One-Niners ("Small Tears"), and when, most recently, a meet with the Irish and the Galindo Cartel goes south and turns into an armed robbery ("Darthy"). "We all want the same thing here!" screams Jax into the escalating heat of this last debacle, perhaps unaware that this may be precisely the root of the problem.

In a world where we where know that others not only have designs on our things but also an excellent chance of obtaining them if we're not sufficiently vigilant, the second of Hobbes's three causes of quarrel kicks in with a vengeance: *diffidence* or *fear*. Needless to say, for the members of an outlaw motorcycle club like SAMCRO, fear will never take the form of shaking and quaking in their boots—or, in Jax's case, in his blindingly white tennis shoes! Rather, the recognition of a serious threat will prompt preemptive action to neutralize the danger. When LOAN shows up in Charming, one of the first things Clay does is to strut into Ethan Zobelle's Impeccable Smokes cigar shop to deliver an intimidating demand for protection money ("Smite"). An even wiser course of action would have been simply to eliminate Zobelle and his cronies without warning in a quick preemptive strike that would have spared the club a great deal of subsequent grief. For Hobbes, the logic of such a first strike can't be denied, given his assumption that as rational actors our chief priority ought to be our own self-preservation. But what makes this logic so cruel and unforgiving is the fact that both our present and potential enemies are doing the same math and, if they're at all sensible, are gearing up for a first strike against us. In a state of anarchy, where everyone is free and equal, each and every one of us poses a constant mortal threat to everyone else.

"Retaliation Must Be Harsh and Immediate"

Once again, Hobbes's point is *not* that human beings are naturally violent, but rather that violence has its own unrelenting logic that explains why it is that, in the words of J.T.'s manuscript, once "you give up the safety that society provides ... violence is inevitable." But perhaps there's a way for us to reduce the risk of being targets for violence in the first place and thereby reduce the necessity of having to resort to a preemptive strike in order to protect ourselves. If a club like SAMCRO can send a credible message to its enemies that it's not only strong enough to survive whatever gets thrown its way but also has the muscle and determination to deliver a devastating retaliatory strike, then that can serve as an effective deterrent against attack. Of course, everything depends on the credibility of the threat of retaliation, which brings us to the third of Hobbes's three causes of quarrel: *glory* or *reputation*.

When Ethan Zobelle's LOAN demonstrates its reach by enlisting members of the Aryan Brotherhood to attack Otto Delaney in Stockton State Prison, Clay convenes a meeting in the chapel to discuss the club's response. "If we don't act now it will be a sign of weakness," he warns the MC. "They'll do it again." A failure to exact retribution will saddle SAMCRO with the ruinous reputation of being a club that can be kicked around with impunity, which only invites more attacks. Consequently, Clay insists, "Retaliation must be harsh and immediate. That's what we do. It's what we've always done." Jax agrees with Clay on all counts—"retaliation is undisputable," he chimes—with the sole exception of the timetable. Prudence dictates that SAMCRO delays retaliation until they better understand Zobelle's game. To act blindly would be courting disaster, but it would be equally disastrous to forego retaliation all together ("Smite").

Significantly, this same episode features a voiceover from J.T., in which he talks about the spiritual toll that the necessity of retaliation had taken on him and laments his "absence of basic human graces. The most obvious was forgiveness. If I was wronged, by anyone, in or out of the club, I had to be compensated—money or blood. There was no turning the other cheek" ("Smite"). It's unclear, however, whether J.T. fully appreciates the extent to which the option of "turning the other cheek" is a luxury that only those who don't live in a state of anarchy can afford to indulge.

Yet another problem with retaliation is that rather than settling scores once and for all, it to tends to fuel a cycle of violence that often spirals out of control. Tig seeks revenge against Laroy Wayne, whom he mistakenly holds responsible for an attempt on the life of Clay, but ends up accidentally killing Veronica Pope, the daughter of Oakland crime lord Damon Pope ("To Be, Act 1"). Himself not one to turn the other cheek, Pope has Tig's daughter Dawn Trager burnt to death before her father's horrified eyes ("Sovereign") and then insists on the life of a Son—which tragically turns out to be Opie—as further recompense for his loss ("Laying Pipe"). In due course, Jax and the Sons exact their revenge on all those responsible for Opie's death: first, Macky, the county jail officer who arranged the attack in which Opie was killed ("Small World"), then T.O. Cross's cousin Randall Hightower, the inmate who delivered the killing blow ("Crucifixed"), and finally Pope himself ("J'ai Obtenu Cette"). Whether the cycle of retaliations is now over remains to be seen. And let's not forget that this whole bloodbath was launched by Opie's attack on Clay in an attempt to avenge the killing of Piney. If retaliation is supposed to be a deterrent to violence, then it seems to get the job done about as reliably as Bobby's old, smoke-sputtering "fat boy" motorcycle on a charity/gun-running outing ("Eureka").

Sons of Anarchy/Sons of Pride

The logic of violence that Hobbes describes pertains to life in the state of anarchy, where everyone, being free and equal, is a mortal threat to everyone else. The only way to escape this logic is to move back onto the social grid, surrendering at least some of our natural freedom in exchange for the security we gain from submitting ourselves to some overarching public authority, as conventional and arbitrary as it must seem in comparison to our natural state. Hobbes's term for this supreme governmental authority is the Leviathan, a name he borrowed from the biblical book of Job, where it refers to a terrible sea monster described as "king over all the Sons of Pride."[10]

From Hobbes's point of view, J.T. was a Son of Pride before he was a Son of Anarchy, for it was pride that planted in his mind that reckless aspiration for "liberation from shackles and restraint of government." The humbling lesson he should have taken from his failed experiment in anarchism isn't that human nature is just too incorrigibly corrupt to measure up to the demands of life "off the social grid," but rather that what such a life demands is that even those who aren't "violent by nature" must submit to the logic of violence inherent in the state of anarchy.[11]

Notes

1. *Mengzi: With Selections from Traditional Commentaries*, trans. Bryan W. Van Norden, (Indianapolis: Hackett Publishing Co., 2008), 144.

2. For an account of the quarrel between Hume and Rousseau, see David Edmunds and John Eidinow, *Rousseau's Dog: Two Great Thinkers at War in the Age of Enlightenment* (New York: Harper Perennial, 2007). Rousseau's dog Sultan may have actually been more of an innocent bystander than a precipitator of the troubles.

3. Jean-Jacques Rousseau, *The Basic Political Writings*, trans. Donald Cress (Indianapolis: Hackett Publishing Co., 1987), 141.

4. John Stuart Mill, *Nature, The Utility of Religion, and Theism* (London: Longman, 1885), 46.

5. Ibid.

6. Emma Goldman, *Anarchism and Other Essays* (New York: Mother Earth Publishing, 1917), 68.

7. Thomas Hobbes, *Leviathan: With Selected Variants from the Latin Edition of 1668* (Indianapolis: Hackett Publishing Co., 1994), 76.

8. Ibid.

9. Ibid., 75.

10. Job 41:34.

11. For a more positive assessment of anarchism, see Chapter 7 by Bruno de Brito Serra.

CHAPTER 6

"The Rat Prince" and *The Prince*

The Machiavellian Politics of the MC

Timothy M. Dale and Joseph J. Foy

In the final minutes of the Season 3 finale of *Sons of Anarchy*, it appears that Jax Teller has betrayed the MC to ATF Agent June Stahl and lived up to the nickname she has for him: "The Rat Prince." But it's actually a set-up to reduce the jail time for SAMCRO members headed to prison and to kill Agent Stahl and IRA leader Jimmy O. Jax's plan is cunning and manipulative: he deceives his enemies and violently retaliates against those who sought the downfall of SAMCRO.

The Italian political philosopher Niccolò Machiavelli (1469–1527) would have been impressed, having famously argued in his handbook on political leadership, *The Prince*, that a virtuous "prince"—his term for the head of a state—needs to be capable of both violence and deception.[1] Much like Jax, Machiavelli's prince is prepared to betray his enemies—and even his allies—in order to maintain and augment his power. The foremost objective of all politics, according to Machiavelli, is the successful use of power. Good political decisions are those that help to maintain control and stabilize the political structure the prince has put in place.

The political structure of a motorcycle club serves many purposes. First and foremost, it encourages solidarity—friendship, camaraderie, and belonging. A spirit of rebellion is also at the heart of an MC. The motorcycle liberates its rider from life's humdrum complications, releasing him onto the open road where the ordinary structures of

Sons of Anarchy and Philosophy: Brains Before Bullets, First Edition.
Edited by George A. Dunn and Jason T. Eberl.
© 2013 John Wiley & Sons, Inc. Published 2013 by John Wiley & Sons, Inc.

domination dissolve into the same blur as the scenery that whizzes by in his peripheral vision. In short, the MC is a refuge from the oppressive order of society, offering its members a source of meaning in the freedom that the club provides. Ironically, however, though the club calls itself the Sons of *Anarchy*, a term that implies the rejection of authority, the MC is itself a system of authority, in which, in line with Machiavelli's recommendations, both guile and force are used to protect the freedom and solidarity of its members.[2] It would seem then that manipulation and violence in the service of acquiring and maintaining power could be a good thing, even when used by a club founded on the rejection of authority.

Another irony of establishing a motorcycle club reflects the central problem of all political institutions. Though they're founded to establish order, the manipulation and violence they require mean that they also tend toward corruption and disorder. This tension between order and disorder is on stark display in SAMCRO. While the MC provides protection and a variety of other services for its members and the town of Charming, it also participates in some rather unsavory activities that have brought violence and destruction to its community. This club, established for camaraderie, harmony, and survival, is also responsible for a lot of isolation, conflict, and death. The lesson seems to be that while manipulation and force are necessary for gaining and maintaining power, they can also generate a great deal of suffering, especially when power is pursued solely for its own sake.

"True Freedom Requires Sacrifice and Pain"

One of the most important characters in *Sons of Anarchy* isn't even alive. John Thomas "J.T." Teller, one of the First 9 who founded SAMCRO, appears only through the book he wrote before he died: *The Life and Death of Sam Crow: How the Sons of Anarchy Lost Their Way*. Along with Piney Winston, J.T. formed SAMCRO after returning from military service in Vietnam. Disillusioned with authority, he was strongly attracted to the idea of anarchism. In "Patch Over," Jax reads about his father's discovery of anarchist political philosophy and the alluring promise of authentic freedom that he tried to implement with SAMCRO. But J.T. also jotted down some serious misgivings that he was to later have about the project he had undertaken:

The concept [of anarchism] was pure, simple, true, it inspired me, lit a rebellious fire, but ultimately I learned the lesson that Goldman, Proudhon, and the others learned. That true freedom requires sacrifice and pain. Most human beings only think they want freedom. In truth they yearn for the bondage of social order, rigid laws, materialism, the only freedom man really wants, is the freedom to become comfortable.

As J.T. realized, founding a club to pursue freedom will inevitably require sacrifice and pain as one confronts a social order committed to keeping everyone in bondage. And, as J.T. also learned, one by-product of the fight for freedom may be the creation of conditions under which violence and corruption can get a foothold.

Machiavelli also understood the dangers of creating a social order. In *The Prince*—his manual for those who aspire to power, as well as those who have power and want to hang on to it—he advises that one must be both a "lion and a fox," capable of both violence and deception. You can flatter and bestow favors all you like, but at the end of the day human beings respond most dependably to violence and intimidation.

Machiavelli's promotion of violence and deception has led to the widespread use of the term "Machiavellian" to refer to ruthless and underhanded scheming, often in the pursuit of purely selfish ends. This is an overly simplistic characterization, however, as simplistic as it would be to say that the members of SAMCRO are all nothing more than immoral criminals. Just as SAMCRO often contributes positively to the community, Machiavellian ruthlessness can also serve a greater good. Consider how Ethan Zobelle, a leader in the League of American Nationalists, uses the term in the episode "Fix," as he explains to Deputy Chief David Hale why he's prepared to flood Charming with drugs in order to undermine the public's tolerance of SAMCRO as the town's self-appointed "protectors":

I understand your anger. And I know you think I'm some kind of devil. For years, I sat back and watched everything I love about this country slowly unravel. Faith, values, morals, decency. It culminated two years ago when my wife was killed in a drive-by. That blood got me off the sidelines and into the game. Now, if that makes me a vigilante, a Machiavellian fool, so be it.

The kindest thing we could say about Zobelle is that he's misguided, but he does nonetheless seem to be genuinely concerned about the erosion of "faith, values, morals, decency" that he perceives in society. His Machiavellianism is, therefore, in the service of what he regards as a greater good.

For Machiavelli, the greatest good is the sustained success and stability of a political regime, for he believes that only under a stable regime will most people be able to live good, decent, productive lives. Similarly, the principle good for the members of SAMCRO is the survival and flourishing of the MC. And, in fact, from Machiavelli's perspective an MC and political regime really aren't that different, for he wrote at a time when governments dealt with each other in pretty much the same way that rival criminal gangs operate today. In Renaissance Italy, rival city-states like Venice, Genoa, Florence, Siena, and Lucca were constantly jousting with each other on trade and diplomatic issues, when they weren't engaged in outright hostilities. Like the Mayans, the One-Niners, and the Sons of Anarchy, Italy's rival city-states found it hard to resist the temptation to encroach on each other's territory. Predictably, they entered into many fragile, short-term alliances that often ended in betrayal. Internal political turmoil was another constant in the lives of these city-states. The most tumultuous was Machiavelli's own city of Florence, which experienced a series of civil wars in his lifetime, resulting in an unstable regime with frequent changes in government.

"Blood Was Every Color"

But the challenge of creating political stability under these turbulent conditions is nothing compared with the difficulties faced by the would-be founder of an entirely new regime. As Machiavelli observes, "there is nothing more difficult to carry out, nor more doubtful of success, nor more dangerous to handle, than to initiate a new order of things."[3] J.T., as the founder of the Sons of Anarchy, came to understand this fact all too well:

> We came to realize that when you move your life off the social grid, you give up the safety that society provides. On the fringe, blood and bullets are the rule of law and, if you're a man with convictions, violence is inevitable. ("Seeds")

Machiavelli's new prince, like the founder of an MC, lives in a world of anarchy. And in such a world, where every individual or close-knit group is responsible for its own safety, the rule of the stronger prevails. Being overly squeamish about the use of violence is not a good way to secure your survival in such a world.

In time, however, J.T. was forced to confront the consequences of the life he had chosen, as violence bred ever more violence and instilling fear became the only way to achieve desired results. "Each savage event was a catalyst for the next," he wrote. "And by the time the violence reached epic proportion, I couldn't see it. Blood was every color" ("Hell Followed). The life of freedom and camaraderie that J.T. sought when forming the MC became increasingly impossible due to the means he needed to employ to secure the club's success. The social order he founded turned out to be incompatible with the very values he intended for it to foster. Does this outcome expose a flaw in Machiavelli's political philosophy? Do Machiavellian methods always undermine the greater good that Machiavelli thought they should serve?

Machiavelli wouldn't accept that conclusion. He would likely argue that the tragedy of John Teller stems from his inability to impose his will effectively on SAMCRO. Ultimately, the outcome of any political contest depends on whether the political actor has sufficient "virtue"—Machiavelli's terms for manly strength, will, and wherewithal—to conquer "fortune," those circumstances that always threaten to get away from us. That J.T. lacked the "virtue" to stay on top of "fortune" is evident in his admission that he "never made a conscious decision to have the club become one thing or another. It just happened before my eyes" ("Hell Followed"). By contrast, Machiavelli declares that the truly great founders of the past "owed nothing to fortune but the opportunity which gave them matter to be shaped into what form they thought fit."[4] In Machiavelli's terms, J.T. lost SAMCRO and eventually his own life because he was overcome by others, such as Clay and Gemma, who were more willful—that is, violent and treacherous—masters of fortune.

"Some Kind of Balance"

Jax is determined not to make the same mistakes as his father, whom he perceives as "weak." But, like his father, Jax wants to find a way to be loyal to those around him while also pursuing what's best for SAMCRO. In his book J.T. had written, "A true outlaw finds the balance between the passion in his heart and the reason in his mind. The outcome is the balance of might and right" ("Fun Town"). Jax shares that commitment to finding balance, but he struggles with making right choices in the face of competing commitments. As he explains to Piney:

> I'm trying to find some kind of balance … The right thing for my family, the club. Every time I think maybe I'm headin' in the right direction, I end up in a place I never even knew could feel this bad. What did I do, man? ("So")

Hearing echoes of J.T. in this speech, Piney responds, "You're loyal, decent. That's who *he* was."

The problem is that Jax recognizes that his loyalty and decency are often liabilities to SAMCRO. Machiavelli would understand perfectly, for he too regards an abundance of moral scruples as a millstone that an effective "prince" can't afford to have around his neck:

> [A] man who wants to make a profession of good in all regards must come to ruin among so many who are not good. Hence it is necessary to a prince, if he wants to maintain himself, to learn to be able not to be good, and to use this and not use it according to necessity.[5]

Jax admits as much to Bobby Munson when, after assuming the presidency of SAMCRO, he announces, "You can't sit in this chair without being a savage" ("Darthy").

In contrast to Jax's pursuit of balance are the actions of Clay Morrow, the youngest of the original founding members. Clay regards an unadulterated show of force as the best way to intimidate rival gangs, though he's also eager to enter into alliances with other gangs when it suits the club's needs. Clay is "Machiavellian" in the sense that he uses manipulation and deceit to maintain his power, following Machiavelli's recommendation that "a prudent ruler ought not to keep faith when, by so doing, it would be against his interest."[6] Machiavellian virtue means knowing when dishonesty is appropriate and being prepared to take ruthless and bold action when it's required to preserve stability and order. But Machiavelli is reluctant to use the word "virtue" to describe the tyrant who betrays even his friends and fellow citizens.[7] Clay's pursuit of naked self-interest at the expense of others in the MC might also fall outside the pale of Machiavellian virtue. Jax, on the other hand, is more commendably Machiavellian when he breaks faith with Agent Stahl and Damon Pope, not in the interests of his own personal agenda, but for the good of his club.

Whereas Clay believes that "might makes right," Jax is much closer to his father when he seeks to balance right and might. Clay embodies the raw pursuit of power for the sake of pure self-aggrandizement, but Jax struggles inwardly, offering us a more accurate depiction of the nuances at the heart of Machiavellian politics. After all, Machiavelli isn't simply an apologist for tyranny. Instead, he advocates the effective use of power as a way to create stable and prosperous regimes. Indeed, Machiavelli criticizes political leaders who achieve empires through the exercise of power, but whose vices prevent them from achieving glory.[8] Most of Clay's "Machiavellian" schemes are in the service of goals that Machiavelli wouldn't deem even remotely worthy. There's nothing glorious or worth celebrating in Clay's amoral egoism.

Jax, on the other hand, values the club in a way that goes beyond self-interest, and it's his "public-spiritedness" that ultimately redeems his actions. Even as he engages in deceit and violence, Jax routinely expresses sentiments that are closely aligned with his father's concern for the well-being of the club and the lives of its members, while many of those around him, such as Clay and Pope, show a callous disregard for life in their reckless pursuit of power.[9] As Jax remarks at one point, "The bond that holds this club together isn't blood or brotherhood ... it's just fear and greed now" ("Out"). Later he complains that he's "tired of being crushed under the weight of greedy men who believe in nothing" ("To Thine Own Self").

"Strength Comes From Good Things"

In his own written reflections intended for his sons, Jax offers this response to the senseless violence swirling around him:

> No matter what, you have to find the things that love you. Run to them. There's an old saying that "what doesn't kill you, makes you stronger." I don't believe that. I think the things that try to kill you make you angry and sad. Strength comes from the good things—your family, your friends, the satisfaction of hard work. Those are the things that'll keep you whole. Those are the things to hold on to when you're broken. ("Sovereign")

As a leader of the MC, Jax must take a manipulative approach to the world, but he does not find the meaning of his life in the pursuit of power or the practice of deceit. Rather, he finds the meaning of his life in relationships built on love.

Notes

1. Niccolò Machiavelli, *The Prince and The Discourses* (New York: Random House, 1950).
2. For further discussion of the concept of "anarchy," see Chapter 7 by Bruno de Brito Serra.
3. Machiavelli, *The Prince*, Ch. 6, 21.
4. Ibid., 20.
5. Ibid., Ch. 15, 56.
6. Ibid., Ch. 18, 64.
7. See Machiavelli's discussion of the tyrant Agaothocles, ibid., Ch. 8, 34.
8. Machiavelli's discussion of Agaothocles is just such an example.
9. According to the show's creator Kurt Sutter, the character of Pope "leads with sheer and utter brutality and then, by contrast, everything else [he does] feels gentle and kind … He starts to play that out on Jax. It starts to be a little bit about, 'let me put my arm around you, son, and you can become just like me if you want to.'" As the season goes along, we'll see an odd mentor dynamic between Pope and Jax. "When you think about in terms of what Jax wants to do, and where he wants to go in terms of taking his club legit, well Pope is the perfect role model for that. He's the guy that has sort of turned all his dirty business into very legitimate things," Sutter says. But, "At the end of the day, it's all really a lot of ego and Pope just assumes everybody wants to be like him." Mandi Bierly, "*Sons of Anarchy*: Kurt Sutter explains last night's death." Available online at http://insidetv.ew.com/2012/09/26/sons-of-anarchy-opie-death-kurt-sutter/ (accessed October 14, 2012).

CHAPTER 7

Chaos and Order
Anarchy in the MC

Bruno de Brito Serra

They are rebellion. They are unbridled freedom. They are the alluring outlaws who capture the imagination of those of us who feel uncomfortably constrained by social norms. Throwing caution to the wind, they are the Sons of Anarchy. Their relationship with their adoptive mother, however, is far from rosy. Momma Anarchy wants freedom for everyone, but the Sons demand obedience to their president; she preaches equality, but the Sons establish a strict hierarchy; she insists on individual autonomy, but lower ranking Sons and prospects simply do what they're told. It sometimes seems that the Sons *of Anarchy* fail to live up to their name.

This dysfunctional family portrait illustrates how the professed anarchism of the founding Redwood Originals—John Teller chief among them—appears to have hit a brick wall. From everything we've been told, SAMCRO has at its heart the will to rebel against the oppression of the state machinery, to reject the supposed authority of politicians and judges, of priests and teachers, of everyone who presumes to tell you what's "best" for you and then tries to *force* you to do it. The cry of the founding Sons of Anarchy was one of utter rejection of the *status quo*, even if that meant life as a social pariah and an outlaw. But SAMCRO evolved into something that mimics the freedom-restricting social structure they were trying to escape. In their attempt to break from society's rules, they evidently felt the need to create some new rules of their own.

Sons of Anarchy and Philosophy: Brains Before Bullets, First Edition.
Edited by George A. Dunn and Jason T. Eberl.
© 2013 John Wiley & Sons, Inc. Published 2013 by John Wiley & Sons, Inc.

Sons of Anarchy, Not Chaos!

To understand this apparent paradox, we first need to figure out what anarchism really means—even if we think we already know the answer. The conventional view is that an "anarchist" is someone who rebels against the Establishment, sticks it to the authorities, disobeys the rules, listens to punk rock, and wreaks havoc. We're all familiar with this popular perception of anarchism: punk bands wildly tearing down the stage with anarchy signs on huge banners in the background; post-apocalyptic Hollywood movies that pan over a devastated urban landscape dotted with crudely painted anarchy signs; news reporters who describe countries plagued by violent civil unrest as having descended into "a state of total anarchy."

Faced with so many instances in which anarchy is presented as a synonym for chaos and disorder, it's only natural that many of us who enjoy *Sons of Anarchy* will tend to regard this definition of an anarchist as the one that best fits an outlaw band of bikers. And, at first glance, the Sons of Anarchy do indeed represent a *violent* liberation from the shackles of social order. They have no qualms about using violence, even in the most seemingly trivial situations. When some random guy on a crotch rocket thinks it's a good idea to sit on Jax Teller's bike, Jax has little doubt that pounding in the guy's face, taking a picture of the beating on his own cell phone, and then riding away with his girlfriend is a proportionate response ("Patch Over"). They fight, kill, and give the insurance companies in Charming ghastly nightmares. They're heroes to some and a scourge to most. Chaos—or "anarchy"—is precisely what they bring forth.

Let's not, however, be fooled by appearances. In fact, anarchy and chaos are far from the same. Simply put, chaos is the absence of order. Anarchy, on the other hand, stems from the Greek *anarche*, which contains the word *arche*—meaning governing principle—preceded by the negative particle *an*. In a political context, "governing principle" means a leader—a source of authority—and "anarchy" is the refusal to accept the legitimacy of this leader. While anarchy literally means "without a leader," it doesn't rule out there being some form of order, though such an order would have to be self-imposed rather than imposed by an outside authority. So anarchism is more complex than its depiction in the popular imagination.

What, then, does anarchism really stand for? What is anarchism's perspective on human nature and existence? How does it envision the relationship between the individual and the community? In sum, what does it really mean to be a Son of *Anarchy*?

Anarchy 101

Encyclopedia entries on anarchism describe it as a complex, subtle, and non-dogmatic philosophy, a dynamic current of thought that doesn't try to impose a fixed doctrine or worldview that's intended to ride roughshod over every other point of view—as is customary with most other political and religious ideologies. But despite the elusive nature of anarchism, it's still possible to identify some key features of this philosophy.

First, true to its etymological origin, anarchism rejects the legitimacy of all sources of authority outside one's self, including the most pervasive authority of all: the state. For the anarchist, the existence of the state oppresses the individual, regardless of whether it's a dictatorship or a liberal democracy. As far as the anarchist is concerned, the only difference between the two is that in the first case we're oppressed by one individual, whereas in the second we're oppressed by many. All governments entail some form of authority and hierarchy that unreasonably deprive us of freedom.

Second, as an alternative to state oppression, anarchism advocates a self-regulating society that relies on voluntary association between free and equal individuals, affording each person an equal shot at realizing his or her potential. The emergence of hierarchies is foreign to this ideal, since they introduce unfreedom and inequality into human relations. Freedom and equality are central notions in anarchist thought, not simply because they represent the liberation of the individual from the shackles of oppressive political institutions, but also because they're the foundation of a truly virtuous political order, in which every individual is autonomous but also sympathetic and able to work cooperatively with others.

Anarchists don't believe that a stateless society would necessarily degenerate into a violent free-for-all,[1] which brings us to anarchism's third key feature: the belief that human beings don't need to be coerced in order to live together in peace. Freed from the pernicious influence of social domination, individuals will spontaneously find ways to coexist peacefully and cooperatively. However, peaceful coexistence requires liberation not only from political oppression, but also from *economic* oppression. The capitalist ideal of the endless pursuit and accumulation of wealth, along with its elevation of private property to the top of our scale of values, is rejected by many anarchists as another source of inequality, injustice, and oppression.[2]

We'll consider some other aspects of anarchist thought later on, but these are the basic tenets by which those who style themselves "anarchists" are expected to live their lives. Do the Sons of Anarchy truly embody these ideals?

The "Rebellious Fire" of the First 9

SAMCRO was co-founded by John Teller and Piney Winston around 1967, when the two returned from serving in Vietnam. In fact, six of the original nine members of the club were veterans. This is a significant factor in the overall attitude and anarchist ideology underlying the early days of SAMCRO. These men were soldiers, trained to obey a strict hierarchy and follow orders unquestioningly. They spent some gruelling years in service to their country, carrying out the missions assigned to them by superior officers. In keeping with the principles of military honor that had been drilled into them, their service should've been rewarded with public recognition and a successful life upon their return home.

What they experienced was very different. A popular revolt against the Vietnam War was underway in the United States and returning veterans were often welcomed home, not with parades and accolades, but with disapproval and disgust. Many of the people for whom the veterans had imagined themselves to be fighting and dying were now shouting insults at them. The government that had sent them to Vietnam in the first place now ignored them and their problems. In the face of all this, something cracked inside them. They'd danced to the tune of political and social institutions for too long, only to be rewarded with disdain and contempt. Enough was enough. They wanted out.

In his revolt against a society that seemed to despise him and his comrades, John Teller turned to a philosophy that resonated deeply within him, one that utterly rejected the need for a state or any external source of authority, advocating complete freedom for the individual. It promised freedom from the stifling domination of parents, from the moldy morals of priests, from the arbitrary laws of courthouses, and especially from the self-serving lies of politicians. All the rebellion welling up inside J.T. and his comrades had now found meaning, focus, and purpose.

John Teller served as a spiritual leader of sorts, providing a vehicle through which others could channel their rebellion. He co-founded SAMCRO, imbuing it with anarchist ideals. He'd already felt the pull of anarchism before he went to Vietnam. In his manuscript he relates how, at the age of 16, he took a hike along the Nevada border and came across a quotation by the anarchist Emma Goldman (1869–1940) written on a wall. Anarchism, said Goldman, "stands for the liberation of the human mind from the dominion of religion; the liberation of the human body from the dominion of property; liberation from the shackles and restraints of government. Anarchism stands for a social order based on the free grouping of individuals" ("Patch Over").[3]

These words "lit a rebellious fire" in young J.T. and planted the seeds of SAMCRO, which underwent accelerated growth after he returned from war in the company of other disgruntled veterans. Their passion for motorcycles and the open road made forming a motorcycle club a natural choice for these men, and J.T.'s anarchist philosophy provided them with an ideal. But the military legacy of its members imbued the club with something foreign to anarchism—a taste for a "chain of command," a hierarchy. Perhaps this is why, from their very inception, the Sons had trouble being faithful to the anarchist aspirations of their founder.

Living Off the Social Grid

There's something enticing about the promises of anarchism, something that's also present in our image of the "outlaw": the seductive ideal of perfect freedom—to roam the land to your heart's content, following no laws but the ones you give yourself, seeking new adventures every day, and ending each adventure by riding off into the sunset. The outlaw biker has the same allure as the outlaw cowboy or gangster—a modern day Jesse James or John Dillinger. Anarchism has the same appeal for someone who feels oppressed by social institutions and expectations. This kind of freedom, however, comes at a cost. As J.T. came to realize, "when you move your life off the social grid, you give up on the safety that society provides" ("Seeds").

Many of the early opponents of anarchism in the nineteenth century offered roughly the same argument: wanting freedom from social and political institutions is all well and good, but it's those "oppressive" institutions that insure that we're not robbing and killing each other all the time. Our baser instincts are kept in check by our system of laws and the punishments that give them teeth. Without these laws, there would be utter chaos. It's this reasoning that informs the popular association of "anarchy" with "chaos" that we noted earlier.

This objection was tackled by Mikhail Bakunin (1814–1876)[4] and Pierre-Joseph Proudhon (1809–1865)[5], two of the founding fathers of anarchism—a sort of Russian J.T. and French Piney, if you will. To them the answer was simple: what we believe to be the "baser instincts" of human nature are actually products of the corrupt social life we're forced to endure in an oppressive society, an idea they inherited from the influential Swiss political philosopher, Jean-Jacques Rousseau (1712–1778)[6]. Vices like greed, vanity, resentment, and envy aren't born into us, but are acquired through living in a society obsessed with wealth, power, and status, whose oppressive nature makes us feel like caged animals.

"Most of us were not violent by nature," wrote J.T. in his manuscript, just before conceding that violence is inevitable for "a man with convictions" living off the social grid ("Seeds"). We can now understand J.T.'s disillusionment. At the heart of anarchism is a profound belief in humanity's inherent *goodness*—we're all innately good, and evil deeds and inclinations are products of nurture rather than nature. Or, if we're not inherently good, at least we're born *morally neutral*, like blank slates with no innate moral dispositions one way or another. Anarchists believe that when freed from the debasing influence of oppressive social and political institutions, individuals will lean toward harmonious co-existence. It's only because of this conviction that anarchists can advocate a life of total freedom without fearing that it will devolve into total debauchery and "a war … of every man against every man," as the English political philosopher Thomas Hobbes (1588–1679) believed.[7]

J.T. must have believed in the inherent goodness of people, for otherwise it's hard to make sense of the disappointment expressed in his manuscript. But does the Sons' adoption of a hierarchical structure and their resorting to violence as a substitute for law mean that anarchism itself is inevitably doomed to failure? And if SAMCRO has indeed "lost its way," as J.T. states in the title of his manuscript, does that necessarily mean it is beyond redemption?

There's No "I" in "Motorcycle Club"

SAMCRO's degeneration from what John Teller originally intended doesn't mean that anarchism is an unrealizable ideal. In fact, anarchist theory itself might be able to help us understand exactly where the club took a wrong turn, for there's an aspect of SAMCRO's evolution that is directly relevant to a debate deep within the heart of anarchism.

The anarchist ideals on which J.T. and Piney founded SAMCRO advocate total individual freedom. But doesn't joining a club replete with officers and rules of conduct seriously limit the very freedom they were seeking in the first place? This question has, in one form or another, been debated by anarchists throughout the history of the movement. On one side is the *individualist* view, according to which an autonomous individual can be truly free only if he maintains his independence from any kind of social order. Taken to an extreme, this view produces an egoist and elitist form of anarchism, for which freedom is the prerogative of the enlightened outlaw but is not suitable for the masses. On the other side is the *collectivist* view that individuals can retain their freedom even when participating in social groups, so long as they are freely and spontaneously joined.

The debate between individualism and collectivism within anarchism allows us to understand SAMCRO's history in a new light. When J.T. started the MC, he probably intended a more individualistic notion of anarchism, with total freedom from social conventions and restraints. But that aspiration will always run afoul of the near impossibility of human beings living in isolation. Either he failed to consider that the Sons of Anarchy as a social unit would not be fully compatible with individualistic anarchism or perhaps he simply desired to belong to a collective of kindred spirits.

When it eventually became clear that the Sons were no longer following the path he'd envisioned, J.T.'s thoughts drifted back to a more pure form of individualism. Becoming Nomad "offered escape and exile" ("Balm"), not just from the dangers he faced, but also from the club he felt had lost its way. Jax, however, seems to adhere to a different kind of anarchism than his father. J.T. left his family for Belfast because he became disillusioned with life in the MC. Jax also considers going Nomad because of his hatred of Clay. However, after learning about Gemma's rape, Jax's deep-seated commitment to *family*—in his mind, *the* indispensable social unit—prompts him to put aside that hatred and stay with the club. Perhaps J.T.'s individualism just doesn't have the same potential for the long haul as Jax's sense of responsibility to the group.

Where else might things have gone wrong for SAMCRO? For one thing, there's the problem of trying to create and maintain a truly anarchistic collective in a world still dominated by corrupt dynamics of power and wealth. Regardless of their anarchist intentions, the MC still has to interact with a world they'd rather reject. They need money for gas and food, tools and parts to maintain their trusted iron steeds, and a place to raise their families. Consequently, they need factories to manufacture those steeds, as well as companies that produce food and refine gas—all of which presupposes an elaborate system of commerce governed by capitalist logic. With their survival dependent upon interacting with the "old" society they're trying to escape, the fall away from anarchist ideals seems inevitable. There's no point in calling yourself "anarchist" if you end up running in the same rat race as everyone else.

Another challenge faced by the club stems from the fact that a lot of the antagonists it faces are decidedly "anti-anarchist" organizations: the ATF, LOAN, a US District Attorney, Charming PD, and the CIA. Most of them represent the establishment and all have the explicit aim either to incarcerate the Sons or to make them follow an agenda that both contradicts their best interests and deprives them of self-determination. Whether forced to dance to another's tune, as when the CIA holds the RICO case over their head, or simply forced to take action to eliminate these outside threats, the Sons are robbed of the autonomy that's indispensable for a truly anarchistic existence.

Of course, many of these antagonists are after the Sons because of their criminal activities, but their antagonistic nature is symbolic of something deeper. The battles that the Sons—and Jax in particular—wage aren't simply to keep them out of jail. They're battles to preserve their way of life, which recall mainstream society's perennial attempts to absorb and neutralize outbreaks of anarchism that it can't afford to tolerate.

In addition to opposition from the outside, the Sons' anarchism also meets resistance *from the inside*. We've already noted the conflict between the club's anarchist intentions and the militaristic craving for a hierarchy of command at its founding. The militaristic mentality of the Redwood Originals has shaped the club's evolution, even though its demand for blind obedience and strict observance of a hierarchical chain of command places it about as far as possible from genuine anarchism. Though important decisions are supposed to be brought to a vote at the table, the Sons have a clear hierarchy that delegates to the president the responsibility to take the initiative in outlining the club's fate and assigns to him the role of commanding officer. When Jax makes a series of deals behind the club's back to get the MC out from under the Galindo Cartel's thumb, he's ultimately congratulated for his leadership despite the undemocratic nature of his secret machinations ("Darthy").

Moreover, the *semper fidelis* mentality underscoring the club's existence, demanding total loyalty to the MC, is not at all in keeping with the spirit of anarchism. To the anarchist, freedom of association is key, and that freedom goes both ways: you should be free not only to associate with whomever you like but also to sever yourself from previous associations without any cause other than your own free will. So the fact that Jax has to negotiate with Clay for a "way out" of SAMCRO is inimical to anarchist principles ("Booster").

Something's Rotten ...

Clay Morrow is one of the coolest characters in *Sons of Anarchy*. People love a bad guy, and Ron Perlman does tremendous justice to the unflinching badass who's desperately trying to get his own before arthritis gets him first. As with any good character, he has layers. We sometimes see his softer side, as when Clay acts as a father figure to Jax and other Sons, such as Tig Trager and Juice Ortiz. What stands out, though, is his role as Jax's adversary over the fate of the club.

Clay isn't just the man who wanted to live John Teller's life and so decided to take it—he's the "anti-J.T." The drama of the show largely turns on the battle for Jax's soul and for the fate of the MC, a battle between the anarchism of his father—the "biker commune" eulogized in his writings—and the more mercenary model of the club proposed by his stepfather.

There's something paradoxical about Clay being the president of the Sons of *Anarchy* when he's clearly *not* an anarchist. His posture as president is authoritarian, and he adroitly exerts his influence to ensure that the outcome of any vote at the table will be in his favor— the close vote for drug-muling in Season 4 impressively showcases his skill at backroom politics. Moreover, his own financial gain is his overriding priority—and a slave of profit is surely not a free man. Nor does he share anarchism's optimistic outlook on human nature. Is there a chance Opie might be a rat? Let's get Tig to waste him. Is Tara Knowles learning too much for her own good? Let's get the Galindo Cartel to waste *her*. Is old Piney becoming too much of a liability? That's nothing a round of hot lead to the chest won't cure.

Clay's guidance has steered the Sons of Anarchy away from the principles of its founder and moved it more and more towards becoming a standard "1%" biker club.[8] The club has become increasingly unworthy of its name—unless we take "anarchy" in its colloquial sense of "chaos" or "disorder." It almost seems as if Clay wasn't happy with simply killing J.T. and taking his place at the table and in his bed, but also felt the need to exorcise J.T.'s guidance of the club. Already in a shambles when he died, the anarchic dreams of John Teller have definitely been trampled underfoot in the years since.

If Jax had been left utterly fatherless, there's no doubt Clay's influence on him would have been hard to escape, but his father managed to speak to him from the grave and stir something within him. As he is drawn more deeply into his father's writings, he becomes increasingly disillusioned with Clay's guidance of the club. Even before Jax learns of Clay's responsibility for his father's murder, the two men seem to be on a collision course. Events occur, however, that place Jax in the midst of an internal conflict between the teachings of his father and the guidance of his stepfather.

J.T.'s idealized version of anarchism is certainly seductive. In its most individualistic form, it offers escape from life's constraints and promises a freedom which we all at one time or another long for. But it may also strike us as the equivalent of taking the easy way out.

When writing his own reflections to pass on to his sons, Jax notes that a true "man" puts aside his selfish desires in order to live for others—which is harder than being selfish and definitely not a path for the weak ("Darthy"). In his mind, J.T. was weak when he retreated to Ireland instead of sticking with the club and trying to make it work. It's clear that J.T.'s vision can't provide practical answers to the real problems Jax faces, such as raising his boys to be better men than him, reconciling his devotion to his family and to the MC, avenging Clay's crimes, and protecting the club from RICO.

Clay's outlook on life, on the other hand, is utterly pragmatic. There's a goal and there are means to achieve it. Whether those means are "right" or "wrong"—or whether they're in keeping with the "spirit" in which the club was founded—are just idle questions that don't concern him. The only "cause" that interests him is himself and maybe Gemma, when she's not in his way. His actions may be harsh and cold-hearted, but they produce results—and that's all that matters in the dog-eat-dog world in which Clay operates. His ideology isn't J.T.'s naive anarchism, but rather stone-cold *egoism*: look out for number one, because no one else will do it for you.

Now that we understand what being a Son of Anarchy *should* entail, it's abundantly clear that SAMCRO isn't living up to its name. Clay, however, has been dethroned by Jax and, as of the end of Season 5, is now heading off to jail. But that doesn't mean he's out of the game: the seeds he planted both in the MC and in Jax's mind may still bear fruit. Jax himself is in a tough situation, having to juggle the deals he's made, the ones Clay made before him, his responsibility to Tara and his sons, and expectations of his fellow club members. Will he grow into another John Teller or will he be forced by circumstances to become a new Clay Morrow, a fear expressed on different occasions by Opie Winston and Bobby Munson? Or will he try to find some middle ground between J.T.'s and Clay's respective visions?

He's definitely giving mixed signals. Contrast the brutality of how he solves the problems with ex-wife Wendy Case and Damon Pope with the clear-sightedness of his dealings with Jacob Hale to ensure economic security for Teller-Morrow Automotive and Opie's family. Is there a middle ground between true anarchism and dealing with the society anarchists reject on principle? It doesn't seem very likely, but we've been surprised before. Whatever comes next, one thing is certain: much like the Sons' motto, if the Reaper doesn't ride *free*, he will eventually die.

Notes

1. For Thomas Hobbes's opposing view that human society inevitably will degenerate into violence without the authority of the state, see Chapter 5 by George Dunn.
2. There is, however, a strain of anarchism that supports capitalism. For recent examples of anarcho-capitalism, see Gerard Casey, *Libertarian Anarchy: Against the State* (London: Continuum, 2012) and Aeon J. Skoble, *Deleting the State: An Argument about Government* (Chicago: Open Court, 2008).
3. Emma Goldman, *Anarchism and Other Essays* (New York: Mother Earth Publishing, 1917), 68.
4. Mikhail Bakunin, *God and the State*, ed. Paul Avrich (New York: Dover Publications Inc., 2003).
5. Pierre-Joseph Proudhon, *What is Property?* ed. Donald Kelly and Bonnie Smith (Cambridge: Cambridge University Press, 1994).
6. Jean-Jacques Rousseau, *Emile; or On Education*, trans. J.M. Cohen (London: Penguin Classics, 1973).
7. Thomas Hobbes, *Leviathan*, ed. Edwin Curley (Indianapolis: Hackett Publishing Company, 1994), 76.
8. An outlaw biker club whose colors include a "1%" patch, referring to a comment made by the American Motorcycle Association that 99% of motorcyclists were law-abiding citizens.

CHAPTER 8

"Another Fun-Filled Day in the Six Counties"
The Real IRA—Terrorists or Freedom Fighters?

Philip Smolenski

If you're Clay Morrow and John Teller, starting up an entrepreneurial outlaw motorcycle club and looking to establish a lucrative gun-running business, who better than the Real IRA to supply you with illegal firearms? Having struggled for liberation for almost a century—a costly endeavour in terms of both money and lives—the Real IRA is more than happy to support "the cause" by working with SAMCRO to deal weapons to rival gangs across the western US seaboard. With their charming Irish brogues, the members of the Real IRA bring a rich and sometimes sinister history to the drama of *Sons of Anarchy*. Since the Irish War of Independence in 1919, the Irish Republican Army has fought a guerrilla war for a free and independent Irish republic. Initially targeting police involved in intelligence work and fortified barracks, the IRA's tactics and choice of targets have become increasingly militant. What began as a band of freedom fighters seeking to liberate Northern Ireland from an oppressive regime has evolved into a more combative force using increasingly extremist tactics.

Is this a good group for SAMCRO to be dealing with? Granted, the MC is an outlaw organization, but there's a difference between living outside the law and directly attacking the state as a *terrorist*. But is the Real IRA just a bunch of cafe-bombing terrorists deserving moral condemnation or are they a liberating force of freedom fighters?

Sons of Anarchy and Philosophy: Brains Before Bullets, First Edition.
Edited by George A. Dunn and Jason T. Eberl.
© 2013 John Wiley & Sons, Inc. Published 2013 by John Wiley & Sons, Inc.

"They Think Every Act of Violence Is Their Republic Duty"

What is terrorism? We typically associate it with airplane hijackers, attacks on buildings, and bombs being thrown into crowded cafes or hidden in metro stations. Does this fit the Real IRA? While the IRA has been known to blow up cars and place bombs on buses, we don't see Jimmy O'Phelan or any of the Real IRA members attacking the civilian population. However, there's more to being a terrorist than just blowing people up. Just because the Real IRA isn't planting explosives all over Ireland's transit system doesn't necessarily mean it is not a terrorist organization.

Michael Walzer, one of the most prominent contemporary philosophers exploring the philosophy of war and armed conflict, defines terrorism as "the random killing of innocent people, in the hope of creating pervasive fear," adding that terrorism involves the "systematic terrorizing of a whole population."[1] The purpose of terrorist acts is to destroy the morale of a nation or class in an effort to undermine its solidarity. When Jimmy O sends his ragtag group of youngsters to throw Molotov cocktails around Dublin, their aim— aside from just destroying property—is to spread fear through the population. While spreading fear is certainly far from morally praiseworthy, must we necessarily condemn it when used as a tactic to oppose an oppressive regime?

Jimmy O and the Real IRA consider the forces of the British Crown oppressive because they've imposed foreign rule over the once independent and united state of Ireland, dividing it in two. The Real IRA wants a united Ireland again. As a localized guerrilla force, the Real IRA has to resort to terrorist tactics because it can't effectively engage the enemy directly. Instead, Jimmy O has to send his boys out under cover of night, destroying property in order to scare supporters of the Crown by demonstrating that their local government can't protect them anymore. (Clay Morrow, perhaps having learned a few tricks from the Irish, uses a similar tactic, staging a series of home invasions in Charming to undermine public confidence in Jax's leadership as president of SAMCRO.) The Real IRA hopes that the local population will be swayed by these attacks to acknowledge their grievances and rally to their cause. Obviously, no one wants to be terrorized, but Walzer doesn't believe that frightening the population is what makes terrorism morally wrong.

According to Walzer, all forms of terrorism involve the random killing of innocent people. By placing explosives on city buses or in metro stations, the IRA leaves people feeling fatally exposed, unsure whether or when they'll become victims. What makes terrorism morally wrong, then, is that it attacks innocent civilians who bear no responsibility for the wrongs that the terrorists want to set right. Jimmy O, however, believes that anyone who shows the least bit of sympathy to the Crown or the Loyalist cause is a legitimate target. As his wife, Fiona, explains, "Jimmy has them all convinced that folks are just fat Irish sheep moving with the loyal herd. They think every act of violence is their Republic duty" ("Widening Gyre").

Jimmy's view, though, doesn't withstand moral scrutiny. Walzer cites the traditional distinction between "non-combatants" and "combatants."[2] The former include both civilians and military personnel not directly engaged in hostilities, such as the medical corps and chaplains. Regardless of whether they show support for one of the sides engaged in hostilities, there is a general consensus that the civilian population ought to be immune from attack. Combatants, on the other hand, have traditionally been thought to comprise only military personnel actively engaged in the hostilities. Walzer, however, broadens the category to include political officials and state agents, such as the police, whose involvement with the oppressive regime makes them legitimate targets of attack. On *Sons of Anarchy* we usually see the Belfast police who are on Jimmy O's payroll—the ones who harass SAMCRO—but there is evidence that other members of the police force actively support the Crown and have used violence against the Real IRA. For example, we see an injured boy brought to the Ashby residence after a run-in with the police during a midnight IRA mission.

The defining characteristic of terrorism is *indiscriminate killing* or failing to distinguish between those who are legitimate targets of attack from those who aren't. Jimmy O is clearly indiscriminate in this sense, endorsing attacks on anyone who shows loyalty to the Crown. But the Irish Kings—the ruling council of the Real IRA—expressly condemn the *randomness* of Jimmy O's tactics, though they don't rule out spreading fear as a legitimate means to an end. It's possible for perpetrators of violence to discriminate between their targets, even when employing traditional terrorist tactics. We can thus distinguish between "terrorists" in Walzer's sense and "freedom fighters."

"We're Not Merchants, We're Soldiers"

Even when civilian populations aren't targeted, any act of political violence committed by a *non-state actor* is condemned by countless legal sanctions. Non-state actors are any political group that acts without the authority of a recognized government. Some of these groups take on a more militant role like the IRA, but not all. For example, Mohandas Gandhi and his non-violent followers were also non-state actors.

The dominant view in philosophy and international law is that states possess a monopoly on the legitimate use of violence and declaring war.[3] It's the job of the state to protect its citizens from harmful attacks, but what if you're a group like the Real IRA and you need protection from the state itself? Is the use of violence morally permissible? Law professor Christopher Kutz asserts that even ununiformed non-state actors can rightfully claim the same kind of privileges as their uniformed state-sanctioned counterparts. Political groups that resort to violence can justifiably be called "freedom fighters," according to Kutz, if they satisfy three criteria: they must have an *internal ordering*, their *aims* must be of the right *character*, and they must have a reasonable chance of *success on the ground*.[4]

Internal ordering refers to a group's ability to regulate its own conduct, some sort of command structure with a hierarchical order of rank, which is necessary if it is to enjoy legitimate combatant privileges. The Real IRA meets this criterion, for it does have a strict, militaristic internal ordering. At the top are the Irish Kings, forming the ruling council. Below them are the likes of Michael McKeavey, Cameron Hayes, and Jimmy O, each possessing the equivalent of the rank of captain or colonel. Finally, there are the foot soldiers carrying out operations.

From their position atop this hierarchy, the Irish Kings have very effective ways of dealing with dissent. Consider how they handle Cameron Hayes after he and his son betray the Real IRA by making a deal to sell guns to groups other than SAMCRO and after Hayes kidnaps Jax's son, Abel. After Father Ashby performs last rites for

Hayes, Sean Casey strangles him and dumps his body in the street—a warning to anyone else who might want to step outside the ranks. While there are serious moral questions concerning whether a man of the cloth should be complicit in an execution, at least internal order is restored and an example set to keep the rest of the troops in line.

Kutz's second condition concerns the *character* of the group's *aims*. Political liberation and national self-determination would seem to be the sort of objectives that can justify violence if anything can. Since the Real IRA is seeking a unified Ireland, free from the influences of the Crown, this criterion seems to be satisfied.

Most problematic for the Real IRA is the final criterion: *success on the ground*. Even a group fighting for a legitimate cause must be morally condemned if the cause is hopeless. You can't sacrifice human lives for a cause that is in vain. As the struggle for Ireland's liberation has lasted close to a century, it's difficult to view the IRA's efforts as having much hope of success.

But even if the Real IRA were able to satisfy all three of Kutz's criteria, Walzer wouldn't be satisfied, since he holds the dominant view that *states* possess a monopoly on the legitimate use of violence. However, while Walzer considers all forms of violence by non-state actors to be wrong from a legal and political standpoint, he concedes that certain forms of "terrorism" may be *morally* permissible. Walzer regards terrorism as a unique phenomenon that emerged as a strategy of revolutionary struggle prior to World War II. Earlier in history, though, there existed a brand of violence by non-state actors which did *not* target civilian populations, which Walzer terms "terrorism" (with quotes).[5]

"Terrorism" is marked by its adherence to a revolutionary "code of honor" that distinguishes between people who can and can't be killed. Walzer designates as "terrorism" violence committed by groups such as the Real IRA that lack legitimate authority but use what he terms "professional revolutionaries." Sean Casey—the Irish Kings' enforcer and resident torturer—epitomizes the professional revolutionary. He's stoic and ruthless, a point made clear when he strangles Hayes and when he tortures Liam O'Neil, the SAMBEL turncoat. Yet his "professionalism" can be seen in the fact that all the violence he commits is against those who'd be considered *combatants*.

Professional revolutionaries don't indiscriminately target whole groups of people, but attack only particular individuals on account of what they've done. Jimmy O would not be a professional revolutionary in this sense, because he urges his supporters to indiscriminately attack anyone who shows sympathy to the Crown. The Irish Kings, however, show a much greater mark of restraint: we never see them sanctioning the killing of non-combatants or attacks on civilian targets. Yes, they traffic in illegal firearms, but McKeavey is quick to point out that this isn't a business for them. The members of the Real IRA aren't gun merchants, they're *soldiers* ("Fun Town"). They sell guns to finance the cause. Those in the Real IRA are thus a good example of Walzer's concept of "terrorists"—revolutionaries who use violence to achieve political goals, but discriminate between targets and adhere to a particular "code of honor."

"The All-Seeing, All-Knowing Wizard of East Belfast"

We've seen some reasons for thinking of the Irish Kings and those they command as "freedom fighters." But what about Jimmy O and his rogue wing of the Real IRA? He doesn't fit easily into either category of terrorist or freedom fighter. Unlike the Irish Kings, he doesn't strike us as the commander of an army striving to free his country from an oppressive force. In fact, his tailored suits and imposing Mercedes make him look more like the leader of a criminal syndicate than of a revolutionary group.

His rhetoric about "the cause" makes Jimmy seem like a committed revolutionary, but his actions cast doubt on his real commitments. He's clearly motivated by the personal fortune he's amassed brokering gun deals stateside, with only a percentage of the profits going to "the cause." In the episode "Home," Jimmy's motives become manifest during a conversation with Fr. Ashby:

JIMMY: This is not about my agenda with the Sons, this is about protecting the progress that we've made.
ASHBY: And the profits you've made.
JIMMY: Aye. Aye, Father, I earn. And it's my bloody efforts that pump cash into our dying fight. And you, you remember that.

Jimmy claims that he wants to cut the Real IRA's ties with the Sons in an effort to curtail reliance on outside elements, shifting the role of the Sons onto "Real Army men." But Fr. Ashby notes that Jimmy isn't commissioning Real Army men to move the cause forward; rather, he's enlisting disenfranchised youth, "recruiting off the streets. Broken kids, some as young as ten, eleven. Promising there'll be a united Ireland, all the cash and prizes that go with it." Ashby correctly concludes, "This isn't a child's war … Jimmy's lost sight of who we are, why we struggle. He's not a soldier anymore, just a gangster" ("Home"). Perhaps at one point Jimmy was truly loyal to the cause of a united Ireland. But now it's clear that his principal concern is making a healthy profit for himself and that he has lost sight of why the Real IRA is fighting in the first place.

"Our Good Priest Getting a Might Too Godly for His Collar"

Fr. Kellen Ashby is a perplexing individual. On the one hand, he's a devout priest. On the other hand, he serves as an advisor to the Irish Kings, sanctioning and even playing a part in acts of violence. Fr. Ashby attempts to walk a moral tightrope, balancing his duties as a spiritual leader with his role within the Real IRA. We see him perform this balancing act most strikingly when he offers Cameron Hayes the last rites just before he's strangled with razor wire. Most priests will, of course, offer last rites to death row prisoners so they can have a last chance for repentance and forgiveness, but they wouldn't necessarily condone the execution itself. Not so for Fr. Ashby.

The good priest is clearly ambivalent about his dual role. He willingly plays his part as an important advisor to the Irish Kings, but he betrays a certain uneasiness about his role when he states, more than a little disingenuously, that he's there only to "offer the guidance of a priest, try to keep us focused on God's will" ("Home"). Was it God's will that Hayes be executed? God's will may be for an independent and unified Ireland, but we might doubt whether that hallowed cause justifies using such brutal means.

Fr. Ashby sees his role within the Real IRA as a spiritual compass, but we should be wary of a supposed man of God whose compass points to the use of violence to further a political cause. Moreover, a priest's involvement with a violent political organization is inherently problematic, since we expect religious leaders to condemn, rather than condone, violence. It's difficult to see how Fr. Ashby can remain faithful to his religious duties while taking up a leadership role within such a violent political organization.

In the end, Fr. Ashby finds redemption and performs his own act of contrition by advising the council to make a deal with Jimmy O to arrange for Abel's safe return to Jax. He agrees to become a hostage in exchange for Abel. All the parties involved know that Jimmy O's going to kill the priest, but perhaps this final sacrifice was the only way Fr. Ashby could find to seek absolution for his past sins of violence ("Bainne").

Terrorists, Freedom Fighters, and Thugs

While the Real IRA is itself a splinter group that broke away from the original incarnation of the IRA that fought the Irish War of Independence—one of many splinter groups, such as the Provisional IRA (Provos)—there's also a division within the group between the forces led by Jimmy O and those commanded by the Irish Kings. By discriminating among their targets and practicing military-like discipline, the Irish Kings gain the status of freedom fighters. Admittedly, their tactics are violent, but groups like the Real IRA resort to violence only because they have no other option for effectively fighting for their political cause. Excluded from the political process and lacking political recognition, they have no way to make their voices heard through official channels. Many have condemned any violence committed by non-state actors, simply on the grounds that these groups don't have the legitimate authority to use violence. But non-state actors may face the same threats that enable states to use violence. That's why some philosophers have concluded that violence may be legitimate for groups opposing an oppressive regime, but only so long as it doesn't directly target the civilian population.

Jimmy O comes closer to being a terrorist in the proper sense of the term—though not in the sense of Walzer's "terrorist"—since he endorses attacks on anyone with Loyalist sympathies. However, his violence on behalf of "the cause" seems to be only a cover. In reality, Jimmy O is a gangster, a criminal kingpin—akin to Damon Pope—who's more concerned with making a profit than promoting real change in Ireland. Perhaps, then, we need a new category beyond freedom fighter or terrorist: *Thug!*

Notes

1. Michael Walzer, *Just and Unjust Wars* (New York: Basic Books, 1977), 199.
2. Ibid., 198.
3. For further discussion of whether SAMCRO can legitimately participate in acts of violence or outright "war," see Chapter 9 by Alex Leveringhaus.
4. Christopher Kutz, "The Difference Uniforms Make: Collective Violence in Criminal Law and War," *Philosophy & Public Affairs* 33:2 (2005): 176.
5. Michael Walzer, "Terrorism and Just War," *Philosophia* 34:1 (2006): 3.

CHAPTER 9

SAMCRO Goes to War

Alex Leveringhaus

References to war abound in *Sons of Anarchy*. In "Old Bones," Clay Morrow and Tig Trager inform Jax Teller that the human remains unearthed on the outskirts of Charming by some water and power workers are the remnants of SAMCRO's "war" with the Mayans in the early 1990s. Later, in "The Pull," the Mayans botch an attempted hit on Clay, prompting him and Tig to remark glumly that it's time for "war." But the Mayans aren't the only combatants against whom SAMCRO goes to "war." In "Call of Duty," SAMCRO and the Galindo Cartel join forces to fight the Lobos Sonora Cartel—with machine guns, rocket propelled grenades, and landmines! A shocked and bewildered Juice exclaims that it's like a scene from a war game on his computer.

But should these conflicts between SAMCRO and its enemies really be described as *war*? It depends on what we mean by the word, which can be used in different ways. On the one hand, "war" can describe any armed conflict between groups or individuals. Using the word in this sense doesn't tell us anything about whether the conflict is right or wrong, legitimate or illegitimate. It simply means that bullets are flying. On the other hand, some philosophers use the term "war" in a way that implies a moral judgment. To classify an armed altercation as a "war" grants it a degree of moral legitimacy that other dust-ups, such as mere criminal violence, may lack.[1] To declare a "war," on this interpretation, one must possess a certain type of authority and only

Sons of Anarchy and Philosophy: Brains Before Bullets, First Edition.
Edited by George A. Dunn and Jason T. Eberl.
© 2013 John Wiley & Sons, Inc. Published 2013 by John Wiley & Sons, Inc.

if one's resort to violence is backed up with that authority can it be regarded as legitimate rather than criminal.

To be sure, SAMCRO can always declare war in the bullets-are-flying sense. That's easy. But could the club also declare war in the other sense: the legitimate use of armed force? If not, then SAMCRO is wrong to bust out the assault rifles against its enemies and its members are murderers. But if they can legitimately declare war, then the Sons of Anarchy may still be bad boys, but at least they're not immoral butchers. To settle this question, however, we need to figure out what counts as a sound moral justification for the use of armed force. Luckily for us, philosophers have been at work on this question for quite some time. So let's ride out and see what they have to say.

"I Don't Recognize Your Bullshit MC"

The questions we're posing fall under the rubric of just war theory, which attempts to spell out the criteria that must be met for the use of armed force to be morally justified.[2] One set of criteria, known as *jus ad bellum* ("justice in the declaration of war"), concerns who can declare war and under what conditions.[3] There are six criteria that must be met:

1. *Just Cause*: Defense against aggression and intervention to halt atrocities count as just causes.
2. *Proportionality*: The declaration of war must not cause more harm than good.
3. *Necessity*: The declaration of war must be necessary.
4. *Last Resort*: War may be declared only after all other options have been exhausted.
5. *Right Authority*: Only those with the appropriate authority can declare war.
6. *Likelihood of Success*: War should be declared only if it's likely to achieve its goals.

To be just, a war must fulfill *all* six criteria. However, even if some armed altercations fall short of fully satisfying all six criteria (for instance, the use of armed force might not be a last resort), we might still call them wars, rather than organized criminal violence, as long as some of the criteria are met. Of special interest is the right authority criterion, regarded by some just war theorists as absolutely essential. Compared with the other criteria, however, right authority proves particularly troublesome for SAMCRO, since it may seem that the club, by definition, cannot fulfill it.[4]

What does right authority mean? Consider how Clay might approach this question. In "Oiled," Hector Salazar, president of the Calaveras MC, gets stomped by the Sons in retaliation for having ambushed SAMCRO during Half-Sack's wake. In protest, Salazar screams, "You can't kill me! I am a patch president!" Clay is not impressed: "I don't recognize your bullshit MC." From his point of view, the Calaveras don't have the same standing as SAMCRO and the Mayans, nor the same rights. They're merely muscle for the Mayans. After he's finished with Salazar, Clay brokers a peace deal with Marcus Álvarez, president of the Mayans, who then strips Salazar of his patch. The Calaveras have no say in the matter. In Clay's world, the presidents of major MCs like the Sons and the Mayans are like heads of states. Hector Salazar and the Calaveras are, by contrast, just fly-by-night thugs.

But when it comes to declaring war, most upholders of the right authority criterion would regard Clay much as Clay regards Salazar, though they might express themselves more delicately. For instance, the influential just war theorist Michael Walzer would probably admonish Clay that, though MC presidents may have the authority to make all kinds of deals, they aren't really heads of states and therefore they lack the authority to declare war. For Walzer, the right authority criterion condition must be met for the use of armed force to be morally justified, and the criterion *defines* war exclusively as a relationship between states. For Walzer, SAMCRO could never declare "war" in the proper sense of the term, since it's a motorcycle club, not a state.[5]

What *is* a state anyway? And why should states, but not SAMCRO, have the authority to declare war? For an answer to these questions, let's turn to Dr. Tara Knowles.

"Can't Get Used to Losing You"

Agent Joshua Kohn has come to Charming pursuing his obsession with Tara. In "The Pull," he breaks into her house, takes her prisoner in the bedroom, and puts on his favorite song, "Can't Get Used to Losing

You," as he prepares to rape her. But Tara is clever. She tricks Kohn into believing that she still loves him and gets him to lower his guard. Tara manages to grab Kohn's gun and shoots him in the stomach. Most would agree that this use of force against Kohn was morally justified as a way to protect her life, her bodily integrity, and the sanctity of her home from a deranged intruder.[6] Given that the physically superior Kohn meant business, what alternative did she have?

This scenario can help us think about the right authority criterion. The state, Walzer claims, is not unlike Tara in her home.[7] Let's suppose the United States is attacked by another country. The aggressor state invading US territory is just like Kohn invading Tara's home and attempting to invade her body. And just as Tara has a right to repel such an invasion, so does the United States. What gives the United States this right is its possession of *sovereignty*, meaning that it's not under the rule of any other state and therefore has supreme authority to enforce the law in its own territory.[8] Not all states are sovereign in this sense. SAMCRO's home state of California, for instance, isn't sovereign, since it's under the authority of the federal government. Because a sovereign state is, like Tara, the boss in its own house, it has the authority to repel invaders, by force if need be. States that aren't sovereign don't necessarily have this authority. California, for instance, lacks the authority to declare war.

Does SAMCRO resemble a sovereign state? On first blush, the comparison doesn't look promising. These are the Sons of *Anarchy*, for crying out loud. Isn't "anarchy" the complete opposite of a state?[9] But on closer examination, it turns out that the club is more like a state than we might initially expect. We can identify four key features of a state: a state is a legal system that (1) rules over people who are (2) located in a certain territory, doing so by (3) making and enforcing laws through (4) state officials.[10] How does SAMCRO measure up?

Like a state, SAMCRO has people over whom it rules: its members, who are subject to the laws of the club. It also has a territory, Charming, that it sees itself as charged to protect (though things get a bit muddied here, since the people under its putative protection, the citizens of Charming, aren't the same as those under its authority). The club makes laws for its members and enforces them through its officials. Step out of line and you might get a visit from the sergeant at arms. Finally, SAMCRO claims a sort of sovereignty, viewing itself as the only body with supreme authority over its members. It has, for instance, the authority to collect club dues from its members and arbitrate their disputes. Fiercely protective of its independence, it respects other outlaw motorcycle clubs on their turf, but in return they had better recognize SAMCRO's sovereignty within Charming. As a mini-state, maybe SAMCRO should consider a name change. But if you want to be a badass biker club, a moniker like Sons of Government really doesn't cut it—I accept that.[11]

Consider SAMCRO's war with the Mayans when they tried to expand their drug operations into the San Joaquin Valley in the early 1990s. Like Kohn breaking into Tara's house or an aggressor state invading US territory, the Mayans encroached on SAMCRO's turf. Or consider what happened when one of SAMCRO's most dangerous enemies, Ethan Zobelle, wanted to take over Charming, full stop! Just as Tara and the United States have the authority to repel those who fail to recognize that they're the bosses of their respective domains, shouldn't SAMCRO have the authority to declare war against invaders like the Mayans and Zobelle?[12] Shouldn't sovereign mini-states have the same authority as their big brothers? It seems like a simple matter of consistency.

Yet, on reflection, the analogy with Tara may seem weak. Tara's interest in her bodily integrity and house are important. She's a living, breathing human being. But states and mini-states aren't. Why should they matter? Walzer's answer is that the sovereign status of sovereign states depends on their ability to protect the communities located within their territory. And communities matter because human beings matter. After all, human beings can only thrive in communities. It's time to bring in an expert on community, Gemma Teller Morrow.

"I Believe in Family"

In "Better Half," IRA gun-dealer Cameron Hayes presses Gemma on her beliefs. Armed with a rosary and having just narrowly escaped death from the Mayan bullet he caught during the botched assassination attempt on Clay, Cameron counts his Hail Marys. Gemma, on the other hand, has no time for religious devotions. What does she believe in? "I believe in family," she replies. And this includes not only her blood kin but also her adopted family consisting of SAMCRO and the community it sustains.

But is this the sort of community Walzer has in mind? Although Walzer is notoriously vague on what he means by community, it's likely that he is referring only to "nations." Sovereign nation-states, according to Walzer, have the authority to declare war on behalf of the nation located within their border.[13] A "nation-state" is a state whose people form a "nation." We shouldn't confuse the two, since there can be nations that don't have a state. The Palestinians don't currently have state, but they're still a nation. The Polish people were a nation even when they lived under Nazi rule. Walzer seems to assume that most states are nation-states whose sovereign authority to declare war stems from the right of those nations to defend themselves against aggressors. So given that SAMCRO is a community, is it also a *nation*?[14] Let's consider what needs to be true to turn an assemblage of people into a nation.

First, members of a nation recognize each other as compatriots and they share certain beliefs. Well, don't SAMCRO's members recognize each other as fellow outlaws? In fact, their common bond is so strong that they refer to each other as "brothers." They also share certain beliefs about the nature of their group. Of course, as the struggle between Clay and Jax makes clear, members of SAMCRO sometimes disagree about the direction of their club. But so do members of nations. Americans, for instance, disagree on a wide range of matters concerning economics and social policies, but that doesn't change the fact that they still regard each other as fellow Americans.

Second, nations are historical communities with identities that stretch into the past. The same is true of SAMCRO, where events surrounding the club's founding continue to play an important role in shaping how members understand themselves in the present.[15] Consider the role that the past often plays in shaping national identity. Because their forefathers toiled hard and maybe even gave their lives in defense of the nation, people often feel that they have inherited an obligation to honor those sacrifices by remaining loyal to their nation's ideals. Jax is the living embodiment of such historical obligations. Does his father's legacy mean that Jax is obliged to stay with the club and fight to restore it to its true purpose? What about the brothers who gave their lives for their club? Isn't he obliged to keep the club running to honor their sacrifices? Given how steeped Jax's identity is with SAMCRO's history, it isn't surprising that he finds it almost impossible to walk away from the club.

Third, nations are active associations that make decisions—or at least their political leaders do. Like many nations, SAMCRO has established decision-making procedures, such as convening for church and observing the rule of one man (or, more precisely, one *rider*) one vote. The decisions made by nations may bring salvation or ruin, but one thing is certain: they shape that nation's identity. Similarly, decisions made during church often have serious repercussions for the club. The decision to mule cocaine for the Galindo Cartel was particularly disastrous. But, good or bad, these decisions indicate that the club is an active group, shaping its own identity.

Fourth, nations are connected to a particular territory. The same is true of SAMCRO, which has deep roots in Charming. Charming is a small town with small-town values and *one* outlaw motorcycle club only—no Mayan infiltration, no crank dealing by the Nords.

Fifth, nations comprise people who share characteristics that set them apart from other groups. The English, for instance, knock politely and then wait until they are asked before entering a room. Germans, by contrast, knock and then barge right in.[16] SAMCRO members are likely first to kick down the door and then knock. There are plenty of other things that set SAMCRO apart from rival groups. For example, members of SAMCRO ride Harleys and wear leather cuts, while One-Niners drive flashy sports cars and wear purple shirts. (Like the Niners, though, Jax wears sneakers—albeit white ones!) Admittedly, differences between groups can be rather fine-grained. Mayans and Sons, for instance, both ride Harleys, but the Mayans have apehanger handlebars. Other differences are more conspicuous. While the Mayans listen to Latino music, we never hear anything but rock and country playing in the Charming clubhouse—though I do sometimes wonder what's playing on Juice's iPod.

Most importantly, SAMCRO consciously maintains an identity that separates it from other groups: all members wear the Reaper tattoo. If you aren't a member of SAMCRO (or one of the club's other charters) you had better not be caught wearing one. As the fate of disgraced ex-member Kyle Hobart attests, sporting a Reaper tattoo as a non-member can be a serious health hazard.[17]

Sixth, nations aspire to be self-determining. They want to make their own laws and decide their own future. The same applies to SAMCRO, which is an active community that makes decisions about its future—for better or worse. An outlaw biker is subject to the rules of his club, which are much more important to him than mainstream social rules that govern "civilians." This is where SAMCRO the nation meets SAMCRO the mini-state. Because SAMCRO's members make and enforce their own rules, it's only fair to consider the club a self-determining entity.

Our conclusion must be that SAMCRO is a mini-nation-state on wheels. But then how can we deny it the authority to declare war against those who threaten its existence? Good news for the club, right? However, this conclusion has radical consequences. Enter ATF Agent June Stahl.

"You Are a Fascist Pig"

In "The Sleep of Babies," Clay accuses Agent Stahl of hating that he and the other members of SAMCRO have good lives and enjoy the same rights under the Constitution as every other US citizen, herself included. Her flippant reply ("Gee, you make me so proud to be an American") causes Clay to snarl, "You're a fascist pig," followed by an implicit threat of violence. Coming from Clay, this is a declaration of war. During this exchange, however, Clay reveals—inadvertently perhaps—a truth about SAMCRO: its members have rights under the Constitution, which means that they're US citizens. And here's the catch: the United States is a sovereign state. As such, it claims supreme authority over its subjects who live in its territory, which, as Clay tacitly acknowledges, include the members of SAMCRO.

Here's the reason why we said earlier that SAMCRO enjoys "a sort of sovereignty." In the shady world of outlaw motorcycle clubs, SAMCRO may be sovereign in relation to, say, the Mayans and vice versa. But even as a "mini-nation-state," it certainly isn't sovereign in relation to the United States. In a way, the numerous run-ins between SAMCRO and members of the law enforcement community can be viewed as conflicts of sovereignty. The United States says, "I am a sovereign state, with supreme authority over those who reside within my borders. I run Charming." In response, our mini-nation-state thumbs its nose and says, "No, you don't. I do!" Conflict between the two is inevitable. So why not take our argument to its logical conclusion? Why shouldn't SAMCRO have the authority to declare war against the United States? No Mayans, no Nords, and no "fascist pigs" allowed to patrol the streets of Charming!

The answer depends on how one interprets the right authority criterion. To have the authority to declare war, does a mini-state or a similar group need to be completely *sovereign*? Or is it sufficient to fulfill the conditions associated with statehood and nationhood? Alas, we can't entirely resolve these extremely important questions here. But it's worth noting that there are real world groups resembling SAMCRO in some ways that also challenge the supreme authority of the states under which they live. Some may be nations seeking their own sovereign state, such as the Palestinians, while others may be insurgent groups that claim to represent "the people" in their struggle against an oppressive government. The right authority criterion matters enormously to how we view the status of these groups. Perhaps at least some of them, even if they're not quite sovereign, should have the authority to declare war against their states.

Of course, it's not clear how the non-outlaw population of Charming would feel about granting SAMCRO the authority to enter into armed hostilities with the US government. Most of them are not citizens of the SAMCRO mini-nation-state. Nor to our knowledge has SAMCRO ever asked them whether they *want* to be defended against the Mayans, the Nords, or the cops. Indeed, public opinion in Charming has turned against the MC from time to time when it seemed to be attracting more violence to this small town than it was preventing. We'll just have to leave it as an open question whether this objection to granting SAMCRO the authority to declare war can be successfully overcome.

Bad Guys or Good Guys?

On balance, our arguments suggest that, in principle at least, SAMCRO does have the authority to declare war against an adversary. The club is not so different from existing political institutions. In fact, the possibility that SAMCRO can satisfy just war theory's right authority criterion should prompt us to question the special status we often unthinkingly accord to the political institutions we live under. Like all great television, *Sons of Anarchy* can teach us a lot about the real world.

That said, we don't need to condone everything SAMCRO does. But we should be careful not to *condemn* everything the club does either, even when it resorts to violence. The Sons aren't unequivocally good or bad. Indeed, it's this moral ambiguity that makes *Sons of Anarchy* one of the best and most exciting shows on television.[18]

Notes

1. Jeff McMahan disagrees; see his *Killing in War* (Oxford: Oxford University Press, 2009).
2. For an overview, see Alex J. Bellamy, *Just Wars: From Cicero to Iraq* (Cambridge: Polity Press, 2007).
3. The second set of criteria—the *jus in bello* ("justice in the conduct of war")—determines how war should be fought. (1) Non-combatant immunity: Belligerents must not kill non-combatants intentionally. (2) Proportionality of means: Belligerents must not use methods that cause more harm than good. According to one view, the *jus in bello* does not determine whether a war is just. It only determines whether it is fought justly. Theoretically, there could be unjust wars that are fought justly and just wars that are fought unjustly. For a defence of this view, see Michael Walzer, *Just and Unjust Wars: A Moral Argument with Historical Illustrations*, 4th ed. (New York: Basic Books, 2006). For a critique, see McMahan, *Killing in War*.
4. See Anthony J. Coates, *The Ethics of War*, 2nd ed. (Manchester: Manchester University Press, 1997) and Walzer, *Just and Unjust Wars*. Some philosophers don't agree that right authority is an essential part of *jus ad bellum*; see Uwe Steinhoff, *On the Ethics of War and Terrorism* (Oxford: Oxford University Press, 2007).
5. For Walzer's views on the related topic of terrorism, see Chapter 8 by Philip Smolenski.
6. For a treatment of self-defense in philosophy, see Jeff McMahan, *The Ethics of Killing: Problems at the Margins of Life* (Oxford: Oxford University Press, 2002) and Judith Jarvis Thomson, "Self-Defense," *Philosophy & Public Affairs* 20:4 (1991): 283–310.
7. Walzer, *Just and Unjust Wars*.
8. See Robert Jackson, *Sovereignty* (Cambridge: Polity Press, 2007).
9. Anarchy comes from the Ancient Greek words *anarchia/anarchos*: without a leader.
10. See David Copp, "The Idea of a Legitimate State," *Philosophy & Public Affairs* 28:1 (1999): 3–45.
11. "Sons of Leviathan," on the other hand, doesn't sound too bad! For further discussion of SAMCRO in the light of Thomas Hobbes's political philosophy, see Chapter 5 by George Dunn.

12. There's one problem with this view. Suppose SAMCRO really does fulfill the right authority criterion because it qualifies as a mini-state. That's no use if there aren't any other parties with whom the club could enter into hostile relations. For Walzer, states have the authority to enter into hostile relations with each other. The United States can declare war against an aggressor state because the latter is also a state. They are both sovereign entities. Are SAMCRO's enemies also mini-states? If SAMCRO is a mini-state, so is the Mayans MC. They may hate each other's guts, but all outlaw motorcycle clubs are similar in their organization. If outlaw motorcycle clubs are mini-states and have the authority to declare war against each other, then there can at least be "biker" wars in the armed-force-is-morally-justified sense. Perhaps some of the other organizations on *Sons of Anarchy*—the One-Niners, LOAN, or the Russian mob—are also mini-states. But let's not dwell on this point here. For now, let's concentrate on biker wars. All I say in what follows could equally be applied to the Mayans.

13. The idea that the nation and the nation-state should be the starting point for just war theory is not endorsed by all just war theorists. For a critique, see Cecile Fabre, *Cosmopolitan War* (Oxford: Oxford University Press, 2012).

14. My description of nationhood closely follows David Miller, *On Nationality* (Oxford: Oxford University Press, 1995). Interestingly, some existing outlaw motorcycle clubs refer to themselves as nations. The Bandidos MC refers to itself as the Bandidos Nation. The Mongols MC calls itself the Mongol Nation. See http://en.wikipedia.org/wiki/Bandidos and http://en.wikipedia.org/wiki/Mongols_motorcycle_club (accessed January 10, 2013).

15. For further discussion of the impact of SAMCRO's history, see Chapters 17 and 18 by Peter Fosl.

16. I should add that I am German but have lived in Britain for most of my adult life. I have been met with bewildered looks when I entered offices in the UK immediately after knocking, without being asked in first. Conversely, I have waited many times in front of German doors because, after knocking, I failed to enter promptly. Fortunately, I have the door situation under control now!

17. For further discussion of the significance of the Reaper and other tattoos sported by characters in *SOA*, see Chapter 10 by Charlene Elsby.

18. I'd like to thank George Dunn and Jason Eberl for their excellent comments on earlier drafts of this chapter.

Part III

"THE CONCEPT WAS PURE, SIMPLE, TRUE"

BIKER IDENTITY AND MEANING

CHAPTER 10

My Skin, My Self
SAMCRO's Ink and Personal Identity

Charlene Elsby

"It's really great to have all this stuff to kinda work with to build a person, you know. They have specific clothing and specific tattoos."
—Katey Sagal[1]

Sons of Anarchy puts us in a world where bikers and other criminal gangs rule, where violence is normal, and where everyone—aside from some of the more strait-laced law enforcement offers—is *tattooed*. The conjunction of these three things calls to mind our tendency to form expectations of people based on their appearance and especially on how they've chosen to permanently alter their bodies, with ink or in other dramatic ways. And, in many cases, this appears to be precisely what the modified individual intends.

Body modification can be a kind of proclamation, a visual representation of things otherwise unstated. The Grim Reaper tattoo, for example, indicates membership of the Sons of Anarchy Motorcycle Club, functioning as a semi-permanent uniform of sorts.[2] The meaning of other symbols can vary from the purely aesthetic to the intensely personal, such as Jax Teller's memorial to his father, John Teller, on his left forearm. Like Tig Trager's "Death Before Dishonor" tattoo from his days in the US Marine Corps, most tattoos are meant to signify some quality that would otherwise remain invisible, such as one's profession, beliefs, accomplishments, or ideals. In most cases, people want their tattoos to be unique, even if what makes them unique has no personal

Sons of Anarchy and Philosophy: Brains Before Bullets, First Edition.
Edited by George A. Dunn and Jason T. Eberl.
© 2013 John Wiley & Sons, Inc. Published 2013 by John Wiley & Sons, Inc.

significance at all. Even when the images are exactly alike, such as the club's Reaper symbol, some choose to display it uniquely: Juice Ortiz has the tattoo on his forearm, Jax has a full backpiece, and Clay Morrow had it on both his back shoulder and upper arm.

How are these tattoos related to the personal identity of the persons they adorn? Are they simply decorations or are they more deeply bound up with each person's selfhood?

I "Ink," Therefore I Am[3]

The French philosopher René Descartes (1596–1650) offered a famous "proof" of the existence of the self, arguing that for the question about the existence of the self even to be asked, there must be a self that's doing the asking.[4] Likewise, if tattoos are a mode of expression, there must be a "self" that's doing the expressing. Furthermore, if tattoos become associated with a particular type of personality or lifestyle, such as that of the outlaw biker, then there must also be "selves" who make those associations. Tattoos thus express one's own self and at the same time shape one's perception of other selves.

Traditional theories of personal identity don't really take into account the choices we make by adorning our bodies with particular images. They focus instead on the *mind* as the locus of individual identity and persistence through time and change.[5] Frequently, such theories don't even refer to the body as part of a person's individual essence (the unique set of defining qualities that makes you *you* and distinct from others). Descartes, for instance, came to the conclusion that if he becomes aware of his self through the activity of thinking, then thinking alone must be his essence ("I think, therefore I am").[6] But this tells us very little about the thing that thinks. The question remains whether the Jax Teller who is thinking about the best way to outwit Agent June Stahl is the same thing as the body that has "Abel" tattooed on its chest.

Philosophical arguments aside, it seems unnatural not to view the body as part of one's identity. In fact, our attitude toward body art strongly indicates that we don't normally think of ourselves simply as minds controlling a machine that does our bidding. While supporters of mind-based theories of personal identity might say that modifying your appearance is a way to express your inner selfhood outwardly, we could instead take tattoos and other forms of body modification as evidence that our bodies are integral parts of our identity. Customizing your body's appearance isn't just a matter of taking an idea and finding a way to express it. The way your body looks affects your self-concept and vice versa. We want our physical appearance to reflect how we see ourselves (or would like to be able to see ourselves), as well as how we want *others* to see us. But customizing your body is not like customizing your Harley with chrome highlights or the Reaper logo, for we see our bodies as *ours* in a more intimate way than how a rider views his bike as *his*. Your body isn't simply a possession—it's *you*!

The fact that many people modify their bodies, whether through tattoos, piercings, or muscle toning and weight loss, betrays the natural identification each of us feels with our body. Of course, there are some physical characteristics we simply can't change, but there are many others that we can and do. I will never be taller, but I can enlarge my breasts, straighten my hair, or get a rose tattoo like the one Tara Knowles wears on her back shoulder in the show's opening credits.[7]

We identify others with their bodies as well, as evidenced by the way we take their body modifications as markers of their identity. We recognize the *Sons of Anarchy* characters in part by their tattoos, which reflect their choices, values, and personal histories. As Ron Perlman explains about Clay's tattoos, "We got a chance to decide how Clay would have adorned himself, which is a great peek into his psyche—or what it was 35, 40 years ago when he first started putting on the ink."

As philosopher Maurice Merleau-Ponty (1908–1961) argued, the body is not just a vehicle we use to express intentions, but itself becomes the expression:

> It has always been observed that speech or gesture transfigure the body, but no more was said on the subject than that they develop or disclose another power, that of thought or soul. The fact was overlooked that, in order to express it, the body must in the last analysis become the thought or intention that it signifies for us. It is the body which points out, and which speaks.[8]

Tattoos are forms of personal expression in which the body itself becomes that expression. We can use tattoos to express our values, personal history, and aspirations, or to alter our perceived identity—and this alteration might be motivated by a wish to be seen as something we think we are or perhaps as something we would like to be. As forms of expression, there are an infinite number of ways to use skin art and, as we'll see in the case of Kyle Hobart, potential for misuse as well.

Badass Aesthetics

Some tattoos are there only to serve *aesthetic* purposes. With their bits of tribal design, what else could Juice's head tattoos be other than a way to look *badass*? But do they really tell us anything about him as a person? One might think that they're intended to show the world that he's dangerous, countercultural, and masculine. Or, like many other body modifications, they could be there just because he thinks they look good. Bobby Munson's forearm tattoo of a skeletal snake is another example of a tattoo that looks extremely cool, while also perhaps associating him with a dangerous form of masculinity. But let's not treat aesthetics as something unimportant. What looks good to Juice and Bobby or how they want to be perceived are very personal considerations, distinguishing them from a whole lot of other people. What's certain is that Juice and Bobby, like anyone else modifying his body, genuinely believe that they're making themselves more visually appealing. Chalk it up to taste. Some people believe that putting any mark on the body mars its natural beauty. Others see the body as a canvass, offering infinite possibilities for aesthetic self-expression.

It might seem easy to dismiss tattoos chosen for their aesthetic qualities as having less significance than others. However, placing an indelible image on your body involves selecting one specific image to express your perception of yourself, while at that same time demanding that others perceive you in the same way. In short, before getting a tattoo, some definite decision has to be made about your private and public *personae*. You start with a general notion of what looks nice and then narrow it down to a very particular image to be inscribed on the skin. We might think that Juice and Bobby wear their tattoos just because they identify themselves as bikers and bikers always have tattoos. But this explanation doesn't suffice to explain why *these* particular images were chosen instead of any of an infinite number of other possibilities. Why didn't Juice choose hearts and flowers for his head? Choosing a particular tattoo is not simply a matter of liking the image, but also weighing what that image conveys to other people. The decision to be tattooed at all is only the beginning of a series of considerations that include what the image should be and where it should be displayed, all of which reflect something about the individual making those choices.

Indelible Images and Inexhaustible Meanings

As we've noted, some tattoos may have no *meaning* beyond expressing one's personal aesthetic. Other tattoos, however, may be a graphic representation of something important to the bearer, like Opie's tattoo of Donna on his upper arm. Do such tattoos reveal aspects of a person's character? At first glance, they seem to do so only indirectly, since they tend to be images of something they want to remember, something they value, or something that inspires them. We tend to judge these kinds of things as more expressive of a person's identity than what they find aesthetically appealing, but it's still the case that what they represent is not the self but *something else*. How do these *other things* define us?

The kind of tattoos someone gets might tell us what he finds beautiful, what he holds dear, or where he's been in life. A tattoo is a way of *personalizing* the body, making it unique to the individual, and indicating something about him. Sometimes the reason for getting a tattoo is as simple as wanting to make your body unique—there may be a lot of women out there matching my general description, but *I'm* the one with *my* tattoos! We don't want to be reduced to some general category or stereotype, so we find some way to set ourselves apart, perhaps by acquiring a distinguishing mark. But when those distinguishing marks are symbols of something we value, they indicate something about our self-identity beyond simple uniqueness. The tattoos I have are indicative of *my* experiences, *my* inspirations, and *my* values.

Let's consider Opie's tattoo of Donna. We can assume from his having her image placed indelibly on his body that he loves Donna. But there's even more that this tattoo might suggest to us. Is there any significance to the placement of the tattoo near his heart? Quite likely. Did he want to tell the world that he's been indelibly marked by this woman? Again, that seems like a reasonable inference. We are able to make these inferences because we associate proximity to the heart with deep love and ink with indelibility, the very associations that Opie probably wanted us to make upon seeing his tattoo. But we can infer other things that go beyond what Opie might have intended when he got the tattoo. After Donna dies, for instance, her image gains a new significance as a connection Opie retains to his past. The intention of the work when it was created, then, does not entirely coincide with its later significance.

Tig's marine tattoo on his forearm tells us that he was a marine who subscribes to the tenet "Death Before Dishonor," but there's not much we can infer beyond that. And then there's Jax's forearm tattoo memorializing his father, which displays his love for J.T. or perhaps his respect for his father's ideals. Or maybe it's just his way of dealing with loss and keeping his father's memory alive.

An image allows for many possible interpretations and the meaning of an image extends beyond what is represented in it. As Kimberly Baltzer-Jaray and Tanya Rodriguez have written:

> a work of art is never fully exhausted by the symbols that carry it, but does not exist apart from those who or that which sustain it. The symbol resonates with suggestions of meanings, and at the same time we are also presented with the notion that not all is given to us. There is an excess of meaning in an artwork, and simultaneously there is the promise of more meaning, and the promise of there being other meanings.[9]

In other words, we don't look at Opie's tattoo of Donna and simply call to mind "Donna," no more, no less, even though that's all that's represented by the image. The image stands for a person, who is much more than a small representation of her face. We also associate the work with his feelings for her, her character, and we never exhaust the possibilities of meaning that Opie may intend with that art. Similarly, we don't know how significant Tig's marine tattoo is to him, what he intended when he got it, or what it means to him now, but it seems likely that it's meaning for Tig has evolved overtime, as he has gone from being a combat marine to an outlaw biker to sergeant-at-arms for Clay. The significance of any work of art is inexhaustible, but this is especially true of a tattoo since it's part of the skin of a living individual who is always undergoing change. As Baltzer-Jaray and Rodriguez argue, "Once the tattoo is executed, it moves with the skin, becomes a part of the flesh, and can even change shape, expression, or color with movement or over time."[10] Not only does the significance of the tattoo change, but even its appearance changes.

"Fire or Knife?"

The Reaper is *the* defining symbol of the Sons of Anarchy Motorcycle Club. Whether in tattoo form or emblazoned on a cut or hoodie, it identifies its bearer as someone closely allied with death, as someone who both shows courage in the face of death and, in warranted circumstances, is prepared to mete it out. While members may choose to place the Reaper in different places on their bodies, the tattoos themselves are almost identical. As a marker of personal identity, the Reaper tattoo indicates that its bearer's identity has a reciprocal relationship with the club's identity. It tells us that this person shares the same interests, goals, and beliefs as other members of the club who bear that tattoo and that his identity depends somehow on that of the community. This relationship is reciprocal, because not only does the club confer an identity on its members, but the nature of the club itself changes as members vote on what its goals and values should be. For instance, SAMCRO's decision to mule drugs was motivated by the personal agendas of a number of individual members, in particular by Clay's greed and Jax's maneuvering to leave the club.

We might imagine that bearing the club's tattoo means that each member's individual identity is completely subordinate to the club. But things may actually be a bit more complicated than that. We can see the tattoo instead as more like the sign of each member's commitment to the club as a community, sort of like a wedding band that can't be easily removed. Receiving the tattoo would be like a conversion ceremony to a religion.[11] The identity of the individual isn't externally defined by the club's ideals, but just happens to be in line with other individuals, who choose to identify themselves as sharing a number of things in common.

In this way, choosing membership in the club is akin to joining a religious organization, in that the member's worldview already aligns with the organization prior to joining. The fact that members choose to demonstrate their commitment with a tattoo is not in itself significant. The permanence of the marking may signify the permanence of the membership in the community, but other ceremonies may signify a similar permanence without producing any actual physical change. Christian baptism, for example, is supposed to provide permanent initiation into the Christian community (at least according to some denominations) even if the convert later becomes an atheist.

Other communities, of course, do require permanent physical changes in order to demonstrate commitment. An adult male convert to some forms of Judaism must be circumcised—and you can't undo that, even with ten laser sessions!

The right to bear the mark of the club is an honor not to be taken lightly. To wear the mark, you must earn it. In Season 1, this point was brought home to excommunicated member Kyle Hobart in a rather dramatic manner. Kyle was supposed to be Opie's getaway driver, but rode off when he heard sirens, leaving Opie behind to face a five-year prison term. Expelled from the MC in disgrace, Kyle should have blacked out his tattoo. He couldn't bring himself to do it, though, perhaps because he wasn't ready to surrender the last vestige of his identity as a member of the MC. After discovering that Kyle still sports his Reaper backpiece, Jax devises a scheme to lure Kyle to Teller-Morrow, where the club provides him with tattoo removal service courtesy of "fire or knife" ("Giving Back").

Earlier, Kyle had remarked on how wearing his cut elicited respect from people. Perhaps it's the respect he misses. Perhaps it's the meaning he received from being part of something larger than himself. Whatever the reason, Kyle still wants to identify himself with the club, but the club does not want its identity sullied by association with his disloyalty and cowardice. "Brothers don't turn on each other," says Jax. As the Sons circle him and force him to remove his shirt, Kyle pleads, "I'm sorry. I'm sorry, Clay. I know I was supposed to black it out and I tried, man, but I went a bunch of times and I … I couldn't do it. This is the only thing I have left, Jax. Please. I'm sorry." Whether because of the physical pain or the pain of ostracism, Opie says of Kyle, "I'd rather be dead than be that guy."

Kyle has, in effect, made an untrue claim about his identity. He might as well have been walking around in a police officer's uniform. Just as impersonating an officer is an offense to someone who's entitled to wear the uniform, so is Kyle's fraudulent wearing of the Sons of Anarchy insignia an offense to the club. Similarly, when A.J. Weston, a "true believer" in the League of American Nationalists, sees that Nord leader Ernest Darby has non-white employees, he tells him not to display his swastika tattoo so proudly since he hasn't "earned it yet" ("Albification").

This insistence on earning one's right to wear a symbol might be motivated by a concern for what happens to the significance of a symbol if it is misused. If outsiders were allowed to wear the insignia of the club, it would lose its meaning as a sign of membership and a token of the other club members' approval. It's even worse when Kyle wears it, since he has been kicked out of the club. The Reaper tattoo has a social meaning recognizable to anyone familiar with the club. You can't put an Oprah's Book Club sticker on any old novel, nor a Reaper tattoo on any old back. The Reaper is a stamp of approval—and without the approval, you don't get the stamp. After Clay is voted out of the MC in "Darthy," he willingly submits to having his Reaper tattoos blacked out, as did a member of the Tucson charter who voluntarily left the club ("Una Venta"). Kyle, on the other hand, continues to make a fraudulent claim about his associations. While it might seem extreme to douse him in liquor and go at him with a blowtorch, it's a surefire way to make certain that he doesn't continue to misrepresent the club and, as a bonus, accomplishes a punitive purpose. Escorting him to a laser technician wouldn't have the same effect.

Nobody Wants to Be a Shithead

Kyle's situation reminds us that tattoos represent *how we want people to see us*. He misses wearing his cut, because everybody knew who he was, but now he's just like every other "shithead." Well, nobody wants to be like every other shithead! We want people to think we're special and we try to make them look at us in the way we want to be seen. Getting a tattoo is one way to do that. Even the simple fact of having a tattoo will cause some people to see us differently. They see us as tough, irreverent, slutty, or a host of other things, although those perceptions may not align with what we intended the tattoo to symbolize.

Kyle wants the world to see him as part of something bigger, something that brings him respect. And he's certainly not the only one. Whenever we declare our loyalty to something, we thereby proclaim ourselves to be part of something bigger than ourselves. And when that thing is terribly important to us, we want to mark its importance by doing something out of the ordinary, making a big deal of our commitment to reflect what a big deal it really is to us. Getting a massive tattoo is the equivalent of shouting something from a rooftop. Not only are we part of something bigger, but we also want others to recognize our commitment and value it as we do.

Bikers are not the only people who do this. Getting a giant Reaper tattoo that transforms one's appearance to reflect one's loyalties is akin to other ceremonies that induct someone into an organization or demonstrate someone's dedication to something. We don't simply state that we are joining a particular religion; we hold a conversion ceremony. We don't simply state that we are committing ourselves to another person, but ask our friends and family bear witness to our devotion in a ceremony that may span several days. The social aspect of the grand gesture reinforces how we identify ourselves and how we want others to identify us. It is, in a sense, a demand that others alter their perceptions of us. And we find it offensive when someone else makes the same demand without exemplifying the same aspect of identity, like poor, cowardly, burnt Kyle.[12]

Notes

1. Transcribed from "Sons of Anarchy: The Ink," a special feature on the Season 1 DVD, 20th Century Fox, 2009.
2. For more on the significance of the Grim Reaper, see Chapter 11 by Kevin Corn.
3. Robert Arp, ed., *Tattoos – Philosophy for Everyone: I Ink, Therefore I Am* (Chichester: John Wiley & Sons, 2012).
4. See René Descartes, *Meditations, Objections, and Replies*, trans. Robert Ariew and Donald Cress (Indianapolis: Hackett, 2006), 16.
5. For an approach to the problem of identity that takes into account both the body and the individual's personality, see Chapter 12 by Minerva Ahumada and Tim Jung.
6. Descartes, *Meditations*, 16.
7. Though we've never seen that tattoo in the show itself.
8. Maurice Merleau-Ponty, *Phenomenology of Perception* (New York: Routledge Classics, 2005), 229–230.
9. Kimberly Baltzer-Jaray and Tanya Rodriguez, "Fleshy Canvas," in *Tattoos – Philosophy for Everyone: I Ink, Therefore I Am*, ed. Robert Arp (Chichester: John Wiley & Sons, 2012), 47.
10. Ibid., 42.
11. For an analysis of the MC as a quasi-religious institution, see again Chapter 11 by Kevin Corn.
12. I would like to acknowledge the helpful discussions I had with Kimberly Baltzer-Jaray and Ferenc Hajos on the ideas for this chapter, as well as the comments of the editors of this volume.

CHAPTER 11

The Faith of Our Sons and the Tragic Quest

Kevin Corn

It is a solemn moment for SAMCRO. Opie Winston has given his life for the MC and it's time for the whole community to honor his sacrifice. Members carry his coffin through the clubhouse, past the glass case holding trophies, an ancient polished Harley, and a wall covered with mugshots of SAMCRO members, both living and dead. They make their way into the "chapel" and lay Opie's coffin on a solid redwood table carved with SOA's Grim Reaper logo. Later, each member of the club places a memento in Opie's open coffin: a rosary, a bottle of tequila, a wrench. Finally, Jax Teller—Opie's best friend—places a photo of the two of them as children on their Huffy bikes, saying, "I'll see you later brother." As the coffin is carried in procession to a hearse, we hear Greg Holden's song "The Lost Boy":

> I will not be commanded,
> I will not be controlled,
> I will not let my future go on, without the help of my soul.

All this solemnity, sacrifice, and concern for the state of the soul might seem a little out of place among anarchists on motorcycles. It looks an awful lot like *religion*. So, should we regard Opie's wake as a religious rite?

Sons of Anarchy and Philosophy: Brains Before Bullets, First Edition.
Edited by George A. Dunn and Jason T. Eberl.
© 2013 John Wiley & Sons, Inc. Published 2013 by John Wiley & Sons, Inc.

The Tragedy of Jax Teller, Prince of Charming

The Sons of Anarchy aren't a Christian sect, nor do they belong to any of the other religious bodies that Americans commonly embrace. And they certainly don't claim any direct revelations from God. But just because they don't attach themselves to some larger religious tradition doesn't mean that they don't share many things with more conventional faiths. Opie's wake is just one among many events, ideas, and artifacts that help constitute the Sons of Anarchy as a community of faith, albeit a very unconventional one.

At this moment in the life of the club, when the whole community must look directly at death, the symbols in the ritual combine to do what the rites of death in any religion must accomplish. First, the symbols frame their collective view of the world they inhabit, particularly the forces that drive them together and that separate them from all other people. Second, they evoke the *ethos* of the whole community— its essential spirit—so emphatically that even in their grief every member knows their club can transcend the death of any one of its members. Third, they make memory of the dead an essential ingredient of that ethos. Opie's death has particular resonance for the club since it was a sacrifice to protect his brothers. There is no doubt that his mugshot will become an icon on SAMCRO's wall, along with those of other honored members who died before him. Anyone who has seen a shrine to the saints and martyrs of any religion can discern the meaning behind it all: to honor Opie is to honor the club and vice versa.

The question isn't whether we can look at the Sons of Anarchy as a community of faith so much as it is how the rites, practices, and symbols of this faith can shed light on the conflicts at the heart of the series. Let's not forget that the drama we're watching has the form of a *tragedy*—that is, a story about characters brought down by some mysterious event in their background or some flaw in their character. On one level, the drama's main character is Jax, who's modeled on Shakespeare's Hamlet. As with Hamlet, Jax's quest to achieve personal redemption moves him episode by episode toward what we fear will be a tragic disaster. But this is more than the story of Jax. His story epitomizes the tragedy of the whole community gathered in and around SAMCRO, the collapse-from-within of their collective values, purpose, and meaning. And if we're to understand the trajectory of this tragedy—and our own attraction to it—the best place to look for clues is in the meaning of the symbols that the Sons use to define themselves and their increasingly threatened ethos.

The Soul of a Man

According to most conventional definitions of religion, SAMCRO is not a religious organization, since the club isn't organized around any relationship with supernatural forces or beings. But conventional definitions of religion can be misleading. To make sense of SAMCRO, we need a broader understanding of what religions do and how they get started.

At the beginning of the twentieth century, French sociologist Émile Durkheim (1858–1917) changed the way scholars understood religion by shifting the focus from supernatural forces to human beings, seeking to understand the way we use religious symbols, beliefs, and practices to bind communities together. For Durkheim, the really interesting questions aren't about what people believe, but rather are about what ritualized religious behavior does for the people engaged in it. And that's precisely what we need to ask about the Sons of Anarchy when we consider the rituals and symbols that bind them together as a club.

Durkheim described a religion as "a unified system of beliefs and practices relative to sacred things ... which unite into one single moral community ... all those who adhere to them." Religions are "social affairs and the product of collective thought," such that every religion in some way reflects the community that gave it birth.[1] Durkheim defined *sacred things* as items that are "set apart and forbidden," meaning that they can't be held or controlled by just any individual, but only by those authorized to do so.[2] All others risk grave spiritual or physical injury. These sacred objects embody the spirit of the group as a whole.

Let's say, then, that a religion is a system of *symbols* that represent a group's collective understanding of life's ultimate value, meaning, and purpose. These symbols can take a variety of forms—words, visual icons, and practices. Taken together, they collectively provide the larger context that gives meaning to each one individually.[3] Like a dictionary that defines each word only in reference to other words— or a motorcycle in which the functionality of each part depends on its relationship to all the other parts and to the bike as a whole—each religious symbol takes its meaning from its contextual relationship with all the rest. This makes religion a sort of *system*.

As a community, SAMCRO certainly has its share of symbols, from the Reaper logo inked into the skin of every member, to the "cuts" that they all wear as a sort of uniform. And in some ways these symbols are regarded as *sacred*. Consider what happens to excommunicated member Kyle Hobart when he neglects to black out his Reaper tattoo. The club "blacks it out" for him with a blowtorch! Or recall how Jax would rather take a bullet to the head from Marcus Álvarez than relinquish his cut. The respect the club shows—and demands that *others* show—for these symbolic objects designates them as *sacred*. And these symbols clearly reflect a shared worldview, one that involves a particular view of *masculinity* and a judgment about the value of *brotherhood*, to which SAMCRO aspires as an ultimate good.

This understanding of masculinity and brotherhood is also tied to a celebration of *transgression*—the willful refusal of each man to submit to the rules and conventions of the larger society. As the song played in the background at Opie's send-off reminds us, the Sons of Anarchy pursue an ideal of not being "commanded" or "controlled." In fact, part of their attraction to us as viewers is that they embody a freedom that middle-class Americans have traded away for the comforts of physical security and social respectability. The MC lifestyle offers the possibility of renegotiating our relationship with society in order to enjoy a degree of freedom that most of us can only imagine.

But the last line of the song suggests that the reason for seeking freedom from the commands of others is to live a life in union with one's "soul." It's that pursuit that sets them at odds with the larger society and that has brought them together to support each other in their struggles. It's for the sake of their "souls" that the brotherhood has become such a priority in their lives. All their other social relationships are secondary, including those with the women in their lives.

MC and MB: Hunters, Warriors, and Bikers

Gender inequality is a common feature of religious life in modern America. The Roman Catholic priesthood remains all male and Orthodox Jews forbid women to lead worship or read publicly from the Torah. In these "all-boy" domains, male bonding becomes a primary good and maybe even something like a religious duty. In this respect, at least, SAMCRO's insistence on male exclusivity is entirely unexceptional.

That men should bond through religious rituals is not surprising, at least from the perspective of German classicist Walter Burkert, who has offered some intriguingly manly speculations on the origin of religion. According to Burkert, religious rituals originated in ancient times within all-male groups of cooperative hunters. His term for such a group is a *Männerbund*, literally an "all-male society." We'll just shorten *Männerbund* to MB, since, as we'll see, these close-knit bands of male predators bore a striking resemblance to our modern-day all-male MC.

These MBs formed as men discovered they could kill animals many times their size, even whole herds of them, if they learned to trust each other and work together[4]—not unlike the way the Sons are able to separate Ethan Zobelle from his large Mayan escort through some very skillfully coordinated action. Such cooperation was no small feat for our ancient ancestors because the human male had already evolved a highly aggressive attitude toward other males in order to compete for the favor of females, an attitude still prevalent today—recall how Jax clobbered the clueless nitwit in Nevada who sat on his bike and then rode off with the bloodied chump's girl. Burkert also describes how early human males learned to cooperate to protect their women and offspring from marauding male outsiders. As these new societies came together and evolved, they began to ritually re-enact their hunting successes in order to transmit to their sons the specialized knowledge they'd acquired and emphasize to the women the enormous gifts their dangerous new business brought for the whole tribe.

Burkert insists that such cooperative engagement on the part of men introduced a new level of stress that had both psychological and sociological repercussions. First, it required an unusual level of repression to get aggressive young males to work together without turning their aggression against each other. We see that also in SAMCRO, where, despite the intensity of the brotherly bond, rivalries, resentments, and assorted "pissing contests" regularly break out in the clubhouse. The contentious relationship between Tig Trager and Herman Kozik is a particularly prominent case in point.

Second, the bond that the MB required of the hunting band divided the loyalties of its members between their male comrades and their families. Again, the same thing happens in the MC. Consider how the often turbulent relationships of club members with their wives, ex-wives, girlfriends, and even children compete with the demands of SAMCRO, seen most dramatically in the strained marriage of Opie and Donna. As with Opie and Donna, such conflicts of loyalty are almost inevitably resolved in favor of the club. In the male-dominated world of the MC, just as in the MB, women are invariably accorded a secondary status. Gemma may be a sort of queen within her community—and she is referred to as such by her husband and club president, Clay Morrow—and she may wield significant power as the club matriarch, but, as she's sometimes reminded, even by her own husband and son, her formal status is simply that of an "old lady," like all the wives and girlfriends of the male club members.[5]

Third, the MB opened up a whole new dimension for conflict with other human beings. The skills and tools you need to bring down a herd of buffalo or a giant sloth are almost exactly the same as those required to kill other human beings, in particular, other bands of cooperative hunters competing for the same game. Battling with other men has the added advantage of allowing one to blow off some of the aggression that has to be held in check in order to hunt cooperatively. In primitive times, great hunters of animals tended to become great killers of men. Similarly, in a world where various MCs and other criminal outfits are constantly competing for turf and moneymaking opportunities, war between rival bands is practically inevitable.[6]

This same dynamic of pent-up aggression and deep group loyalty that was present in these ancient hunting bands is at work among the Sons of Anarchy, shaping their "souls" and, as we'll see next, reflected in the symbols through which the club expresses its understanding of life's ultimate value, purpose, and meaning.

The Grim Face of the Sons of Anarchy

The most prominent and ubiquitous symbol for the Sons of Anarchy MC is its Grim Reaper logo. The Reaper is a hooded skeleton who carries a scythe with which he harvests the souls of the dead. Also known as the Angel of Death, the Reaper has been a familiar symbol of death in Western civilization since the fifteenth century. He's frequently conceived of as a *psychopomp*—a figure who conducts souls from the world of the living into the realm of the dead. His scythe shows that he's a harvester, coming to collect souls that will inevitably mature and die, unless, of course, they die prematurely through external causes, such as a bullet in the skull. The Reaper logo associates the Sons of Anarchy with death, emphasizing both the dangers of their profession—as we've seen, members of the MC have a distressingly high mortality rate—and their own willingness to act as "Men of Mayhem," agents who bring the disruptive power of death into the world.

But the Sons have tweaked the Reaper's form significantly to reflect their club's particular characteristics. Like the classic image of the Reaper, the club's logo holds a scythe in his right hand, but it's fixed like a bayonet to the end of an M16 rifle. The M16 hearkens back to the origins of the club as an organization formed by members of an army airborne unit that fought in Vietnam. From its beginnings, the club has been a band of warriors. The rifle also reflects the club's core business—selling illegal guns, mostly military weapons, to various criminal organizations.

The Reaper's left hand holds an orb, an ancient symbol of sovereignty over the world. Innumerable works of religious art depict God or Jesus Christ holding just such an orb. However, the Sons have marked their orb with an Λ for "anarchy," thereby announcing their rejection of *any* claims to authority over them. Far from submitting to authority, they are dedicated to flouting and subverting it. Scoffing at the official law enforcement agencies, they administer their own brand of justice, dealing death to their enemies just as they did in Vietnam. Beyond that, as we know, they sell guns to others who operate outside the law.

Beneath the orb are the letters MC, for "motorcycle club." A banner on top says "Sons of Anarchy" and a banner below indicates the name of the chapter or the area in which the chapter of the club is located—California in the case of the logo that adorns the meeting table used by SAMCRO in its "chapel."

In all these respects, the club's logo operates as a religious *icon*. It's crowded with visual symbols and words that appear in a set form that is not to be tinkered with. As with many other sacred symbols and objects, it's reproduced in precisely the same form wherever it appears, even when used by the Belfast chapter. Only the chapter's location in the bottom banner changes.

Hierophanies of Death: SOA's Reaper and the Cult of Santa Muerte

Despite the Sons' use of iconic symbols like the Reaper, one might still object that they're simply too transgressive to be taken seriously as a *religious* community. They're *criminals*, after all! And while it's not uncommon for religious people and institutions to be embroiled in criminal activity, crime is usually not their *avowed* profession. But consider the Mexican cult of Santa Muerte, "Holy Death" in Spanish, which is strikingly redolent of the world of the Sons.[7] Not only is the figure of Santa Muerte a variation on the Grim Reaper, but the veneration of this "saint" is especially popular among criminals involved in the drug trade and associated branches of organized crime. While outwardly resembling the veneration of saints as practiced by Roman Catholics in Central America, the cult of Santa Muerte is quite separate from the official church and has provoked strong denunciations from church authorities.

Like the image of Santa Muerte, the Reaper logo is what scholars of religion call a *hierophany*. Hierophanies connect human beings to an order of being that transcends ordinary reality, set apart and out of reach for all but the initiated.

The Reaper logo is the club's most sacred symbol and the degree to which other symbols and objects are sacred to the club can be seen in their proximity to the logo. There are strict rules about when and where the logo can and must be displayed, as well as who can and must display it.

We find the logo in three major settings. First, it's carved into the table around which the club meets to take votes and conduct other important business—the same table on which Opie's body is laid in state. Second, new members have the logo tattooed into their flesh. Getting such tattoos is both expensive and painful, and, of course, it's not something you can ever cleanly undo. The permanence of the tattoo is a reminder of their commitment to their new identity. It represents an ultimate pledge in which the new member makes visible his understanding that his new life is essentially tied to the club. Nevertheless, we have at least two cases of members who are expelled and consequently forbidden to wear the logo. Despite being one of the original members of the club and president of it for most of his adult life, Clay Morrow had to have his Reaper tattoos blacked out with ugly botches of black ink: permanent marks of his humiliation. In another case, mentioned earlier, Kyle Hobart makes the mistake of returning to town without having had the Reaper logo on his back blacked out. He's offered a grim choice for its removal: fire or knife.[8]

Because the Reaper logo is on each member's cut, the cut is also *sacred*, a hierophany connecting the wearer to the collective spirit and identity of the Sons of Anarchy. The cuts of prospective members don't display the Reaper. But when Half-Sack Epps, a prospect, is killed defending Tara, the club honors him by placing a newly minted member's cut draped as a pall over his coffin—just as veterans have an American flag draped over their coffins or Christians have a white cloth symbolizing their hope of bodily resurrection.

Members are expected to wear their cuts in most public situations, making it difficult for them to establish an identity separate from the club. And club rules dictate that they never enter the clubhouse without their cut. After Piney Winston nearly shoots Clay for his role in Donna's death, Clay rebukes him: "Hey old man, don't ever come into this clubhouse without your cut" ("The Culling"). An attempted homicide is of less gravity than the ritual infraction.

The clubhouse itself is another hierophany, insofar as the club itself is sacred. It's set apart from other spaces and reserved for club members and their invited guests. And, of course, the most sacred space in the clubhouse is the "chapel," where official business is conducted.

The Tragic Flaws in the Faith of SAMCRO

There's something rotten in Charming. Season by season, we watch the shadow of tragedy grow darker, hovering over all the main characters on *Sons of Anarchy* and over the club as a whole. These are violent people who make a lot of enemies and attract a lot of attention from law enforcement agents who want to put them away. But the club's ability to withstand these external challenges depends significantly on the unity they maintain in the face of adversity. However, tensions within the club keep eroding the bond of brotherhood and with it their faith, which has always been a faith in each other first and foremost. Using Durkheim's ideas as our guide to the religious dimension of the Sons of Anarchy and understanding their faith as an outgrowth of their community, the breakdown of community that we witness over the course of the series is tantamount to a failure of their faith. And we can improve our understanding what ultimately brings SAMCRO down by considering the symbols and practices of their faith.

The root conflict of *Sons of Anarchy* is between Jax and his stepfather, Clay, which mirrors the central conflict in Shakespeare's *Hamlet*. In the play, Hamlet discovers that his uncle and stepfather became King of Denmark by murdering Hamlet's father. In *Sons of Anarchy*, Jax discovers that his stepfather became president of SAMCRO by murdering Jax's father, John Teller. Hamlet's quest for vengeance eventually destroys not just his stepfather, but his mother, himself, and much of the royal court. If Jax's quest for revenge follows this Shakespearean script, then it's bound to rebound in one way or another on the entire MC.[9]

Ultimately, this conflict at the heart of SAMCRO's tragedy is embodied in its most basic symbols and what they represent. In holding as sacred the flouting of all rules, they undermine the sanctity of their own union, which is nothing if not bounded by rules. If the orb in the middle of their icon represents the triumph of anarchy throughout the world, how can we not expect there to be trouble in the clubhouse? If you make the Grim Reaper your central symbol, it should be no surprise when death makes frequent visits.

Moreover, the symbol of the Reaper suggests more than death. It represents SAMCRO's commitment to vengeance. The Sons of Anarchy claim vengeance not only as their right, but as their *moral obligation*, their ethic of brotherhood being grounded in the duty of each member to help the others to avenge the wrongs done to them, as both Damon Pope and the prison guard involved in Opie's murder had to learn the hard way. Even when reason argues for caution, vengeance remains the priority. After an attack on club members by the Nords, Clay states unequivocally, "Retaliation must be harsh and immediate. That's what we do" ("Smite"). When it's vengeance against outside enemies, the act of retaliation can reinforce the unity of the group. But when vengeance becomes the routine way to resolve internal conflicts, like the quarrel between Jax and Clay, the community is set on a tragic path of destruction.

To be sure, the fat lady has not yet sung. Though SAMCRO has had to bury far too many brothers since Season 1, at the end of Season 5 most of the principle characters still remain above ground. There's still time to subvert Hamlet's logic and still time for SAMCRO's members to find their collective soul without more bloodshed. Jax has had numerous opportunities to kill Clay outright, but so far he has only connived to put a price on his head for the murder of Damon Pope and packed him off to prison. Tara might still persuade Jax to walk away from his *Männerbund* and find domestic happiness in Oregon—assuming she survives her own trip to the slammer.

Is that what we really want for them, though? Of course, even if it is, the Reaper might have other plans.

Notes

1. Émile Durkheim, *The Elementary Forms of the Religious Life*, trans. Joseph Ward Swain (Hollywood, FL: Simon & Brown, 2013), 53, 17.
2. Ibid., 53.
3. For a detailed breakdown of the categories of religious symbols and behaviors, see Ninian Smart, *Dimensions of the Sacred: An Anatomy of the World's Beliefs* (Berkeley: University of California Press, 1996).
4. Walter Burkert, *Homo Necans*, trans. Peter Bing (Berkeley: University of California Press, 1983).
5. For further discussion of the women of *SOA*, see Chapter 15 by Leslie Aarons and Chapter 16 by Leigh Kolb.
6. For more on the inevitability of war, see Chapter 5 by George Dunn.
7. For information on the cult of Santa Muerte, see R. Andrew Chestnut, *Devoted to Death: Santa Muerte, the Skeleton Saint* (New York: Oxford University Press, 2012); Tony Kail, *Santa Muerte: Mexico's Mysterious Saint of Death* (La Vergne, TN: Fringe Research Press, 2010).
8. For more on the significance of the Reaper tattoo and tattoos in general, see Chapter 10 by Charlene Elsby.
9. For more on Shakespearean themes in *Sons of Anarchy*, see Chapter 14 by Andrea Zanin.

CHAPTER 12

Once a Biker Slut, Always a Biker Slut
Narrative Identity in Charming

Minerva Ahumada and Tim Jung

When we first meet Tara Knowles, she is wearing her scrubs and saying things like "congenital birth defect" and "gastroschisis." Dr. Knowles explains to Jax Teller and Gemma Morrow the frail condition of Jax's newborn son, Abel: born ten weeks premature to a junkie mother, Abel will need all the medical help he can get. It's a good thing that the accomplished Dr. Knowles has volunteered to be on Abel's watch, since she seems to care deeply about Abel and Jax. But when Gemma lifts Tara's shirt to reveal a tattoo on the small of her back (the type sometimes called a "tramp stamp"), we get a fuller glimpse of who Tara Knowles is—or should we say was? Tara asserts that she's not the same person she was ten years ago when she left Charming for college and then medical school, saying about her tattoo, "I leave it there so I remember all that shit's behind me" ("Pilot").

How can Tara claim to be a different person with that ten-year-old tattoo displayed so prominently on her lower back? There's something paradoxical about Tara still being *Tara*, the girl who left Charming so many years ago, but nonetheless claiming that she's *not* the same person as that 19-year-old girl who got the tattoo. This is the sort of question that gets under the skin (so to speak) of philosophers. It's a question about *identity* or, more specifically, about *personal* identity.

Sons of Anarchy and Philosophy: Brains Before Bullets, First Edition.
Edited by George A. Dunn and Jason T. Eberl.
© 2013 John Wiley & Sons, Inc. Published 2013 by John Wiley & Sons, Inc.

"What Have You Done With *Tara*?"

Questions of identity involve the attempt to determine what exactly makes a person or thing what it is—what makes Tara *Tara* or what makes Charming *Charming*? The answer often involves an attempt to pinpoint those aspects of a thing or a person that remain the same across time, even as other aspects have changed. For example, let's say you've lived in Charming for the past three years. What changes has Charming undergone? Quite a lot, actually! There have been outbursts of violence, a cigar store has opened and closed, the local PD was replaced by the San Joaquin County Sherriff's Department, the development of Charming Heights has begun, a barber shop window has been replaced—maybe more than once!—and Lumpy Feldstein along with many other residents have died. Is Charming still the same town as three years ago? Yes, of course it is. It's not like it's moved from California to New York! But what makes Charming *Charming*?

Or consider another case. Over the past few seasons of *Sons of Anarchy*, we've seen a number of members come and go. As of Season 5, SAMCRO has lost Opie Winston, Piney Winston, Half-Sack Epps, and Clay Morrow. The club has gained and lost Herman Kozik, as well as some other prospects and nomads. It won't surprise us at all if the club gains and loses even more members over the course of the next couple of seasons. And, of course, this change of membership is nothing new. When the series began, Clay and Piney were the only original members still with the club. Now, the club has none of its original members. So how is SAMCRO the same organization now as it was when John Teller founded it if none of its original members are alive or, if still among the living, welcome in the clubhouse?

The changes in the MC and Charming are similar to the changes Tara has undergone since she got that tattoo on her back. Of course, Tara can't be anyone but *Tara*, yet many of *Tara*'s qualities, both physical and psychological, have changed significantly throughout the years.[1] She initially made the decision to leave Charming and go to college and then to medical school to become a neonatal surgeon. Lately, however, Tara isn't looking like a doctor so much as she's looking like Gemma! She also seems to spend more time in fights than in the operating room. So, how do we solve the paradox of someone undergoing so many personal changes but still remaining the same person? Imagine that we were friends with Tara in medical school and that we came to visit her in Charming. We might end up exclaiming, "Who are you? And what have you done with *Tara*?" And yet there is another sense in which, despite those radical changes, she still remains the same person.

The philosopher Paul Ricoeur (1913–2005) attempted to solve this paradox of personal identity by pointing out that when we talk about the identity of a person, we're actually talking about two different concepts: identity as *sameness* and identity as *selfhood*. Tara is the *same* in some respects, but different in others. She retains her *selfhood* through many of these changes, yet the person she was once isn't entirely the person she is today. Ricoeur describes how we weave these two types of identity, *sameness* and *selfhood*, together to form a *narrative*, a story that allows us to understand how we are able to preserve our identities through time. Let's see whether Ricoeur's ideas on personal identity can help us make sense not only of Tara's identity, but also of how SAMCRO and some of its members maintain their identity across time.

"Well, I Guess Someone's True Colors Finally Bled Through"

Ricoeur's word for that aspect of identity that concerns *sameness* is *idem*-identity. It concerns the attributes that a person has that make her unique and different from others, such as her physical qualities and unique genetic code.[2] It is *idem*-identity that allows us to identify a person based on his or her dental records or—to SAMCRO's consternation—from the semen found in some undocumented migrant's remains. In the criminal world, it's the job of professional "cleaners" like Bachman[3] to make any evidence of that sort of identity disappear. *Idem*-identity is also what Gemma invokes when she lifts Tara's shirt to reveal her tattoo. So what does Tara mean by saying that she's not the *same person*? It can't mean that she doesn't have the same *body* or many of the same physical characteristics.

Ricoeur would say that she is talking about *ipse*-identity, which refers to her *selfhood* or personality. By distancing herself from the *Tara* who got the tattoo, Tara disavows her younger self's character and personality, things she changed when she moved to San Diego and decided to hit the books. Tara is claiming that she's no longer that teenager who was running around with Jax when they were kids. She's now the doctor with the promising career—albeit also the doctor who risks her career by choking and punching the hospital administrator, Margaret Murphy, after she suspended Tara's medical privileges for coaching Chibs to fake symptoms in order to stay safely in the hospital.

This is where the paradox hits: Tara is different—at least to some extent—in terms of her personality, but she's physically the same in that she has the same tattoo. So, is she the same person or not? The truth of the matter is more complex than that simple either/or. Ricoeur's *idem*- and *ipse*-identities are both constitutive of Tara's identity because they intertwine with one another. When Tara—or anyone—asks "Who am I?" a complete answer needs to take into account both *ipse*- and *idem*-identity. Time weaves these two components together into a single *narrative*. For Ricoeur, the coming together of these two components of identity in story form is most apparent when we look at a person's character and examine the practice of keeping one's promises.

"What Kind of Nasty Shit Did Your Momma Do to You?": Tig's Character

Ricoeur claims that our *ipse*-identity is largely made up of the "values, norms, ideals, models, and heroes" with which we identify ourselves.[4] Take Tig Trager, for example. Tig is someone who at one time played his part without question as sergeant-at-arms for Clay. During much of Season 1, Tig's values are clearly aligned with his position as Clay's right-hand man, which constitutes the "ideal" or "model" through which Tig recognizes himself. Ricoeur would argue that Tig's identification with the values of the club is what allows him to put the "cause" of SAMCRO above his own survival.[5]

Sure, Tig is a little bit out there: he routinely bites the person he is fighting, was arrested for public nudity (was a chicken involved?), and has expressed an interest in necrophilia and alluded to bestiality. It's no surprise, then, that Clay at one point asks Tig, "What kind of nasty shit did your momma do to you?" Given his overactive and highly imaginative libido, not to mention his going rogue and inadvertently killing Damon Pope's daughter, Tig *might* be described as somewhat impulsive.

Tig's character is for the most part impetuous, wild, and troubled. We recognize Tig through his dispositions and habits: there's a certain Tigness to the way he approaches Venus Van Dam, the transsexual southern "belle who does not tell," as well as a Tigness to his doll phobia. So, what's our reaction when Tig eats some hallucinogenic mushrooms, begins to weep, and commences apologizing to a small doll without recoiling in fear? ("Balm"). No longer recognizing that familiar Tigness in his actions and dispositions, we might conclude that Tig is "acting out of character."

Ricoeur describes *character* as the "set of lasting dispositions by which a person is recognized."[6] In a way, character belongs to the realm of *ipse*-identity, since one's character is what marks one's personality as, for instance, loyal, upbeat, or disorganized. But these traits get identified with one's body:

> Precisely as second nature, my character is me, myself, *ipse*, but this *ipse* announces itself as *idem*. Each habit formed in this way, acquired and become a lasting disposition, constitutes a *trait*—a character trait, a distinctive sign by which a person is recognized, re-identified as the same— character being nothing other than the set of these distinctive signs.[7]

The habits that form one's character (*ipse*-identity) are not accidental— they've been acquired through time and acted out countless times. And, of course, *someone* acts them out, so they are credited to a body, to an *idem*-identity. Habits become part of your identity—for both you and others—to such a degree that when you fail to perform according to habit, everyone notices the difference.[8]

Even Tig notices that he's been acting out of character. "Sorry, I'm not myself," he tells Gemma in the next episode ("Service"). After helping her collect guns, Tig finds himself in a compromising situation with Gemma, but he stops the amorous encounter from going any further when he sees the family photos on the wall. Is this the same Tig we've come to know? The same Tig who, despite his phobia of dolls, is aroused at the sight of one of Georgie Caruso's business ventures: life-like sex dolls?

Consider also when Tig confesses his crime to Opie in the same episode. Opie throws Tig around like a rag doll, frantically demanding "What did you do?" while Tig listlessly responds, "Stahl made you a rat, Opie." Unlike the Tig we knew from the first season, this Tig doesn't fight back, but instead allows Opie to use him as a punching bag. When the rest of the MC shows up and Clay angrily asks, "What the hell did you tell him?" Tig simply explains, "I don't know who I am anymore, man."

There's a certain stability that comes with your character: your habits, dispositions, and moods are all part of what makes you *you*. When your habits, dispositions, or moods change severely or unexpectedly, you may end up acting very differently from who you normally are. Tig exemplifies the disturbance of this stability in his guilt over killing Donna, since he's not the kind of person who'd kill the innocent wife of one of his brothers. Tig feels like he doesn't know himself anymore, revealing that his *ipse*-identity includes a moral compass, albeit a strange one. Tig's moral compass may allow for being nude in public, ingesting hallucinogenic mushrooms, killing rival gang members, biting people in fights, and sleeping with everything that moves (and even perhaps some things that don't), but it definitely does *not* allow for the killing of Donna.

"I Got This": Opie's Promises

While Tig helps us to see the importance of *character*, the life and travails of the late Harry "Opie" Winston can teach us much about the role that *promise keeping* plays in the narrative form of personal identity. When the show began, Opie has just spent five years in the Chino State Penitentiary for a botched arson job for SAMCRO. Understandably, his wife, Donna, wants nothing more than for Opie to leave the club. For a while, Opie tries to be half-in, half-out, but both sides pressure him to declare an allegiance. As he did when he was 16 and left his mom's home to come back to Charming, Opie chooses the club. To get proof of Opie's commitment to SAMCRO, Clay asks him to kill Brenan Hefner, the Oakland Port Commissioner who had killed Real IRA member Michael McKeavey. When the time comes to pull the trigger, however, Opie can't do the deed. Bobby Munson does.

When a witness identifies Bobby and someone who looked a lot like Opie, ATF Agent June Stahl seizes the opportunity to pit the Sons against each other. Her insidious plan involves making it look like Opie has ratted on SAMCRO. The Sons reel in shock upon hearing the news. Could Opie really be a rat?

Jax stands by his best friend. Opie can't be a rat. It just doesn't add up, not only because of his *character*, but also because he *promised* to be fully in the club again. From Clay and Tig's point of view, however, it seems that Opie *might* be a rat. This possibility arises from the competing claims that Opie juggles: the promises he's made to both Donna and the MC. If Opie is more serious about his promise to Donna, then maybe he could be a rat.

According to Ricoeur, your disposition to keep your promises makes who you are. In fact, keeping promises is precisely what makes you a "*who*." When somebody breaks a promise to you, you may not recognize that person as *whom* they've been to you. For example, when Opie learns that his second wife, Lyla, had an abortion and is on the pill, he doesn't recognize her as the same Lyla he married. Promise keeping differs from character, though, because it involves deciding in the present to respect a pact you made in the past. When married couples respect their vows ("I promise to treat you as good as my leather and to ride you as much as my Harley"), their identities become anchored on that promise, expressing *self-constancy* or our ability to remain through time who we once were.[9] While character may evolve and new habits emerge over the years, which make them appear to be always moving toward the future, promise keeping anchors your identity in a recognizable moment in the past. A person who keeps the promises he's made exhibits "the perseverance of faithfulness to a word that has been given."[10] Promises allow us to identify a person as being the same person.

Opie suffers not only because Donna was killed by Tig, but also because he lost part of who he thought he was when she died, since her death represents his failure to keep her safe and to be the sort of husband he promised to be. Ricoeur points out that events have meaning and significance only after they take place, when we look back at them and integrate them as part of our present identity. As these events were taking place, we couldn't foresee how influential they would be in determining Opie's identity. Now we can't imagine him without calling these two promises—to Donna and to the club—to mind; nor could we imagine how Opie's life and death could've been any different.

Opie demonstrates how damaging not keeping some of our promises can be to our *ipse*-identity. He also reveals one of the most fascinating aspects of Ricoeur's theory of personal identity: when Opie struggles to make sense of who he is after Donna's death, he can only come to terms with it by creating a narrative that integrates this horrible blow with other events in his life. Ricoeur notes that our "temporal totality"—that is, our sense of the meaning of our lives as a whole—can be "threatened by the disruptive effect of unforeseeable events," such as the death of Donna.[11] Who you are at any given moment has to do with how you deal with and incorporate these events into a coherent story of your life. This is one reason why our identity is never static, but is in constant flux, incorporating daily life occurrences that are beyond our control.

Opie may not always be able to keep his promises, but we still recognize him as someone who doesn't promise things in vain. So, when Gemma points out that the reason Opie head-butted Sherriff Roosevelt was to keep his promise to "stay close" to Jax, we fear that what he must do to keep that promise won't be easy to watch. Our fears are well-founded, for when Pope demands that Jax hand over "a dead Son," Opie steps up and says, "I got this."

"Once a Biker Slut, Always a ..."

Opie isn't the only person in Charming who cares deeply for Jax. Although Tara left Charming for at least ten years, when she returns it's evident—at least to creepy Agent Joshua Kohn—that she's still in love with Jax. Tara tried to change who she was in those years away from Charming, and initially she clings to her new identity as the committed and respected physician who just *happens* to volunteer to care for Abel. She can cling to her new identity-in-scrubs as long as she stays away from Jax, but when she must call him to help her deal with Kohn after she shoots him in the stomach, the distance between the two former lovers begins to break down. Kohn makes us wonder if it is true that "once a biker slut, always a ..." Hmm, wonder how he was going to end that sentence?

Of course, Kohn's judgment doesn't take into account the ways that Tara's choices over the past ten years have fundamentally altered who she is. Still, our own choices aren't the only things that influence our identity. Once she's back in Charming, Tara's identity undergoes some fairly dramatic changes due to her interactions with her new associates, which is why hospital administrator Margaret Murphy tries to convince Tara to forget about Jax. Ricoeur also recognizes how our identity is affected by others, for as much as we are *agents* who act and make choices, we are also *patients* who endure the actions of others in ways that come to define who we are. This is very clear in Tara's case: the things she's endured and the suffering that's befallen her have had a huge impact on her personal identity.

Ricoeur speaks of the way in which our "life plans take shape—a shape that is mobile and, moreover, changeable—thanks to a back-and-forth movement between more or less distant ideals, which must now be specified, and the weighing of advantages and disadvantages of the choice of a particular life plan on the level of practices."[12] Tara's "more or less distant ideals" involve a happy life that includes practicing medicine, raising her kids, and being with Jax.

Her attempt to fulfill this life project lets us see something no other character's story arc has shown up to this point: what it costs someone to choose to become part of SAMCRO. In particular, we get to see the "back-and-forth movement" between Tara's ideals and the practical consequences of trying to fulfill them within the world of SAMCRO. We meet most of the other characters when they are already fully involved with the club. By contrast, Tara wasn't even interested in being associated with SAMCRO at first—unlike Opie, Jax, and even Cherry, all of whose life projects are inseparable from the MC world. Nonetheless, once she has become Jax's old lady, her character, her life plan, and her ethics all acquire new dimensions, as she, for instance, uses her medical abilities to help SAMCRO in various ways, such as mending gunshot wounds or reaching out to Otto Delaney in prison. She does this not only for the benefit of SAMCRO, but primarily as a means to achieve her own ideal life.

Just as with Tig and Opie, Tara's character and her ability to keep promises will keep grounding her identity and re-identifying her with the Tara we knew before. But she will most likely continue to do things, such as providing Jax with the injection to kill Clay, that create conflicts with her former identity. Like the rest of us, Tara often finds herself torn between who she was in the past and what she does in the present. It's only after we have looked back at what we have done that we can really understand who we are. Looking back helps us to create our own identities and organize our life by assigning greater importance to certain events than to others. The past events that we emphasize in the narrative we construct of our lives are the ones that come to define us.

Ricoeur also says, "It is precisely because of the elusive character of real life that we need the help of fiction to organize life retrospectively, after the fact."[13] Consequently, we may look to characters in *Sons of Anarchy* to help us find answers to the question of who we are. That might help explain why law-abiding viewers who've never sat on a Harley are so fascinated by the lifestyle of outlaw bikers.

The Death of John Teller and the Life of SAMCRO

Narrative identity links up *character* and the anchor of *promise keeping*. But a narrative identity, according to Ricoeur, always has an ethical aim, namely, "the good life with and for others in just institutions."[14] A just institution looks out for its members. In the world of *Sons of Anarchy*, John Teller, who we meet only through his writings, is the one who pushes for a *just institution* and a *good life with and for others*. According to him, SAMCRO should be a just institution for its members, providing them with the opportunity to enjoy a certain lifestyle with economic security, which would count for them as a "good life." It's the idea of leading a good life that made Teller disavow the gun-running in which SAMCRO is involved. Someone like Tara could flourish in the type of club he envisions, instead of being drawn into activities that eventually lead her to prison and a total disruption of her life plans.

But we know about John Teller's ideas only through his manuscript, which highlights a point Ricoeur makes about how our narrative identities don't receive *closure*, even after we die. "As for my death," writes Ricoeur, "it will finally be recounted only in the stories of those who survive me."[15] Reading John Teller's memoir and taking its message to heart, Jax bring his father's character to life, continues his story, and becomes a thorn in the side of Clay, whose idea of a "just institution" centers on accumulating wealth for himself.

The mysteries of John Teller's death and the discovery of his writings have played a key role in how things have gone for the club. As Ricoeur notes, our lives are not solitary ones: "the life history of each of us is caught up in the histories of others."[16] The life history of John Teller is delicately intertwined with the fate of every member of SAMCRO, for better or worse. Let's hope that his influence prevails before the body count gets too high.

Notes

1. She could change her name, of course, but that in itself wouldn't make her a different person.
2. Paul Ricoeur, *Oneself as Another* (Chicago: University of Chicago Press, 1995), 117. Objects also have *idem*-identity, as defined by each object's unique set of physical qualities, including its location and extension in three-dimensional space.
3. Played by Stephen King in "Caregiver."
4. Ricoeur, *Oneself*, 121.
5. Ibid., 122.
6. Ibid., 121.
7. Ibid., 121.
8. For further discussion of the cultivation of character traits through habituation, see Chapter 1 by Jason Eberl.
9. Ricoeur, *Oneself*, 121.
10. Ibid., 123.
11. Ibid., 147.
12. Ibid., 157–158.
13. Ibid., 162.
14. Ibid., 180.
15. Ibid., 160.
16. Ibid., 161. For further analysis of how the history of SAMCRO, from its original founding through Clay's presidency, has an impact on the club's future under Jax's presidency, see Chapters 17 and 18 by Peter Fosl.

CHAPTER 13

SAMCRO and The Art of Motorcycle Maintenance

Massimiliano L. Cappuccio

Yeah, darlin' / Gonna make it happen / Take the world in a love embrace / Fire all of your guns at once / And explode into space.
— Steppenwolf, "Born to Be Wild"

Jax Teller, Clay Morrow, and the other members of SAMCRO aren't just outlaws. They're first and foremost bikers and mechanics who fix bikes. Their garage is, after all, their official—though certainly not their most lucrative—source of income. For the Sons and others who ride thousands of miles each year on Harleys, motorcycles aren't just vehicles: they are symbols of a certain lifestyle and its values. In the episode "Sovereign," Jax reflects on the significance of flying down the open road on his Harley:

> Something happens at around 92 miles an hour. Thunderheaders drown out all sound. Engine vibration travels at a heart's rate. Field of vision funnels into the immediate. And suddenly you're not on the road— you're in it, a part of it. Traffic, scenery, cops—just cardboard cutouts blown over as you pass. Sometimes I forget the rush of that. That's why I love these long runs. All your problems, all the noise, gone. Nothing else to worry about, except what's right in front of you.

It's not uncommon to hear bikers compare riding to sex, a thoroughly absorbing experience that resembles dissolution into the warm embrace of orgasmic ecstasy. Riding, among other things, can reconcile

Sons of Anarchy and Philosophy: Brains Before Bullets, First Edition.
Edited by George A. Dunn and Jason T. Eberl.
© 2013 John Wiley & Sons, Inc. Published 2013 by John Wiley & Sons, Inc.

you with the world, producing a forgetfulness that frees you from the fierce bites of apprehension and remorse. Many bikers experience riding as *therapeutic*, since a good ride can help a suffering soul to forget the worries of life.[1] Jax's words suggest that this forgetfulness involves a sense of unity with the world, so that when he's totally absorbed in this flux he can no longer tell whether he's steering or being steered by the bike.

Robert Pirsig, in his famous *Zen and the Art of Motorcycle Maintenance*, reveals why the experience of riding is so unique.[2] Unlike a bicycle, a motorcycle allows the rider to transcend the usual status of pedestrian, but, unlike driving a car, the rider doesn't lose the immediacy of his contact with the road—his view of the landscape isn't constrained within the TV-like frame of car windows. A car has an inside and an outside, but a motorcycle rider is always outside, exposed to the world. Jax knows that his sneakers can brush against the ground at any moment, that he could fall on the asphalt, that he could be drenched by rain, that wind blows against his face, and that both sun and moon shine on his leather cut. Jax must also continuously adjust where he places his body's weight while changing his angle of inclination to avoid becoming more intimate with the road than he'd like.

A rider is deeply absorbed in the world, participating in a broader reality where awareness of one's identity as a separate being can easily be lost. This loss of self-awareness, the forgetfulness of one's own mind, explains why riding can offer relief and liberation from the burdens of life. What happens in Jax's mind that allows him to experience this liberation? The answer is suggested by an interesting debate in contemporary philosophy of mind.

Zen and the Art of Brawling, Riding, and Picking Up Girls

Hubert Dreyfus builds on the ideas of German philosopher Martin Heidegger (1889–1976) to develop an influential theory about the processes that occur in the mind when one acts "pre-reflectively"— that is, in a way that involves a self-forgetting absorption in the task at hand.[3] This pre-reflective attitude doesn't prevent one from acting skillfully—quite the opposite! It's often when we overcome the awareness of our own actions that we perform best. Skilled performers and trained professionals know that you're not going to perform well if you're consciously thinking about what you're doing. A *skill* is effective only when explicit thinking is absent, when it automatically prompts us to adapt fluidly to real-life circumstances. When the ATF agents who torment SAMCRO were still rookies at the academy, they had to learn certain tactical operations—like how to break into a house occupied by armed drug dealers. When they initially practiced this joint action, they were instructed to forget their goal and focus solely on performing each step of the process. But once their training is over and the time comes to do it in the field, they need to forget about all the procedural steps and focus on the goal. They direct their concentration towards the desired outcome, and those hard-won skills kick in automatically.

The experience of forgetfulness during motorcycle riding also involves a lack of conscious self-monitoring. As with other embodied skills—as displayed by Tara Knowles performing surgery, Tig Trager firing a gun, or Bobby Munson imitating Elvis—riding involves a set of complex capabilities that require training and adaptive responsiveness to a quickly changing environment. When Jax's son Abel first learns to ride a bike, he'll have to pay careful attention to his body's position and movements. While still a novice, he'll have to decide the best strategy to handle a stiff curve or a slippery road. But, once he acquires a more confident expertise, he'll know how to manage these situations automatically, without consciously paying attention to his own actions. At that point, he'll be an expert like his father.

Dreyfus' theory is a part of the "embodied approach" to the mind, which stresses that we can't understand how the mind functions without considering the crucial role the body plays in grounding our intellect in real-life circumstances.[4] Chibs Telford's options in a pub brawl in Belfast—parrying an incoming upper-cut or responding with a fast jab—are directly afforded by the world, not decided in the solitude of his mind. What he sees, hears, and feels determines what he'll do next, not some rule stored in his mind like a computer program. Riding, brawling, or shooting a gun doesn't involve intellectual representations of stereotyped contexts or predefined rules. While some practical principles guide our skillful movements and prevent us from committing rookie mistakes, these principles are so implicit in our behavior, so unconscious, that it's hard to describe them—imagine asking Chibs to teach you how to brawl.

No set of rules or instructions can tell us how to behave in the hugely complex universe of real-life circumstances. For example, no instruction manual could ever lay out everything you need to know to approach a girl successfully. Somebody like Jax has a knack for that particular activity, but there's no fixed procedure or "magic formula" that works for all occasions. Jax might give a beginner a few tips based on his past experiences, but following those tips as if they were strict rules would likely lead to huge catastrophes: each situation is unique and each of us must find our own way. That's why the "artificial intelligences" that run computers aren't even remotely able to replicate the flexibility of complex social behaviors—like picking up a girl—that someone like Jax finds extremely natural and intuitive. Computers run on very sophisticated, but necessarily limited, representational models and lists of instructions, which allow them to solve complex calculations but leave them totally inept in real-life situations.

Heidegger on Hand-Jobs

Martin Heidegger argues that practical skills, such as the ones Tig needs to repair bikes in the Teller-Morrow garage, are the most fundamental form of knowledge. Even Tig's more intellectual knowledge of motorcycles—such as his ability to understand the blueprints of a Harley-Davidson V-twin engine—derives from his practical skills as a mechanic. Intellectual knowledge is reflective in nature, relying on abstract concepts, technical definitions, and explicit bits of information. However, the effectiveness of such knowledge requires a background familiarity with the practical world of screw-drivers, clefs, and other tools used to repair such engines. This physical familiarity isn't all that different from riding a motorcycle. In both cases, it's a pre-reflective, non-conceptual skill that operates without conscious awareness or deliberation.

Chuckie Marstein, SAMCRO's perverted and mutilated accountant, might deny the primacy of practical over intellectual knowledge, since he's an office worker who uses rational procedures more than practical skills. Office work, operating with stored information (documents, computer files, and noisy calculators), typically requires only attention to the rules. There's usually little or no involvement in manual practices—though Chuckie's compulsive masturbation disorder definitely involves a "hand-job" of a worrying kind. Be that as it may, from the point of view of someone like Tig, who makes skillful use of his hands to fix motors, Chuckie's work seems abstractly intellectual and less immediately effective. The other members of the club would probably agree, as almost all of them work outside and on the open road, not stuck in stuffy offices, earning their money with the sort of skills one doesn't learn in school but through practice in the real world. This doesn't make intellectual work less valuable or important than manual activity. However, intellectual work wouldn't even be possible if it wasn't scaffolded by our practical engagement with the world, because our most fundamental relationship to things is practical, not conceptual.

Most jobs require a mix of practical and intellectual skills. Consider Tara's profession as a surgeon. It obviously required a great deal of book learning, but that intellectual knowledge is virtually useless once her hand is smashed. And the knowledge embodied in her hands didn't come from just reading books, in any case. It's a practical know-how, similar to Jax's ability to ride and Chibs' ability to brawl. And without some embodied capabilities, even more purely intellectual activities wouldn't be possible. Juice, the "intelligence officer" of the club, must have the practical prowess to operate a computer. And even the "impractical" philosophers who contributed chapters to this book can't do their jobs without practical skills like finding books in the library and knowing how to type.

On one interpretation, Heidegger's opposition of practical and intellectual capabilities is best understood if we posit a third mode of engaging with equipment somewhere between practical, hands-on engagement and the intellectual detachment. Each mode involves a particular attitude toward reality and a specific perception of things. The first mode, called *readiness-to-hand*, is practical and unreflective. Tig is absorbed in *readiness-to-hand* when he becomes so engaged in his task that he's one with the repairs he performs and with the motorcycle engine he's repairing. The opposite mode of interaction, called *presence-at-hand*, traffics in isolated facts and bits of information abstracted from their practical significance. When Tig consults a parts catalogue to place an order, he evaluates an objective set of properties, features, and specifications in a neutral, detached way, approaching them as *present-at-hand* but not as objects with which he's practically engaged. The intermediate mode, called *un-readiness-to-hand*, arises from the need for practical problem solving in the face of unexpected circumstances. When Tig's screwdriver breaks and becomes *un-ready-to-hand*, he has to improvise a different repair strategy with a different tool. He's still using his familiar repertoire of repair possibilities, as in *ready-to-hand* interactions, but now he must step back a little from his previous absorption in his task in order to reflect on the situation and bring reason to bear on his problem.

The Problem of Dirty, Oily Hands

According to embodied theories of mind, it's during practical activities (*readiness-to-hand*) that things really matter to us and acquire their familiar meanings. Their significance affects our attitudes and behaviors in an *immediate* fashion, without the intervention of intellectual reflection and deliberation (*presence-at-hand*). Like everything else, motorcycles have different meanings for us depending on whether we approach them as *ready-to-hand*, *un-ready-to-hand*, or *present-at-hand* pieces of equipment. Many people buy motorcycles simply because they want to ride and forget their worries during a long trip—a concrete, *ready-to-hand*, embodied activity. But there are other ways to interact with motorcycles. Bikers also study pictures of models they'd like to own and accessories with which they'd like to customize their own bikes. This is a *present-at-hand* approach to engaging with motorcycles, much like fantasizing about the biker life style while watching *Sons of Anarchy*. Even the Sons partake of this mode of engagement. They proudly display a classic Harley Panhead in the clubhouse and enjoy collecting old Harley manuals.

The problem is that motorcycles—and technology in general—tend to break down, which is a real pain. Think of Bobby's beloved but somewhat dilapidated old Fat Boy, which starts spewing black smoke and causes Tig to crash ("Eureka"). Switching out the hog's oil pump isn't nearly as exhilarating as riding it into the breeze of the first day of spring or passionately conversing about the new catalogue of Harley accessories. This mode of encountering a bike—the intermediate, *un-ready-to-hand* mode—is linked to the frustrating experience of malfunction and failure, which is especially vexing when the bike leaves you on foot at the side of the road.

Many bike owners don't feel confident when they have to do repairs and finally face the dreaded encounter with the *un-ready-to-hand*. But this isn't true of everyone. SAMCRO supports itself partly through a legitimate automotive repair shop and some members collect Harley manuals and enjoy working on older models. Opie even starts rebuilding a '65 Panhead Electra Glide as a form of therapy after Donna's tragic death ("Albification"). The Teller-Morrow garage is not only a source of income for the club, but also provides an outlet for the members' love of working on bikes. Owning a Harley inevitably means having to take care of its maintenance once in a while, and many owners aren't afraid of dirtying their hands. Solving repair problems gives them the satisfaction of having surmounted a challenge. And even if they can't be sure of succeeding, there's value in just rising to the challenge. It's possible to feel at peace even in the midst of a world of troubles, so long as we keep dealing with them head-on and skillfully.

In *Zen and the Art of Motorcycle Maintenance* Robert Pirsig notes, though, that many bike owners are afraid to get their hands dirty with engine oil. What is it that people find repulsive about repairing an engine? For starters, there seems to be a general repugnance for technology. Pirsig remarks that the feeling of unease—even the sense of *threat*—that comes from technology is something deep and universal. He suspects that it's motivated by an unconscious fear of "something undefined, but inhuman, mechanical, lifeless, a blind monster, a death force. Something hideous they are running from but know they can never escape."[5] The risk of *alienation* affects our view of technology regardless of whether our technological devices are working or not: their very presence makes us feel uncomfortable.

Porn Stars and Other Mounts

Alienation occurs when we're compelled to serve as slaves to those industrial machines that we originally created to serve us. Karl Marx (1818–1883) believed that technology enslaves its human creators in societies dominated by the greedy ideal of consumerism, where workers are exploited in titanic factory assembly lines.[6] Heidegger thinks that the risk is even greater than the exploitation of workers: technology can lead to an unprecedented catastrophe for humanity, namely, the loss of the very concept of *humanity* itself.[7] Alienated people aren't simply overpowered and controlled by machines. They can get to the point where they forget they're alive, overlooking the fact that there's much more to life than efficiency, productivity, pre-programmed procedures, arid calculations, instrumental rationality, and predefined norms. Technology is the mechanism by which people every day become prisoners without realizing it, following automa-tized procedures with pre-programmed sets of rules.

Motorcycles perfectly epitomize how human beings both rely on their technological creations and constantly revolt against them, as we both desire to control the powerful mechanisms that decide our fate and recoil from them in fear. A malfunctioning motorcycle can evoke strong irritation or repulsion, especially if we're required to put our hands on its engine. Yet the Sons' motorcycles, customized to represent the character, personality, and style of each of their owners, are like the steeds who loyally accompanied the journeys of noble knights in earlier times. More than just shiny pieces of equipment, motorcycles represent a set of values centered on rebellion against the highly controlled tech-nological reality of our alienated society. They're symbols of an anarchic aspiration to freedom, a lifestyle that seeks liberty at any cost, maybe even John Teller's romantic ideal of a "Harley commune" ("Pilot").

How can a motorcycle both free a biker from alienation and poten-tially be a cause of that very alienation? This is the fascinating double nature of the Sons: they're outlaws, rebels who disregard social rules, but they're also mechanics who follow the rules necessary to repair a Harley and members of a club with its own set of bylaws and rituals. As motorcycles can be symbols of both rebellion and rule-following, they show us that the essence of technological alienation lies not in our everyday practices and tools per se. According to Heidegger, the real source of the problem lies in our technological ambition to exploit things *instrumentally*, to treat them as mere means to an end with no intrinsic value of their own. Tools, practices, the natural world, and even other people become a mere "standing reserve" of stored wealth or energy disposable at will and potentially available for any purpose, blinding us to the unique significance of the little things around us and the real meaning they have for our lives. For example, the porn actors working at Cara Cara and the "companions" employed at

Diosa could be understood as using their own bodies *instrumentally* for a business that has nothing to do with real sentiments of love and sex. But this is just one of many examples that could be given of how we delude ourselves and impoverish our existence if we view everything in our lives as mere "stuff" to be exploited.

Heidegger is adamant that using things instrumentally isn't always bad. The problem isn't technology itself, but what Heidegger calls the "technological attitude" of those who think that a thing has no value unless it can be exploited to achieve some result. This "calculative thinking" reduces everything to a balance of costs and benefits, emptying the world of any intrinsic meaning. It's truly catastrophic when calculative thinking comes to be regarded as the *only* desirable form of thinking, for then everything has a price but nothing has any real value. This seems to be the sort of alienation that John Teller feared, anticipating that SAMCRO—under Clay's leadership—would pervert its original aspiration to freedom into a greedy, brutal struggle for power. This actually happens when a blind monetary calculus induces Clay to enter into a deal with the Galindo Cartel, enslaving the club to a huge criminal apparatus that jeopardizes its very survival.

Heidegger notes that friendship and wildness escape calculative thinking. A *friendship* of the sort shared by Jax and Opie can't be bought or sold. It's value lies in its intrinsic nobility, not in its usefulness to achieve something else. This is also true of *wildness*. Consider the free-spirited nature of a wild horse, untamed and unavailable to be used as a means to an end. It will never belong to us as long as it remains wild. If we ever find a way to make it submit to our calculative designs, turning it into a workhorse or a show animal, it is no longer wild. The members of SAMCRO also exemplify wildness, while enjoying a strong bond of friendship. Their bikes are like wild horses, emblems of self-sufficiency and spontaneity.

The Buddha and the Biker

Pirsig believes that most people have a snobbish and suspicious attitude toward technology due to their fear of things that are unfamiliar, inaccessible, or mysterious. When technology is viewed as an inflexible cage imposed on our lives and controlled by a few specialized experts, alienation is the inevitable result. Think of how people dread having to call tech support to resolve a computer glitch. But this view reflects a refusal to experience technology as a form of *care*. Repairing a motorcycle, for example, is an activity that requires dedication, attention, constant creativity, and personal investment, both intellectually and emotionally—just like raising a child, writing your memoirs, or winning the respect of other bikers. It's also possible to develop a deep and sincere love for a piece of technology. Recall Opie's desire to restore a classic Harley that he purchased after Donna's death, as an outlet for the selfless commitment, loyalty, and zeal that he'd once dedicated to his wife. Maintenance is another way that the feeling of care can be expressed, as it requires dedication and active engagement with technical problems that require both skillful expertise and intelligent reflection to be solved. The problems that arise in motorcycle maintenance don't discourage the biker from caring about his bike. Rather, the problems motivate him to care even more.

Caring for a piece of technology is exactly the opposite of treating it instrumentally. Opie isn't addressing mechanical problems simply to find a solution and achieve the most efficient result. He wants to solve the problem because it's worth doing for its own sake, because it's how he cares for the old bike he's restoring. Realizing that maintenance is a form of care suggests why the *unready-to-hand* plays such a crucial role in restoring a non-alienated meaning to technology. People who are disdainful of technology are afraid of moving beyond familiar *ready-to-hand* or *present-at-hand* situations. They don't realize that the peace they enjoy while riding a bike can also be experienced while repairing it when it breaks down. In both cases, our embodied activity is a form of caring, bestowing the sort of love and attention that give our actions meaning.

Even if he's an outlaw like the Sons, a true biker is *purified* as he finds peace in both his hands-on knowledge of his vehicle and his awareness of the problematic technology that makes it function and, at times, malfunction. As Pirsig explains in *Zen and the Art of Motorcycle Maintenance*, even fixing a mechanical problem can become an occasion of participation, unity, and reconciliation with the world: "The Buddha, the Godhead, resides quite as comfortably in the circuits of a digital computer or the gears of a cycle transmission as he does at the top of the mountain, or in the petals of a flower."[8]

Notes

1. See, for example, Jeremy Kroeker, *Motorcycle Therapy: A Canadian Adventure in Central America* (Bloomington, IN: Trafford Publishing, 2009).
2. Robert Pirsig, *Zen and the Art of Motorcycle Maintenance: An Inquiry into Values* (New York: William Morrow & Company, 1974).
3. The most relevant text on this topic is Hubert L. Dreyfus and Stuart E. Dreyfus, *Mind over Machine: The Power of Human Intuition and Expertise in the Age of the Computer* (Oxford: Blackwell, 1986). As for Heidegger, his phenomenology of practical skills is offered in his philosophical masterpiece *Being and Time*, trans. John Macquarrie and Edward Robinson (London: SCM Press, 1962). For more on Heidegger, see Chapter 18 by Peter Fosl.
4. One of the most enlightening books in this field is Shaun Gallagher, *How the Body Shapes the Mind* (New York: Oxford University Press, 2005).
5. Pirsig, 15.
6. For more on Karl Marx, see Chapter 18 by Peter Fosl.
7. Martin Heidegger, "The Question Concerning Technology," in *Basic Writings*, ed. David Krell (New York: HarperCollins Publishers, 1993), 321.
8. Pirsig, 16.

Part IV

"THE PASSION IN HIS HEART AND THE REASON IN HIS MIND"

SEX, LOVE, AND GENDER

CHAPTER 14

Sometimes a Motorcycle Is Just a Motorcycle
Freud and Hamlet Come to Charming

Andrea Zanin

Sons of Anarchy offers us a weekly spectacle of arson, gun-running, murder, kidnapping, drugs, blackmail, porn, prostitution, and sundry other violent or unsavory activities, but it's the relationships that really drive the show. It's a drama about families, both blood relations and the brotherhood within the MC, showing how such relationships can be crazy and perhaps a little strange or even warped. One famous (often infamous) thinker who knew all about crazy, strange, and warped was Sigmund Freud (1856–1939), the father of *psychoanalysis*, a theory he developed to explain disturbances in human thought and behavior.[1]

The ideas that informed Freudian psychoanalysis are dramatically illustrated in the works of the playwright William Shakespeare (1564–1616). Shakespeare created some of literature's most powerful and memorable characters, many of whom have inspired the creation of protagonists regularly seen in film and on television, including *Sons of Anarchy*. Shakespeare used grand themes—the corruptions of power, unchecked ambition, sex, revenge, justice, tyranny, betrayal, and, of course, family—to mold his characters into forces of nature that transcend time. Through the men and women in his plays, Shakespeare shows that strength and power don't preclude pathology. To the contrary, power invites pathology.

It's no secret that *Sons of Anarchy* is influenced by Shakespeare's *The Tragedy of Hamlet, Prince of Denmark*. Jax Teller is the tormented

Sons of Anarchy and Philosophy: Brains Before Bullets, First Edition.
Edited by George A. Dunn and Jason T. Eberl.
© 2013 John Wiley & Sons, Inc. Published 2013 by John Wiley & Sons, Inc.

Prince Hamlet. Gemma Teller Morrow, who abandons all moral restraint and allegiance to truth in an effort to win her son's affection, is the capricious Queen Gertrude. Clay Morrow is the greedy and murderous King Claudius. And Tara Knowles, who starts out as a damsel in distress, is a gutsier version of Hamlet's beloved Ophelia.

Through these characters and others, *Sons of Anarchy* exposes the bloody, misshapen core of the human condition. Applying a little Freudian philosophy to these Shakespearean characters can provide insight into some of the core questions raised by this epic television show: Why are the protagonists so defiant in their attitude to authority? Why do they engage in subversive criminal activities when there are other ways for them to survive? What's with the chain-smoking? (Freud has an answer.) And how can we make sense of Gemma's rivalry with Tara or Jax's rivalry with Clay? Freud would have a field day with these characters and all their mommy issues, daddy issues, and just plain *people* issues. Let's jump in and see what a Freudian analysis can come up with.

"What Kind of Nasty Shit Did Your Momma Do to You?"

According to psychoanalytic theory, one cause of the craziness of human behavior is a fixation in one of what Freud calls the "psycho-sexual stages of development." Each stage corresponds to a different period of physical growth. Fixations—or obsessive attachments—occur when a child can't successfully overcome the challenges presented in one of these stages, leading to weird or deviant behavior in adult life.

There are five psychosexual stages of development—oral, anal, phallic, latency, and genital—but the one that seems to incite the severest form of pathology is the phallic stage. Psychoanalytic theory holds that, from ages three to six, children become aware of their bodies and especially their genitals. As they become curious about the differences between boys and girls, exploration and innocent probing may occur. A fixation in this phase will likely result in what's known as the "Oedipus complex," named for the Greek king who unknowingly killed his father and married his mother.[2] Freud says that during the phallic stage, a boy competes with his father for his mother's affection, focusing his libidinal energy—Freud's term for the sex drive—on his mom and becoming jealous of his dad. He fears that if his dad found out about the boy's "mommy lust," he'd take away what the son loves most at this stage—his penis. This is called "castration anxiety." Freud believes that most boys eventually resolve their Oedipus complex by coming to identify themselves with their fathers and mimicking their masculine behavior, which keeps castration anxiety at bay.

Does an unresolved Oedipus complex fit any characters on the show? You bet. Jax is a mommy's boy, even when he self-deludedly claims—in a conversation with Nero Padilla, his mother's lover, with whom Jax is brokering a deal that includes Nero staying away from Gemma—"I untwisted my mommy thing a long time ago" ("Stolen Huffy"). The show's popular anti-hero is pinned beneath the thumb of Gemma's claustrophobic love, which is expressed in many ways, including hugs, kisses, babysitting his kids, lies, and manipulation. And Jax is okay with that—for a while, at least. But why does it take Jax five seasons of Gemma's incessant meddling for him to get a freaking clue? Only when Gemma risks the lives of his sons by crashing her car while high does Jax cut her out of his life—but not for long. He offers her a deal to let her earn her way back into the family by betraying Clay. We might wonder whether this deal was, in fact, just an excuse to let Gemma back in without pissing off Tara or seeming unmanly. Freud would have his suspicions.

One psychoanalytic hypothesis might be that Jax is fixated in the phallic stage and still lusting after his mom. To understand the inner dynamics of Jax's fixation, we first need to consider the three parts of the human psyche posited by Freud: the Id, the Superego, and the Ego. The Id contains our basic instinctual drives, including our drive for sex and pleasure, but also an aggressive drive for destruction that we'll discuss later. The Superego is our internal voice of authority and morality, punishing our bad behavior with feelings of guilt. And wedged uncomfortably between them is the Ego, always looking for ways to satisfy the Id without antagonizing the Superego or otherwise coming to grief.

With respect to Gemma, we can imagine Jax's Id saying, "Hell, yes, mama!" while his Superego admonishes, "No, Jax! Incest is wrong!" Meanwhile, his poor Ego spends a lot of time in mediation. When the Id goes toe-to-toe with the Superego, the voice of morality is usually the victor. But the Id is sneaky and can often find a back entrance when refused admittance at the front door. That may be why Jax grants Gemma dictatorial rights over his life. He wants her close but he needs an acceptable manner of gratifying this desire, so he allows her to be an overbearing mother because, unconsciously, it gives him pleasure.

Jax's fixation also explains his intense rivalry with his stepdad Clay. Jealous of Clay's relationship with his mom, Jax contends for the spot of "alpha male," which he finally achieves at the end of Season 4 by displacing Clay as president of the club ("To Be, Act 2"). But at the end of Season 5, who's standing beside him as his "old lady"? Not his wife, Tara, but his mom, Gemma, who tells him sweetly, but with a dark undertone, "I'm here, baby" ("J'ai Obtenu Cette"). All his reasons for banishing her from the family are seemingly forgotten. Season 4 ends with a tableau of Jax sitting at the head of the table as the new president of SAMCRO, with Tara behind him, protecting her man. Season 5 repeats that tableau but with Tara replaced by Gemma, who has her arm around Jax and with Abel included in the frame. Jax replaces Clay and Tara replaces Gemma, but then Gemma supplants Tara as Jax's "old lady" and mother to his sons. All a little too Freudian, wouldn't you say?

But don't worry, Jax! Hamlet had the same issues. Heir to the throne of Denmark, Hamlet is hell bent on avenging the death of his father at the hands of his uncle, Claudius, who's now married to Hamlet's mom, Queen Gertrude. In a parallel situation, Clay kills Jax's father and marries his mom. Like Hamlet, Jax learns of the treachery and things don't seem likely to turn out well for Clay. But is it just a need for righteous justice that fuels Hamlet's hatred for Claudius and Jax's hatred for Clay? A famous (and somewhat infamous) book, titled *Hamlet and Oedipus*, by Freud's colleague and fellow psychoanalyst Ernest Jones (1879–1958) suggests otherwise.[3] Jones argues that Hamlet's inability to resolve his Oedipus complex means that Hamlet's repressed erotic affection for his mother complicates his desire for revenge when Claudius usurps the spot for which Hamlet has unconsciously always yearned. He longs to slay Claudius not only to avenge the slain king, but because Claudius is Hamlet's mother's husband and an object of jealousy. And that's why Hamlet treats Gertrude with such vitriol in the famous "closet scene" (Act 3, Scene 4), chastising her for her adulterous ways, which Hamlet describes as incestuous:

> She married. O, most wicked speed, to post
> With such dexterity to incestuous sheets!
>   (Act 1, Scene 2, 156–157)[4]

Of course, Jones believes that Hamlet is the one with the incestuous desires that he projects onto his mother.

Jax handles his mother's infidelity differently, using her to gain secrets from Clay as a condition for gaining access to her grandchildren again ("Ablation"):

JAX: You want to fix the damage you've done? ... He'd do anything for you, let him in. Get his trust ... I want you to be with him, sleep with him. Make him feel like a king. The dirty secrets will start to flow just like they always did.

GEMMA: What if I can't do that?

JAX: Then get used to living in a brothel, because hookers and bangers are going to be your only family.

Jax's ultimate goal is Clay's downfall in revenge for his father's death. But Freud might postulate a subconscious enjoyment on Jax's part in making his mother's sexuality the means of attaining this goal, despite his unawareness of his mother's role in his father's death. Gertrude may be insecure and in need of love, but she's guiltless of her husband's murder. And this is where she and Gemma part ways. Gemma is also insecure and starved of love, but she's not at all innocent of murderous intentions *and* actions.

"I Learned From the Best"

Gemma is street-wise, fierce, passionate, intrusive, manipulative, and violently protective. Gemma isn't yet wringing her hands in soap and water, trying to wash away phantom spots of blood, but her ambition and penchant for "playin' the game" smacks all too much of a Lady called *Macbeth*, whose lust for power came at a steep price—the loss of her sanity, husband, power, life, and everything. Like Shakespeare's character, Gemma connives and schemes with her partner to dethrone the rightful king. Id defeats Superego, immorality destroys the natural order, and chaos ensues. Scotland, the land filched by the Macbeths' evil scheming, is swept into disarray, while SAMCRO and Charming likewise descend into an abyss of death and despair. As Wayne Unser says, "I'm not sure which cancer is worse: the one in me or the one in Charming" ("Out").

And it's not just Charming that pays penance for Gemma's lust for power and unquenchable thirst for affirmation. Her family suffers too. Gemma just cannot—or *will not*—back off. She involves herself in every one of Jax's decisions, which becomes a major point of contention when Tara enters the picture. There's no doubt that Gemma loves Jax, but her love is pathological, rooted in a desire to possess, as though Oedipus were strangely inverted and Gemma fell in love with her son. With Gemma and Tara in competition for his love, Jax's life is an emotional war zone. Gemma's boundary issues escalate the situation so severely that Jax must choose between his mom or his wife. Tara and Gemma simply can't co-exist, not even for the sake of Jax. *Share?* Puh-lease!

In spite of their volatile relationship, Tara and Gemma turn out to be incredibly similar. Initially, Tara seems to be the antithesis of Gemma: gentle, kind, righteous (even self-righteous), morally sound—all the characteristics required of a doctor who values the lives of her patients. Consider the different ways that Gemma and Tara engage with the violence, disrespect, and bigotry doled out by SAMCRO: hard-ass Gemma surrenders to the biker creed, while Tara learns to understand it but fights it nonetheless. At least, that's how it starts. Tara's love for Jax means that the strong ethical code that constitutes the core of her being is repeatedly challenged by the vice and villainy enveloping the SAMCRO lifestyle. In the end, she compromises her values to be with Jax—another victory for the Id!

Tara's character development can be tracked in the changes she makes to her appearance. The mild-mannered Dr. Knowles of Season 1 has traded in her scrubs for hardened biker chick chic by Season 5. She's adopted Gemma's biker style and has the attitude to match. She hits, threatens, manipulates, and protects with a fierceness rivaled only by her mother-in-law. "Quite the secret-queen lately," remarks Gemma to Tara upon learning that she's pregnant but hasn't told Jax. "Yeah, well, I learned from the best," Tara replies ("Turning and Turning"). So it turns out that Jax did marry his mom after all—in the guise of Tara. No big surprise there. Freud would conclude that Jax has betrayed his unconscious lust for his mom by marrying someone just like her. Well done, Ego! Nice way of satisfying the Id without doing anything actually icky! We'd rather see Jax in the sack with mom-look-alike than his *actual mom*, after all. But Kurt Sutter always has a twist: Tara may be Jax's wife, but, in true Gemma style, mother-in-law has the last word when Tara exits the stage and enters prison in the Season 5 finale.

The love-triangle between Jax, Gemma, and Tara is a major plot device in *Sons of Anarchy*, hammering home the idea that families can get pretty weird. (We won't even mention Jax's near-incestuous encounter with his half-sister Trinity Ashby.) The question is: how far are we willing to go to make our families work? The situation in Charming has yet to resolve itself, but if the show's Shakespearean motifs are any indication, doom and death are waiting ahead.

"It's Just Fear and Greed Now"

Freud believed that the Id housed two competing instinctual drives: the *libido* or *sex drive*, on the side of the preservation and propagation of life, and the *aggressive instinct* or *death drive*, a self-destructive force that wants to restore us to the state of non-living from which we emerged. These two instincts are in constant conflict. Freud believed that unless the aggressive instinct was controlled, psychosis would result. So, in addition to the Id's battles with the Superego, it's also embroiled in its own civil war between the death drive and the libido. Our souls are a regular WWF showdown. And so is the town of Charming. Let's see if we can use Freud's concepts to shed some light on what's going on.

SAMCRO exists on the show as a protagonist in its own right. It's like a deity or a religion, worshipped, revered, and lauded by its members. The club's religious significance isn't lost on its members, who attend "church" at the sacred table to decide, debate, and declare.[5] But what kind of god is SAMCRO? The death and destruction wreaked in the club's name doesn't call to mind a good god. Eris, the Greek god of strife and discord, is a more apt counterpart to the club.[6] SAMCRO is a sex, drugs, and rock 'n' roll kind of god. Deluged in a sea of illegal enterprises, the men of the club are bidden by their god to act out violent and sexually deviant fantasies—and not just Tig!—wallowing in illicit activity, all in the name of SAMCRO.

In psychoanalytic terms, SAMCRO is pure Id, a symbol for the aggregate neuroses and psychoses of the men who kneel at its altar. The Id says, "Do what you want, when you want," and the club obliges. The club is a whirling vortex of pandemonium, offering its members a way to live out all their repressed urges rooted in anger, lust, greed, and frustration. Of course, psychoanalytic theory holds that, without the Superego and the Ego to keep the Id in check, people's urges will run riot. We need to repress our urges in order to maintain order within our individual psyches and society as a whole. But if that's the case, SAMCRO has gone seriously awry. The club is like a devil that woos men with promises of brotherhood, home, and family, topped off with lots of guaranteed pleasure. But the devil always asks a price. And his currency is souls.

While SAMCRO works as an illustration of the Id, conflicts among various protagonists manifest the struggle among the three elements of Freud's model of the psyche. Clay is the Id, embodying everything SAMCRO represents: unbridled pleasure and chaos on two wheels. With each passing season, it becomes more and more clear that Clay's Superego is seriously defunct. Greed, power, and desire run rampant. As president of SAMCRO, Clay digs the club deeper into criminal activity and tramples on the bonds of friendship and family that have always sustained the club. He's responsible for the deaths of John Teller, Donna Winston, and Piney Winston, as well as plotting to kill Tara and fostering violent home invasions in an attempt to unseat Jax from the presidency. All of Clay's heinousness, however, is encapsulated in one action: his beating the shit out of Gemma. The one person who should escape Clay's violence *doesn't*. Gemma's bruises attest that Clay is out of control and, as Gemma herself puts it, "can't be saved" ("Hands"). For him it's all about self-gratification and the means totally justify the end—which is money.

At the opposite end of the spectrum is Tara, little Miss Superego, voice of morality and antithesis to the chaos. In the middle is Jax, mediating between the Id (Clay) and the Superego (Tara). Jax is the voice of reason. As vice-president, and later president, Jax aims to legitimize SAMCRO, seeking a middle ground where the club can exist as neither dangerous nor degenerate, an ideal inspired by the manifesto left to him by his father. "The bond that holds this club together isn't blood or brotherhood," laments Jax, as he contemplates leaving SAMCRO. "It's just fear and greed now" ("Out"). But instead of leaving, he decides to stick around and try to fix things.

Jax wants to help the club retreat from chaos and restore order. Hamlet attempts to do this for Denmark by killing his father's murderer; and ultimately Jax may be destined to do the same. But Hamlet's quest for order through revenge cost him his life and the eradication of the royal family. Will Jax pay a similar price? We know from Season 5 that Jax has already turned a dark corner upon ascending to the presidency of the club, telling Bobby, "You can't sit in this chair without being a savage" ("Darthy"). Though Jax may have started out as the rational Ego, the battles he's fought to save his club have rendered him little more than a savage Id. Even Tara, our avatar of the Superego, the moral voice whispering in Jax's ready ear, gives in to the impulses of her Id as she transforms into Gemma Mark II—fierce "mamma bear" and "old lady" fiend, who doesn't hesitate to smash in the face of a woman who tried to kill Jax, while Gemma looks on approvingly at her protégé in action ("Stolen Huffy").

Despite his surrender to the Id, however, by the end of Season 5 Jax has killed, beaten, blackmailed, and, with great genius, manipulated SAMCRO into a better position than it was in when he took office. Has he accomplished what he set out to do, restoring SAMCRO to a "brotherhood," rather than a club fueled by "fear and greed"? No, he hasn't. Fear still reigns supreme and trust is non-existent.

What's With All That Chain Smoking?

SAMCRO clearly attracts a certain personality type: reckless, careless, defiant, rebellious, aggressive, and domineering. Witnessing this mayhem, Freud might wonder whether Tara was the only one properly potty trained, for fixations in the oral and anal stages of psychosexual development would go a long way toward explaining the immoderate behavior of the Sons and some of their old ladies.

The anal stage lasts from about one to three years of age and marks a shift in the child's erogenous zone from the mouth to the anus. A fixation in the anal phase occurs when a child can't overcome the challenges associated with toilet training. Neuroses can result from training methods that are either too strict or too lax. An approach that's too lax would give the child too much room to rebel, by soiling his or her pants or using the toilet at inappropriate times. The resulting fixation produces what's called an "anal expulsive" personality:

reckless, careless, defiant, unorganized, rebellious, and generous—personality traits that seem endemic to the Sons. The anal phase is about learning to control behavior and accept boundaries, which is important to the development of the Id, Ego, and Superego. If children go through the phase without understanding the need to delay gratification, you end up with men in a biker gang who can blame their parents for the giant chips on their anarchistic shoulders.

Then there's the "oral aggressive" personality type—common among the club members, all of whom Freud would suspect hadn't been breastfed enough at the oral stage. During this stage, which occurs from birth until the age of two, the focus is the mouth. Babies gain libidinal gratification from breastfeeding and will explore their environments by placing objects in their mouths. A fixation due to too much or too little gratification in this stage may result in the need to chew on things (gum, pencils, plastic, nails), chain smoking, excessive drinking, and compulsive eating, kissing, and oral sexual practices—all symptoms of a libidinal oral craving that wasn't satiated as an infant.[7] An unsatisfied craving can also result in aggressive, controlling, and domineering behavior; so all those murders ... yup, they're mom's fault.

While all the Sons seem to be affected by oral and anal fixations to a greater or lesser degree, the specific neurotic behaviors resulting from these fixations depend on the outcome of the battle between the libido and the aggressive instinct raging in the Id, with one drive on the side of life, while the other is on the side of death. We see this same battle raging in the lives of those associated with SAMCRO, which is itself is a total life-and-death fest. Porn in the morn, a little lunchtime murder, and a beating or two for tea—it's all par for the course for the MC. In a world immersed in violence, death, and destruction, sex is the cure-all for those enveloped in the folds of SAMCRO's deadly cloak. Season 5 starts with Gemma on a rampant sex binge. She bones anything that moves, perhaps to help her feel alive. Beaten by her husband, no longer an old lady, and now second fiddle to Tara, Gemma can find no better way to assert herself in the world than to fornicate with it. Her life instinct is operating at full throttle.

However, Freud never says that pleasure is bad. Libido is good as long as it operates within the confines of societal mores and values. And it's not only for the sake of society that we need to keep it in check, but also for our own sakes. If the extreme urges that well up from a hyperactive Id aren't repressed, we get hurt. And, soon enough, Gemma's Ego and Superego reassert themselves to do some damage control. She's one temperamental lady, though, and her aggressive instinct is as impressive as her libido. This woman pummels anyone who gets in her way. In Season 1, Clay's roadside fling, Cherry, has her face rearranged courtesy of Gemma and a skateboard ("AK-51"). Death threats from Gemma are a regular occurrence—sometimes with the means taken from the pages of The Good Book—as are hand-to-throat and fist-to-face salutations. While the libido serves a positive function, Freud regards aggression as always negative and destructive. It is antilife and pathological.[8]

Jax's Ego seems to have a pretty good handle on his libido. Except for that one indiscretion with Ima that he deeply regrets, he's remained faithful to Tara and doesn't seem tempted to stray. On the other hand, his aggressive drive is pathologically robust. But does he exercise it gratuitously? Life in the MC has nurtured a keen survival instinct that uses violence as a means to an end—to keep Jax and his club alive. But looking at how routinely Jax resorts to lethal means, Freud might argue that Jax must gain pleasure from killing. It gratifies an urge, for otherwise his aggressive instinct wouldn't outweigh his libido so massively, as it apparently does. Jax's behavior suggests an unconscious death wish, though consciously he perhaps sincerely believes that violence is merely a tool to survive. Is it his unconscious instincts or his conscious reasoning that pulls the trigger? Freud would go with instinct.

"Balance"

According to Freud, a healthy soul requires the Ego to perform a careful balancing act between the claims of the Id and the Superego. Sadly, not all of our Egos are that well-balanced—and certainly not those of the Sons! Yet, even John Teller recognized the need for balance when he wrote, "A true outlaw finds the balance between the passion in his heart and the reason in his mind. The outcome is the balance of might and right" ("Patch Over"). In the end, Teller might agree with Freud that true freedom isn't simply surrendering to the Id and its errant urges, but rather learning to control our aggressive drives and impetuous desires, and making due with lustful, violent fantasies.

Anyone complaining? Yes. The anarchist—he's complaining bitterly. The irony is that Jax and company become entrapped by what's supposed to set them free: SAMCRO. The anarchy unleashed by a pathologically fixated Id on a rampage is the very thing that binds Jax, Gemma, Clay, Tara, and all the Sons to a life of fear, death, and loss. On the plus side, though, there's lots of opportunity for sex and killing. But is it worth it?

Notes

1. Sigmund Freud's most important psychoanalytic concepts are contained in his *The Essentials of Psycho-analysis* (London: Vintage Books, 2005).
2. Robert Graves, *Greek Mythology* (London: Book Club Associates, 1985), 129–133.
3. Ernst Jones, *Hamlet and Oedipus* (New York: The Norton Library, 1976).
4. William Shakespeare, *Hamlet* (Hertfordshire: Wordsworth Classics, 1992).
5. For more on the religious dimension of SAMCRO, see Chapter 11 by Kevin Corn.
6. Robert Graves, *The Greek Myths, The Complete and Definitive Edition* (Harmondsworth: Penguin Books, 2011), 12.
7. With all those cigars he smokes, Clay apparently wasn't breastfed; and Ethan Zobelle not only smokes cigars, he sells them too! But maybe this is making too much of innocent details. Freud might agree; after all, he said, "Sometimes a cigar is just a cigar."
8. Johan M.G. van der Dennen, "Psychoanalytic Theories of Aggression." Available at http://rint.rechten.rug.nl/rth/dennen/a-panal.htm (accessed April 30, 2013).

CHAPTER 15

When a Charming Woman Speaks

Leslie A. Aarons

On *Sons of Anarchy* power is in the hands of the men. It's their votes that count in the clubhouse and the women must strategize from the outside looking in. The men of SAMCRO know that violence gets things done. Adept at manipulation, they don't shy away from exploiting whatever and whomever they can. But the male members of the MC are only one part of the story, as the Charming women play equally pivotal roles in the action.

These women, too, have shrewd powers of manipulation. However, though women like Gemma Teller Morrow and Tara Knowles are strong and resourceful, most of their identity, focus, and energy are devoted to the men of the MC. It's difficult to know who Gemma is—or would be—without SAMCRO. And though Tara is a practicing physician, her dedication to her profession diminishes as the story progresses, taking second place to her commitment to Jax and the MC. As with Gemma, it becomes difficult to understand who Tara is apart from her connections to the men in her life. So consuming is her relationship to Jax that one wonders whether she would've even pursued and achieved her medical degree and career if she hadn't ended her teenage romance with him.

Feminist philosopher Luce Irigaray argues that in the modern world a social hierarchy still prevails in which men are the dominant subjects and women are significantly subordinate to them, due to deeply rooted conscious and unconscious social habits. Our definitions of gender

Sons of Anarchy and Philosophy: Brains Before Bullets, First Edition.
Edited by George A. Dunn and Jason T. Eberl.
© 2013 John Wiley & Sons, Inc. Published 2013 by John Wiley & Sons, Inc.

roles are governed by a long-standing social bias that recognizes the value of only one sex: the male. Irigaray calls such a biased society "patriarchal," arguing that "all the systems of exchange that organize patriarchal societies and all modalities of productive work that are recognized, valued, and rewarded in these societies are men's business."[1] Our shared values create enduring, organized patterns of relationships through which we define and understand ourselves and interact with one another in ways that tend to devalue qualities associated with women. According to Irigaray, we exist in a culture that perpetuates a male-dominated attitude to such an extent that we have not yet reached a place where women can envision and speak about themselves as independent subjects, rather than simply in terms of their relationships to men.

Where is the place in Charming where the woman's vote counts? Where is the church that provides a clandestine roundtable for them to meet, debate, and consult with each other? Where is their political voice and power? To answer these questions, let's take a look at the women of Charming to see how they wield their power, what they do with it, and how it's limited by the world in which they operate.

"She's Just an Old Lady?"

SAMCRO is a central and vital part of Gemma's life. She has dedicated herself to the club, though as a woman she is not—and never will be—a member. Nonetheless she still finds ways to influence the club's business from outside by shrewdly inducing others to do her bidding. As a strong-willed, assertive person with deep convictions of her own, she passionately serves and protects both the club and her family in her own skillful ways. Gemma's strengths make her a valuable asset to the MC. She has strong connections to the club through her husbands John Teller and Clay Morrow, both former presidents, and through her son Jax, the current president, over whom she exercises considerable influence. In short, Gemma's much more than just an old lady—or so she at one time believes.

When Jax is planning to leave SAMCRO, he's asked by both Tara and Clay how Gemma will react, since they both know she won't be pleased. Jax responds bluntly, "She's just an old lady, not a member" ("Out"). In the episode "Hands," Gemma confronts Clay about taking all the money from the household safe, which we know he used to pay a hit man to kill Tara. Not wanting to be answerable to his wife, Clay puts her in her place:

CLAY: What did I tell you about diggin' into club business?
GEMMA: It's not club money.
CLAY: That's right! That's my money. And as long as you have enough to take care of the house and *amuse yourself*—you don't need to worry about it.
GEMMA: Did you really just say that to me?
CLAY: Maybe I should be saying shit like that to you more often. Reminding you that you are *not* a member of this club— you're just an old lady! And don't forget it!

Gemma is deeply insulted and hurt by Clay's condescending attitude. Although she embraces her role in the club as an old lady—the president's old lady—she evidently views her marriage as more open, equal, and respectful than Clay does. It appears that when the worth of a person is brought to the bar of judgment in SAMCRO, women just don't measure up. Irigaray wouldn't be surprised by these conversations. "Women are not worth listening to," she says, characterizing the harmful mentality of a male-dominated culture with its dismissive attitude toward women.[2]

The often-conflicted relationship between Jax and his mother follows a Freudian script. In his lecture on "Femininity," Sigmund Freud (1856–1939) states:

A mother is only brought unlimited satisfaction by her relation to a son; this is altogether the most perfect, the most free from ambivalence of all human relationships. A mother can transfer to her son the ambition which she has been obliged to suppress in herself, and she can expect from him the satisfaction of all that has been left over in her of her masculinity complex.[3]

This "masculinity complex" to which Freud refers is part of his theory of psychosexual development, according to which girls at an early age identify with their fathers before (in cases of "healthy" psychosocial development) they eventually assume the female social role. Freud understands women as being in a natural state of dereliction, lacking a phallus, ineligible for the active male social role, and thus destined to search for ways to compensate for their lack. From his perspective, the closest a woman can come to satisfying her own ambitions is by giving birth to a son—sort of a substitute phallus—and developing a nurturing bond with him.[4] This may be why we find Gemma and other women associated with the club constantly strategizing to position themselves in relation to the men, often in competition with each other, in order to remain present in the scenes at all. It's also telling that Gemma and Tara both have two sons and no daughters. When Tara tells Gemma that she's planning to take Abel and Thomas away from Charming, Gemma threatens to expose her as an accessory to murder. Tara threatens back that Jax would kill her, but Gemma responds that she'd be "dead without my boys" ("J'ai Obtenu Cette").

In "The Pull," Jax argues with Gemma about his rekindled relationship with Tara. Gemma is, as always, ferociously protective of her son and seemingly jealous of another woman entering Jax's life—especially one who has hurt him before:

JAX: What happened with me and Tara is ancient history, Mom.
GEMMA: She hurt this family—tried to pull you away.
JAX: I didn't leave, did I?
GEMMA: But she did. Broke your heart.
JAX: I guess.
GEMMA: You guess? She crushed you, Jax.
JAX: I was nineteen. It was first love bullshit. I grew up. I got over it. It's time you got over it too.
GEMMA: Somebody hurts your baby, you never get over it.

At the end of Season 5, it appears that Gemma has made good on her threat to implicate Tara in the murder committed by Otto Delaney and has her sent off to prison.[5] Having been on a downward spiral for most of the season, Gemma is now seen revitalized in her renewed alliance with Jax. Her realignment with her son restores her vitality and confidence. Wouldn't it be nice, though, if Gemma could have a respected voice and identity of her own, so she wouldn't need to employ her admittedly impressive skills as a schemer to position herself next to Jax?

"Family Is Everything"

When not maneuvering situations to her own personal advantage, Gemma believes her best course of action is to use her powers of manipulation and seduction to orchestrate the best possible outcomes to protect her family. She's focused and confident as she craftily executes her plans to protect the ones she loves. But Gemma's sense of love is disturbingly twisted and has left a legacy of one disaster after another. Moreover, Gemma's conception of who's *part* of her family shifts wildly with each thickening of the plot.

Take Piney Winston. He was an original member of the club and her late husband's best friend. Gemma and Piney had history and they were "family." But in "Kiss," with her old friend's bloody murdered body lying only a few feet away, she persuades Wayne Unser to cover up the truth about Piney's murder by Clay. "He's like a wounded animal, Gemma. He's gonna rip apart *anything* that comes too close," says Unser, explaining why he wants to turn Clay in to the authorities. Unser adds ominously that, otherwise, "the next corpse you're gonna be standing over is the mother of your grandchild. Are you ready for that?" But Gemma placates Unser, agreeing that Clay is dangerous but arguing that he's in need of their help now more than ever. "What kind of wife would I be if I turned on him now?" she asks.

Gemma declares her love for Clay, which to her means she must protect him at all cost. She also acknowledges her culpability in Clay's murder of her former husband. "I supported Clay's decision," she confesses. "I knew it was the best thing for the town and the club and my family." But this admission raises the very same question Gemma had just asked: What kind of wife would conspire with her lover to murder her husband, the father of her son, and then justify such savagery? John Teller *was* her husband—her *family*. Gemma's changing sense of family makes her dangerous and unpredictable. She's unshakably loyal to whomever she considers family, but as the shape of her "family" shifts, so do her allegiances.

Nothing shows Clay's lack of respect for Gemma more blatantly than what he does in "Kiss." The conclusion of this episode finds Gemma and Clay alone together, with Gemma being uncharacteristically vulnerable. She confesses to Clay, "I live with so many lies, Clay. So many things I can't ever speak of. I'm okay with that. I do it to protect what we have. But I can't lie to you. You're the only truth I have." This is a profound and intimate moment for Gemma. She admits the difficult truth that she has irrevocably compromised herself and professes her love to Clay. She then lets him know that she found Piney's murdered body and tells Clay that she understands why he killed him. Visibly alarmed, Clay coldly responds, "So what do we do with this 'truth'?" Gemma promises that she'll handle everything. The incriminating information contained in the letters thought to be in Tara's possession will be destroyed so she can't "hurt this club or our family." Gemma then makes him promise that he won't hurt Tara. "I promise," says Clay. "I won't hurt Tara. I love you Gemma. Everything I do is for you." For a few precious moments, as love, respect, and honesty are shared between husband and wife, there's hope that Gemma got through to Clay. But just as Gemma leaves, Clay makes the call to put out the hit on Tara.

"[I]n this culture the only sex, the only sexes, are those needed to keep relationships among men running smoothly," writes Irigaray.[6] If women's primary role is to serve and service men, true love and mutual respect with their male partners is rendered difficult, if not impossible. Healthy relationships require mutual respect and care. The partners need to know from the words and the deeds of their lovers that they're appreciated and respected—physically, mentally, and spiritually. Love in this sense requires mutually autonomous subjects who embrace reciprocal appreciation, respect, and honor for themselves and for each other. It soon becomes apparent to Gemma that she doesn't have this with Clay.

In "Hands," a brutal fight erupts between Gemma and Clay over his broken promise not to harm Tara. Gemma fires a gunshot that misses Clay, screaming, "You stay away from me you son of a bitch! You stay away from *my* family!" Now, Clay is *outside* the family because of his attempt to kill Tara, whom Gemma now considers *inside* the family. In "To Be, Act 1," we witness in deed William Congreve's (1670–1729) famous phrase, "Heaven has no rage like love to hatred turned, Nor hell a fury like a woman scorned." Gemma rises to her powerful best, cunningly avenging herself on Clay. Sitting at the table in the clubhouse's "chapel," she tells Jax, "Clay Morrow killed your father—stole that seat away from this family. Gunned down your father's best friend. He tried to kill your wife. He's a murderous traitor. And there's only one thing to do now Jackson, for your father, your family, and your club."

"Men Need to Own Their Pussy"

Irigaray argues that even today women tend to be objectified and treated like commodities to be exchanged between men. Consider Cherry, who leaves her abusive husband and burns down her condo, only to end up with the Devil's Tribe MC in Indian Hills, Nevada. When Uncle Jury, the club president, offers her to Clay for sex in "Patch Over," Cherry can't refuse despite her romantic feelings for Half-Sack Epps, since she's a "sweet butt" who's job is to be available for sex with club members and, evidently, anyone else the club asks her to do it with. Though most women have more autonomy than Cherry, Irigaray still believes they're treated like objects to be exchanged by a society that expects them to adopt their husbands' names to indicate which man has title to them. Referring to the way some cultural theorists have described the emergence of a system that treats women as marketable items, Irigaray writes, "Without the exchange of women, we are told, we would fall back into anarchy ... The passage into the social order, into the symbolic order, into order as such, is assured by the fact that men, or groups of men, circulate women among themselves."[7] Irigaray wrestles with how to emancipate women from this objectified commodity status, so they can achieve their own unique identities as subjects independently of how the male-dominated culture identifies them. Gemma, on the other hand, doesn't wrestle with female emancipation at all and accepts being commodified, telling her lover Nero Padilla, "Only men need to feel loved. Women need to feel wanted" ("J'ai Obtenu Cette").

Tara would appear to be a woman who's achieved her own identity. She certainly has had more choices than Gemma. The distance she gained from Jax and his criminal enterprises during some formative years yielded her a medical degree, which she parlayed into a successful practice as a neonatal surgeon. When Tara and Jax reunited, she was dedicated to her career and was found most often at the hospital, working in her capacity as a surgeon. But as their relationship became more serious, she attended less to her career and was seen more often patching bullet wounds at the clubhouse than saving newborns at St. Thomas Hospital. She also has made a number of decisions that jeopardized her freedom, safety, and career—because, after all, you can't perform surgery from a prison cell. Tara's waning dedication to her hard-won, high-level career continues as she involves herself in illegal activity for the sake of the club that ultimately results in her arrest. When we last see her in Season 5, she's on her way to prison.

Tara further compromises her independent identity in her response to Jax's struggles with leaving SAMCRO. One reason he's remained a member for longer than he would have otherwise has been his anticipation of making that final deal that would allow him to cash out. After all, he has no livelihood or lucrative skills outside the MC. He adamantly rejects the sensible alternative of Tara supporting their family. In "Out," Jax explains why he's not ready to leave the club until he's made enough money running guns with the Irish:

> JAX: I don't have any skills, Tara. I'm an okay mechanic with a GED. The only thing I ever did well was outlaw.
> TARA: Jax, I can go anywhere. I make good money.
> JAX: I'm not gonna live off my wife. I can't.

It's customary in Western cultures for the man to be the family's principal provider. Jax is proudly resolute in his rejection of allowing his old lady to support him. It also seems natural and right in a male-dominated society that Tara, as a wife and mother, should be the one to sacrifice for the good of the family, tolerating Jax's criminal activities to spare him the indignity of being supported by his wife. But it seems absurd for a skilled, practicing surgeon to defer to the business of an outlaw—that is, until we take into account who's who in the gendered equation.

Irigaray describes how women have historically been limited by the demand that they defer to men. "Woman, for her part, remains in unrealized potentiality—unrealized, at least, for/by herself," she writes. "*Is she, by nature, a being that exists for/by another?* And in her share of substance, not only is she secondary to man but she may just as well not be as be."[8] At the end of Season 5, Tara seems poised to realize the potential that she'd been willing to let languish for Jax's sake, finally realizing that her role as an old lady is to be strong where Jax is weak—namely, in his inability to cut ties with SAMCRO for good. But her escape from Charming was thwarted by a combination of her own past mistakes and interference from Gemma, who, knowing only how to exist for others, had good reason to fear losing everything.

"You Don't Have a Normal Life, Baby–You Have This One"

The stories told on *Sons of Anarchy* are familiar to us. The character's lives ebb and flow with hopes and fears, gains and losses, friendship and enmity, love and resentments, and regrets and triumphs that we can identify with. The existential dramas portrayed there resonate with us. We ride alongside the characters as they strive for the ideals that make life worth living, such as friendship, love, and happiness, though none of the characters seems to have achieved these ideals perfectly in their lives. If we haven't either, then perhaps part of the reason lies in the way we've organized our society.

Irigaray calls for a profound restructuring of the distribution of power between men and women. She imagines a radical shift in our understanding, language, and social practices that would realign the position of centrality from being exclusively male to one that would recognize sexual difference, thus creating a place for women to speak and act independently. In our most sacred texts and throughout the history of ideas, we've envisaged ourselves as being of two different sexes and yet we're imprisoned within a social network that, according to Irigaray, is terribly out of balance, as it's been defined and appropriated by only one sex. Our relation to language, our bodies, politics, and the earth is warped and biased by the fact that the masculine sex alone has usurped and dominated the economy of meaning for millennia.

The question remains, if a woman could speak with words and meanings that emanate from her own unique and distinctive feminine voice, what would she say? More to the point, what would Gemma say?

Notes

1. Luce Irigaray, *This Sex Which Is Not One* (referred to hereafter as *TS*), trans. Catherine Porter (New York: Cornell University Press, 1985), 171.
2. *TS*, 90.
3. Sigmund Freud, *New Introductory Lectures on Psychoanalysis*, trans. James Strachey (New York: W.W. Norton & Company, 1965), 165.
4. For more on Freud's psychoanalytic theories, see Chapter 14 by Andrea Zanin.
5. In an interview with TVLine, Kurt Sutter, the show's creator, said the following in response to a question about whether Gemma ratted Tara out: "My intention was to definitely put that out there as a possibility, and I think we'll reveal how that happened. I do want the audience coming away with, 'Wow, did she actually follow through on that threat? And what does that mean for Gemma and Jax if he finds out?'

I definitely wanted to create that discussion." Available at http://tvline.com/2012/12/04/sons-of-anarchy-season-5-finale-spoilers-kurt-sutter/ (accessed May 1, 2013).

6. *TS*, 192.
7. *TS*, 170.
8. Luce Irigaray, *Speculum of the Other Woman*, trans. Gillian C. Gill (New York: Cornell University Press, 1985), 165.

CHAPTER 16

Mothers of Anarchy
Power, Control, and Care in the Feminine Sphere

Leigh C. Kolb

The women of *Sons of Anarchy* have pivotal, powerful roles in the drama, despite not being official members of the MC. Consider the pilot episode. Jax Teller's pregnant ex-wife, Wendy, is injecting herself with a syringe full of meth—a fallen mother. Jax's mother, Gemma Teller Morrow, finds Wendy in a pool of blood and rushes her to the hospital. At the hospital, Tara Knowles, a neonatal surgeon and Jax's ex-girlfriend, tends to his newborn son, Abel, delivered ten weeks premature because of his mother's drug abuse. Here we have three images of motherhood: the bad mother (few things are considered worse in our society) who endangers her child, the powerful matriarch who comes to the child's rescue, and the mothering healer who is responsible for keeping Abel alive. Each is defined in that pilot episode by the way she cares for or neglects the child, Abel.

In contrast, the men of *Sons of Anarchy* are engaged in club warfare from the get-go, committing brutally violent crimes as they navigate troublesome waters of gun-running and, in later episodes, drug-muling, porn, and prostitution. The *masculine sphere*, as depicted in *SOA*, is powerful and aggressive, but, compared to the *feminine sphere*, it deals in matters that are less essential to true human flourishing. Even though matters of life and death are part of the club's daily agenda, SAMCRO's allegiances and dealings tend to be more profit-driven than motivated by a concern for the essentials of living a good life. The feminine sphere, while perceived by the club members as less

Sons of Anarchy and Philosophy: Brains Before Bullets, First Edition.
Edited by George A. Dunn and Jason T. Eberl.
© 2013 John Wiley & Sons, Inc. Published 2013 by John Wiley & Sons, Inc.

important and less powerful, deals in matters of giving and sustaining life and in maintaining caring relationships. When Jax comes to the hospital to visit his son, he has blood on his clothes from a raid on a Mayan warehouse in which he shot a member of the rival MC. Tara tells him to clean himself up—then he can see his son. Tara, who gave Abel his heartbeat, is in control in this sphere.

Beyond the pilot episode, *Sons of Anarchy* follows its women with a watchful eye and critiques the unequal power of the feminine and masculine spheres. There is a persistent tension between the feminine sphere, historically focused on care, nurturance, and home-making, and the masculine sphere, historically focused on politics, justice, and competition. Gemma cares for her husband, Clay Morrow, by giving him injections for his arthritic hands, thus allowing him to ride his motorcycle toward yet another violent encounter. Sometimes, these altercations end in fiascos that result in one of the Sons or their allies needing medical care from Tara back at the clubhouse. In many ways, it's the women who keep the world of SAMCRO running, though they exercise no formal power in the club. Feminist philosophy can help us get a better understanding of the power dynamics depicted in the show, as well as some of the key motives that drive the women and men of SAMCRO.

"Gemma? She's Just an Old Lady"

The famous Greek philosopher Aristotle (384–322 BCE) once made an infamous observation, claiming that in almost all animals:

> the female is softer in disposition than the male, is more mischievous, less simple, more impulsive, and more attentive to the nurture of the young: the male, on the other hand, is more spirited than the female, more savage, more simple and less cunning ... Hence woman is more compassionate than man, more easily moved to tears, at the same time is more jealous, more querulous, more apt to scold and to strike. She is, furthermore, more prone to despondency and less hopeful than the man, more void of shame or self-respect, more false of speech, more deceptive, and of more retentive memory.[1]

Aristotle viewed men as fully human and women as somewhat less so, even though he acknowledges that women are "less simple," more cunning, and have superior memory. His overall contention was that women and men were meant to inhabit different spaces: a woman's main place being the home, *oikos*, and a man's being the city, *polis*, which gave men overall authority.

This ancient idea that men and women inhabit different spheres based on their biological makeup is deeply rooted in Western culture. The Victorian era of the nineteenth century embraced this idea of "separate spheres": a man's was public and political; a woman's was private, inside the home, and maternal. In *Sons of Anarchy*, the men live in a world of assault rifles, motorcycles, drugs, political alliances, and power plays. The women stay at home or in the clubhouse—raising children, healing, protecting, and feeding. When the MC goes on lockdown in anticipation of a confrontation with the League of American Nationalists (LOAN), Clay tells all the members and their families, "If you have a safety concern, you talk to Piney who raises his hand holding a shotgun]. If you have a comfort concern, you talk to my Queen [indicating Gemma]" ("The Culling"). The different spheres reflect a gender-based division of labor.

Twentieth-century philosopher Hannah Arendt (1906–1975) saw a need to keep the public political and private domestic spheres separate for society to function properly:

> Since the rise of society, since the admission of household and housekeeping activities to the public realm, an irresistible tendency to grow, to devour the older realms of the political and private as well as the more recently established sphere of intimacy, has been one of the outstanding characteristics of the new realm ... The private realm of the household was the sphere where the necessities of life, of individual survival as well as of continuity of the species, were taken care of and guaranteed. One of the characteristics of privacy, prior to the discovery of the intimate, was that man existed in this sphere not as a truly human being but only as a specimen of the animal species mankind. This, precisely, was the ultimate reason for the tremendous contempt held for it by antiquity.[2]

For Arendt, it's only in the public, or political, realm that we are truly human and not mere animals concerned with physical survival. The (historically female) domestic sphere, the realm in which we eat, reproduce, and sustain the other necessities of life, is tethered to the needs of the *body*, while it's in the (historically male) rough-and-tumble world of politics, competition, and conquest that the human *spirit* is able to find its greatest satisfactions. "This Life," the *Sons of Anarchy* theme song, celebrates the nobility of "ridin' through this world all alone." It doesn't say anything about the innumerable things that must happen in the domestic sphere in order to make "this life" possible, since they contribute only to the preservation of our animal life, not to its human nobility.

Arendt is alarmed that the wall that separates the public and private realms seems to be collapsing in the modern world into a new "social" realm where activities that were once relegated to the domestic sphere have become public. And this, she fears, threatens the inherent dignity of the public realm, which depends on its separation from the lowly activities that serve the preservation and reproduction of life:

> The social realm, where the life process has established its own public domain, has let loose an unnatural growth, so to speak, of the natural; and it is against this growth, not merely against society but against a constantly growing social realm, that the private and intimate, on the one hand, and the political (in the narrower sense of the word), on the other, have proved incapable of defending themselves.[3]

While Arendt doesn't view these spheres as necessarily gendered, it's difficult to imagine Western society keeping them separate while dissolving gender-based norms and expectations. And, as long as this historically female domestic sphere is devalued as being good only for sustaining "mere" animal life while the male public world is where the human spirit is nourished, their separation affords women a permanently second-class status. So it's not surprising that other feminist thinkers—and most probably Gemma and Tara if we were to ask them—disagree with Arendt. On the surface, the men and women of SAMCRO appear to be firmly planted in an authoritarian form of patriarchy, where women are "just" old ladies, as Jax and Clay have both reminded Gemma. The contributions of women, however— especially the matriarchal figures of Gemma and Tara (ever notice that Chibs Telford often calls Gemma "mom"?)—have been vital to the club's existence and efficient functioning. While the Mothers of Anarchy, on the surface, have no control, in reality they use their power in the private sphere to influence the public sphere and effect great change, albeit with little public recognition for their efforts.

Just look at how Gemma handles her rape by A.J. Weston and those other goons from the LOAN. She's lured into the enemy's hands when she's stopped on the road by Polly Zobelle, who's pretending to be in a panic because her baby's not breathing. Pulled by her maternal instincts, Gemma rushes out of her car and into Polly's van, where there's just a baby doll. Knocked unconscious, Gemma is taken to a warehouse and raped as part of an effort by the LOAN to demoralize and destroy SAMCRO. The way that she deals with the assault— keeping it secret in order to protect the club, yet helped by Tara medically and emotionally—is painful and courageous. She finally decides to tell her family about the rape only when she learns of Jax's plans to leave the club and go "nomad" because of his conflicts with Clay ("Balm"). As Gemma explains the assault to Clay and Jax at the family dining table, Patty Griffin's song "Mary" plays softly in the background, conjuring the image of that archetypical suffering mother. Gemma, however, isn't the pure and perfect image of virginity. Far from it! She's real, complex, damaged, and yet able to be strong when others need her to be. Gemma's decision to tell Clay and Jax about the rape has the desired effect, as Jax puts his VP patch back on. Damon Pope will later tell Jax that turning one's pain into an advantage "makes players into kings" ("Laying Pipe"); by using her rape to bring Jax and Clay—and in fact the whole club—closer together as they take on the LOAN, Gemma shows that she really is the undisputed "queen" of SAMCRO.

Gemma is not just the biological mother of Jax—she is a mother to all the Sons. While the traditional masculine and feminine spheres are firmly in place within SAMCRO, with the men making all the decisions about the club's future behind the closed chapel doors, the power this mother wields is monumental. Gemma has orchestrated the club from its beginning, having brought the club to her hometown of Charming in the first place. As Chief Wayne Unser notes, Gemma left Charming when she was 16 and returned "ten years later with a baby and a motorcycle club" ("Eureka"). And yet both her son and her husband still seem to regard her as "just an old lady."

"God Wants Me to Be a Fierce Mother"

The two most prominent women on the show are both mothers. Motherhood is firmly rooted in the feminine sphere—from inside the womb to inside the nursery—and is focused on *care* and *family*, the most basic form of community. Gemma lives by the creed, "Family is everything." But concern for family isn't exclusive to the women. One way their influence is seen is in the way Jax's priorities shift as he and Tara start to build their own family. As Jax comes to view the well-being of his family as being of paramount importance, he appreciates more and more the wisdom of his father's original vision for the club; he recognizes how the club's current path imperils what he has come to care about most. Like his father, Jax becomes highly introspective and, like his father, he wants to move the club away from the violent path it's on and toward a more communal future driven less by individual greed. He complains to Clay at one point, "I'm tired of being crushed under the weight of greedy men who believe in nothing" ("To Thine Own Self").

Ironically, though, while Tara ultimately decides that she, Jax, and their boys need to leave Charming and SAMCRO behind, Gemma's maternal instincts drive her to manipulate Jax into seeking greater power as president of the MC, which, in her mind, entails not only deposing Clay but also killing him. It just goes to show that maternal instincts don't exclude complex motivations that may be as influenced by the agenda of the public, masculine sphere as many of Jax's public decisions are influenced by his domestic concerns. Whether Arendt likes it or not, these spheres already mutually influence each other.

The foremost maternal archetype in Western culture has long been the Virgin Mary, but, as noted earlier, Gemma may be a mother on a mission ("God wants me to be a fierce mother," she says in "The Culling") but she's no Virgin Mary. *Sons of Anarchy* does a commendable job of avoiding the "virgin–whore" dichotomy that has shaped many of our ideas about femininity and motherhood. Gemma is a vivacious woman who desires sex—one episode even deals with her battling vaginal dryness after menopause ("AK-51")—but that isn't treated as something that in any way compromises her maternal role. Other mothers on the show are also depicted as sexual creatures. Opie's girlfriend and eventual second wife, Lyla, is one of the stars of a porn production company with which SAMCRO becomes affiliated. She has a son of her own and is compassionate in her role as stepmother to Opie's children, taking responsibility for them after his death ("Stolen Huffy").

Lyla also is the catalyst for conversations on the topics of abortion and birth control. Motherhood isn't only about mothering children.

It can also be about making choices concerning what's best for the entire family, which sometimes means not having more children. In Season 3, Lyla becomes pregnant and does not want to be, in part because her relationship with Opie isn't solid, but also because pregnancy would end her career in the porn industry and she feels the need to work a few more years. Tara, who is also pregnant, offers to take Lyla to an abortion clinic and, while there, decides that she also wants to schedule an abortion ("Lochan Mor"). The entire scene is without judgment or negativity—it's a clean clinic and a simple procedure. Rarely is abortion presented in as realistic or shame-free manner in popular culture. The notion that women are the standard-bearers of religion and morality make the subject of abortion more toxic than the violence that bloodies so many episodes of modern dramas. Later, when Opie discovers Lyla had an abortion and is taking birth control pills, he's angry and ends their marriage ("With an X"). But Lyla is mothering the best she can and her decision not to have another child at this time appears to be a moral choice born out of care. Tara ends up not having the abortion she scheduled, but only because subsequent events persuade her this is the right time to welcome a new child into the world. She's abducted and almost killed by Hector Salazar. After the ordeal, she and Jax see the unharmed baby on an ultrasound scan and reconcile.

These examples of "fierce" motherhood illustrate the modern feminist philosophy of *care*, which insists that caring relationships—best exemplified by the mother–child relationship—should be the driving force behind modern ethics, more so than the masculine justice that has historically been associated with the public sphere. Feminist psychologist and philosopher Carol Gilligan describes some of the aspects of the moral sensibility that she thinks women's historical role as caregivers in the domestic sphere has fostered:

> Since the reality of interconnection is experienced by women as given rather than freely contracted, they arrive at an understanding of life that reflects the limits of autonomy and control. As a result, women's development delineates the path not only to a less violent life but also to a maturity realized by interdependence and taking care ... [W]omen perceive and construe social reality differently from men, and ... these differences center around experiences of attachment and separation ... [B]ecause women's sense of integrity appears to be intertwined with an ethics of care, so that to see themselves as women

is to see themselves in a relationship of connection, the major changes in women's lives would seem to involve changes in the understanding and activities of care.[4]

Whereas men tend be more concerned with issues of justice, in which the protection of individual rights is paramount, Gilligan's research has revealed that women often approach moral issues with an overriding concern to foster and maintain the sorts of relationships in which care is given. Caring for those to whom we are connected by love and affection—and, in particular, for those like children, the sick, the disabled, and the elderly who can't care for themselves—takes precedence over assertions of individual autonomy. From this feminine "care perspective," we never ride through this world "all alone."

As the series progresses, the ethic of care becomes increasingly important and the mother–child bond frequently acts as a catalyst for action. And there are some notable examples of empathic bonding and expression of care besides the mother–child connection, such as when Tig Trager rescues and cares for an injured fight dog ("J'ai Obtenu Cette"). When the ethic of care is absent—as when Wendy uses drugs while pregnant or the Real IRA uses Abel as a pawn to get Jax to kill Jimmy O'Phelan—the villain is clear ("Turas"):

GEMMA: Who the hell are these people? Using a baby like a goddamn poker chip.
JAX: It's not just them. This happened because we deal guns with the Irish. Let's not kid ourselves we're the victims here.
GEMMA: Maybe that profound awareness helps relieve your guilt, but now is not the time for soul searching. You focus on the hate you need to kill all these Irish pricks.

Gemma, in her need to care for her grandson, encourages her son to rage and kill without thought. She even goes so far as to put a gun to another baby's head and threaten a group of nuns for information on his whereabouts ("Bainne"). Her own use of a baby as "goddam poker chip" is rewarded in this instance, which drives home how complicated and problematic it is to try to combine the care ethic with the violent criminal world that Gemma inhabits. This situation reminds us of why many proponents of the care ethic insist that we need to transform the public sphere to make it more hospitable to the care ethic and to ensure that no one's flourishing or well-being needs to be sacrificed.

When Gemma isn't holding a gun to someone's head, she also lives the ethic of care in a more traditionally domestic manner: she cooks big family meals, cleans up Jax's house and his room at the clubhouse, and does whatever she must to protect and emotionally support her "boys." Tara also grows into her matriarchal role within SAMCRO, initially by serving as the club's on-call doctor, bringing back to life men who would otherwise have died. After initially resisting the club's hierarchical structure, Tara grows into her role as an "old lady" and accepts her rank among the women of SAMCRO, which is derived from the rank of the men to whom they're connected. We see this hierarchy in action when Tara is approached during a "lockdown" at the clubhouse by a lower-ranking "croweater"—one of the women who hang around the club and may sleep with members—who offers to get her a coffee. Tara demurs, but Gemma advises her:

> They need to do that—show respect … You've earned that, sweetheart. You're not just some crow eater. You're Jax Teller's old lady. And that means something—in this clubhouse and in this town. People need to show you respect. And you don't take shit from anyone. ("The Culling")

Gemma and Tara certainly are deserving of respect. But equally deserving of respect is the ethic of care that motivates them and that has sustained the club from behind the scenes from its beginnings.

"My Job as Your Old Lady Is to Be Strong When and Where You Can't Be"

Whereas Gemma ran away from Charming as a teenager and returned with a motorcycle club, Tara left and came back with a medical degree. Tara represents a new generation of female power. Her professional training has empowered her to be able to support her sons on her own if need be and to move away from Charming to start a new life. She could be her family's ticket out of the violent life of SAMCRO. Jax seems to understand that, on his own, he can't be. "I'm an okay mechanic with a GED," he concedes. "The only thing I do well is outlaw" ("Out"). When Tara decides that the time has come for her and the boys to leave, she tells Jax:

I used to think if I gave up on the club, or Charming, I'd somehow be betraying you and I didn't want to do that. And then I realized my job as your old lady is to be strong when and where you can't be. That's what this is, baby. I took that job in Oregon. It starts in two weeks. The boys are coming with me. And if you love them, and if you love me, you'll follow us up there. We both know if we stay here we'll end up like the two people we hate the most. And our boys will be destined to relive all of our mistakes. ("J'ai Obtenu Cette")

Writing about the theater in his *Poetics*, Aristotle says, "Each kind of character may be effective, for both woman and slave may be effective [or good for dramatic purposes] even though one is perhaps inferior and the other generally base."[5] In Aristotle's view, the role of a woman (or a slave) in a drama can only be supportive, since, after all, in his opinion that's all they can ever be in real life. He might have been forced to reconsider this view, however, if he had been given an opportunity to watch *Sons of Anarchy*. Despite her apparent "inferiority" to Jax within the hierarchical, male-dominated structure of the MC, Tara has a power all her own. She can do precisely what Jax wants to do, and knows he must do, to properly care for his family. In addition, she understands that she can prompt Jax to act by issuing her ultimatum. It's thus truly tragic that Sheriff Roosevelt shows up seconds later to arrest her for conspiracy to commit murder—a position she's in because she put her role in the club above her responsibilities as a caregiving healer and mother.

Gemma cares deeply for her family, but a lifetime of male-dominated influence has led her often to express her *care* in the hardened masculine form of *retributive justice*—exemplified by her drive for vengeance when she exhorts Jax to depose Clay from the presidency of SAMCRO and to kill him for the murder of his father, John Teller:

Clay Morrow killed your father, stole that seat away from this family, gunned down your father's best friend and he tried to kill your wife. He's a murderous traitor and there's only one thing to do now, Jackson—for your father, your family and your club. It's in you. It's who you are. Clay has to die ... You kill Clay before he's on his feet and strikes first. And when it's done? You take your place at the head of this table where a Teller belongs. Where you belong. ("To Be, Act 1")

Of course, we understand that it's not so much revenge for J.T.'s death that Gemma is seeking—given her own complicity in her first husband's murder—but for Clay having brutally assaulted her. Gemma cares for Jax more than anything and wants to see him take the president's gavel, but she's also motivated by justice in the most classical sense of "an eye for an eye."

According to Annette Baier, a contemporary moral philosopher and leading proponent of the care ethic:

> It is clear, I think that the best moral theory has to be a cooperative product of women and men, has to harmonize justice and care. The morality it theorizes about is after all for all persons, for men and for women, and will need their combined insights ... Then, once there is this union of male and female moral wisdom, we maybe can teach each other the moral skills each gender currently lacks.[6]

Gemma's particular combination of care and justice doesn't seem too harmonious—particularly since her extreme maternal care for Jax and her grandsons also apparently leads her not only to seek revenge against Clay, but also to turn Tara in to Sheriff Roosevelt in order to keep Jax and the boys in Charming. After Tara's taken away, Gemma repeats the now-familiar tableau: standing behind Jax with her arm around him protectively, saying, "I'm here, baby" ("J'ai Obtenu Cette").

Yet Gemma may be softened in the long run by her relationship with "companionator" Nero Padilla. Like Jax, Nero wants out of the violent life of justice-as-vengeance he's led, although forces keep conspiring to pull him back in. His dream is one that is infused with the care ethic—to build a peaceful home in order to care for his disabled son. Thus far, *Sons of Anarchy* hasn't depicted a successful marriage of the ethics of justice and care, nor even a very consistently attractive picture of either of them individually. We see Gemma's *care* for Jax turn her into a manipulative mother and the *justice* enacted by the Sons typically only taking the form of revenge. Perhaps healthier forms of these respective ethics could be harmoniously merged, but it's clear that a marriage of justice and care can never happen without overcoming the resistance of the old guard, who seek to preserve the dominant masculine model that treats the concerns of the domestic sphere as second rate.

Notes

1. Aristotle, *The History of Animals,* in *The Complete Works of Aristotle,* ed. J. Barnes (Princeton, NJ: Princeton University Press, 1984), Book IX, Part 1.
2. Hannah Arendt, *The Human Condition* (Chicago: University of Chicago Press, 1958), 45–46.
3. Ibid., 47.
4. Quoted in Annette C. Baier, "The Need for More than Justice," in *Ethics: Selections from Classical and Contemporary Writers*, 9th ed., ed. Oliver A. Johnson and Andreus Reath (Belmont: Thomson/Wadsworth, 2004), 509.
5. *Aristotle's Poetics*, trans. Kenneth A. Telford (Chicago: Henry Regnery Company, 1961), 27.
6. Baier, "Justice," 516.

Part V

"EACH SAVAGE EVENT WAS A CATALYST FOR THE NEXT"

THE HISTORIC AND THE HOMERIC

CHAPTER 17

Sons of History
How SAMCRO Lost and Found Its Way

Peter S. Fosl

Sons of Anarchy—what a great name for a motorcycle club! It paints its members as outlaw brothers, bound in deep solidarity. Their name also proudly declares them to be the offspring of something that preceded them. The past is, indeed, so essential to the club that they might just as well be called the Sons of History. Consider just a few of the ways that the members' histories play into the club's present life.

Of course, much of the series centers on Jackson (Jax) Teller wrangling with *The Life and Death of Sam Crow*, a manuscript written by his father, John Thomas (J.T.) Teller, which Jax discovers in the detritus of historical storage.[1] But that's just the tip of the iceberg. J.T.'s murder two decades ago at the now trembling hands of Jax's stepfather Clay (with the presumed help of Jax's mother, Gemma) looms forebodingly just below the surface of current events, as large as the berg that sunk the Titanic. Looming there too are J.T.'s Irish lover, Maureen Ashby, and their love child, Trinity, along with those pesky letters on which no one can seem to get a proper grip. Jax's wife Tara Knowles (whose name calls upon a knowing, royal Irish past) also emerges from his romantic history, just as psycho-ex Joshua Kohn stalks his way out of hers.

Then there's Juice Ortiz's secret past in the form of his African-American father, which is also a reminder of the racist history of the United Sates. Not only is that racism inscribed in the club's rules and in the disturbing lack of "color" that Sheriff Eli Roosevelt observes in

Sons of Anarchy and Philosophy: Brains Before Bullets, First Edition.
Edited by George A. Dunn and Jason T. Eberl.
© 2013 John Wiley & Sons, Inc. Published 2013 by John Wiley & Sons, Inc.

the mugshots adorning the clubhouse wall,[2] but it also feeds the club's ongoing conflicts with "black" and "brown." Tig Trager's past returns through his daughters and their issues. Chibs Telford is literally marked by his past association with the Real IRA. It would take a full chapter even to begin to plumb the depths of Big Otto Delaney's troubled history, which drags behind him, heavier than the chains of Marley's ghost (not Bob but Jacob, the other Marley). And, of course, it's SAMCRO's history of criminal activity that makes possible the RICO prosecution that threatens the club's existence.[3] There's no mistaking the fact that history casts a long shadow over SAMCRO and its members.

Philosophers are also concerned with history, in part because of an old dictum inscribed on the gateway to Apollo's temple at Delphi: "Know thyself" ("γνῶθι σεαυτόν" or "gnōthi seauton").[4] Coming to terms with our histories is one of the main ways people come to know themselves. Therefore, understanding history and how it generates meaning is an important dimension of philosophical inquiry, as well as a matter of deep importance for people generally.

"For Ten Years I Gave Up on this Club. Rode My Limit Just to Keep the Patch"

There are lots of ways to look at the movement of history. Some see history largely as decay, a decline from what the Greek poet Hesiod (active between 750 and 650 BCE) called a Golden Age through successively more degenerate periods—Silver, Bronze, and Heroic ages—culminating at last in his own era, the Iron Age.[5] One can only speculate about what he would have called our era: the Carbon Age?

Certainly, one could look at the epic history of SAMCRO as a trajectory of degeneration. The MC's origins might be regarded as a golden age—the period when J.T., Piney Winston, and the rest of the First 9 established the Sons of Anarchy Redwood Originals back in 1967 as a sort of hippie commune on wheels and thundered like gods along the majestic coast of northern California between Eureka and Big Sur. By comparison, the age of Clarence "Clay" Morrow looks profoundly diminished.[6] Clay's age isn't properly an age of iron, even though the club and its businesses do sling a lot of ferrous around.

It's an age of something far more base and weak, an Age of *Clay*. The organization headed by Clay has feet of clay, leading it into an age not only of iron (in the guns they haul) but also of cocaine, war, murder, internecine strife, government prosecutions, and disintegration, culminating in near annihilation. Like post-1960s and post-Vietnam America generally, SAMCRO finds itself on a downward slide away from its founding ideals and into something much less inspiring. It's the decline of the West (and I don't mean just northern California) in microcosm.

The rise of Jax and Tara, however, suggests that the club's history doesn't have to be one of inexorable decay after all. Even the couple's first initials tellingly (pardon the pun) reestablish the presence of J.T., as does the ending of Season 4. After Jax deposes Clay, the mournful tableau of Tara standing behind Jax with her hand on his heart morphs nostalgically into an old photo of J.T. and Gemma. Meanwhile, a dirge-like "House of the Rising Sun" is heard on the soundtrack, as if the original couple had been resurrected, rising again at the dawn of a new day for the MC. Of course, with the closing of Season 5, that sun seems to have set, signaled by a third, more foreboding repetition of the ruling couple's tableau. This new iteration features a darker Gemma displacing the now-arrested Tara and standing behind a darker Jax. Might the age defined by this new ruling pair become the worst of all?

Time Wounds All Heals

The Italian philosopher Giambattista Vico (1668–1744) wouldn't be at all surprised by the return of a heroic past that had seemed obliterated but that is then followed by a new round of degeneration. For Vico, history moves neither simply downward nor upward but in cycles—or through what he calls in his *New Science* "*corsi*" and "*recorsi*." For Vico, the human world begins in an act of imagination (*fantasia*) and then becomes increasingly reflective and rational. The movement of reason and reflection as they emerge out of the imaginative worlds of faith and poetry marks a kind of relative progress for human institutions—such as motorcycle clubs—out of a primitive or "barbarous" condition into one of rationality, conceptual clarity, and scientific rigor.

But the rational human world is deficient without imagination. It's therefore subject to new forms of barbarism peculiar to reason itself. Human beings don't live in a world of abstract, detached, universal concepts. We live as located beings, in particular situations, socially linked and related to others through imaginative tropes, images, metaphors, sympathies, and narratives. For Vico, it's imagination that locates us, creating the common sense and common places or topics of communal thinking, feeling, and acting, without which we are lost.

Reason cut loose from the humanizing and gathering guidance of imagination quickly becomes individualistic, violent, and self-destructive. Without imagination, the social order collapses and becomes vulnerable to external assaults until the cycle begins again in a new moment of imaginative re-founding. Vico writes about people who succumb to what he calls the "barbarism of reflection," comparing them to "so many beasts, [who] have fallen into the custom of each man thinking only of his own private interests and have reached the extreme of delicacy, or better of pride, in which like wild animals they bristle and lash out at the slightest displeasure."[7]

So it goes with the MC. SAMCRO initially understood itself as rooted in J.T. and the rest of the First 9's heroic and founding act of imagination, which created a new world for them to inhabit after the barbaric anarchy they had suffered during the Vietnam War. But Clay's more rational and ambitious outlook was seductive to Gemma. She believed she'd found in Clay Morrow a better tomorrow than the one promised by the more poetic J.T. And for a while it looked like she was right. The club prospered through its lucrative, albeit illegal, business of gun-running, while Charming remained relatively free from the crime, drugs, and social tensions that afflicted so many other US communities. It was the American dream—or rather the American *scheme*. But it wasn't to last. "Men first feel necessity," says Vico, "then look for utility, next attend to comfort, still later amuse themselves with pleasure, thence grow dissolute in luxury, and finally go mad and waste their substance."[8]

As if following Vico's map, Clay eventually risks the club's very existence by muling cocaine for the Galindo Cartel so he can maintain his personal life of wealth and comfort into old age.[9] Into the cozy order that Clay's calculations had established, there irrupts in due course madness (Joshua Kohn), addiction and regret (Wendy Teller), sadism (Agent June Stahl), racial discord (Ethan Zobelle), and ambition and revenge (the Mayans). Had J.T.'s imaginative vision endured, it's unlikely the MC would have become vulnerable to these threats. But these destabilizing intrusions aren't just forces of irrationality. Rather, they're degenerate forms of rationality and order: degenerate criminal law equals Kohn and Stahl, degenerate moral rectitude equals Zobelle, degenerate marriage and parenthood equals Wendy, and degenerate inter-MC solidarity equals the war with the Mayans.[10]

What Vico writes about the free imperial cities of the Holy Roman Empire applies just as much to Charming and SAMCRO: "But as the popular states became corrupt, so also did the philosophies. ... [A]s furious south winds whip up the sea, so these citizens provoked civil wars in their commonwealths and drove them to total disorder. Thus they caused the commonwealths to fall from a perfect liberty into the perfect tyranny of anarchy, or the unchecked liberty of free peoples, which is the worst of all tyrannies."[11] The same disorders plague SAMCRO and Charming. Conflicts among club members mount, as brothers turn murderously on each other. Charming, too, loses a sense of its traditional identity, becoming vulnerable to wealthy developers and other ambitious outside forces as it turns against SAMCRO.[12]

For the Vichian cycle—the *recorsi*—to start again, a re-grounding act of imagination and faith is required. Jax and Tara seem poised to generate this sort of imaginative restoration in their vision of a new life. Of course, if their saga is just a part of a cycle, then history will open a new wound in the order Jax and Tara build, and it will collapse into a new barbarism. Indeed, one of the couple's deepest fears is the same as one that J.T. confessed to Maureen in one of his letters—that the new generation will succumb to the errors of the past and that their own sons, as well as the Sons as a club, will reprise the cycle of decay. As the famous criminal attorney Clarence Darrow once remarked, "History repeats itself; that's one of the things wrong with history."

But there's reason to hope, too, that the return of J.T. in Jax doesn't mark a *recorsi* of the sort Vico described or just a moment of respite on the highway to some fresh hell with Gemma by his side. Things may in fact move forward. There are other philosophies of history that explain how the past may return in the present and in the future, but in a progressive way.

"Who's That Writin'?"

Christianity offers one of the most popular of the progressive theories of history.[13] Most Christians view history as a path that leads down and then up—an initial fall from a pristine condition, followed by a return to the heights, to a restored condition of wholeness that is perhaps even an improvement over the original Eden. Central to this restoration is the bloody death of a Son. This Christian graph of history plummets downward with the fall but then winds progressively upward toward a redeemed reign of righteousness through the Second Coming of that slain savior, the Son of the Creator.

Similarly, in the beginning J.T. and SAMCRO co-founder Piney motored through stands of towering, ancient pines (hence Piney's name) along the northern California coast. Young, strong, and beautiful, they inhabited one of the loveliest and most immaculate parts of our world, their own Garden of Eden. But then the club fell into a world of betrayal and violence, as J.T. succumbed to the adulterous temptations of Maureen Ashby and Clay's adulterous relationship with Gemma led to their murdering J.T. (which rhymes with J.C., Jesus Christ).

The rise of the anointed son, Jax, seems to signal the coming of the MC's redeeming savior. Faithful but weak Bobby Munson is betting on it, and the show itself plays on this theme. Jax even saves Tig from the judgmental (anti-)Pope who consigns Tig's daughter to a pit of Hell-like flames, meting out an eye-for-an-eye justice (the *lex talionis* of the Old Testament, Exodus 21:23–25) that shadows the Sons if they don't mend their evil ways.[14]

The closing episode of Season 1, called "The Revelator," uses Curtis Stigers & the Rangers' powerful rendition of the traditional song, "John the Revelator," to identify John Thomas Teller with St. John, author of the Bible's Book of Revelation. The connection is made even more forcefully when Jax retreats to a cemetery—a necropolis, a "city of the dead" where the past lies buried—and ends up sleeping on the porch of a Greek-styled mausoleum, the family name of which is emblazoned on its architrave: "Patmos." Patmos is also the name of the island in the Aegean on which St. John (sometimes called "John of Patmos") is said to have lived and received (or at least written) his revelation of the end times.

The message is clear; the Truth has now been revealed to Jax (his name is even a kind of Christogram),[15] and it falls to him to do what must be done to restore justice to the club. We feel that justice in his stride as he marches like history through the cemetery (albeit with his stupid white sneakers—what biker would wear shit like that?) to confront his stepfather at Donna's funeral. The title of John Teller's revelatory manuscript tells it all: *The Life and Death of Sam Crow: How the Sons of Anarchy Lost their Way*. Yep, they once were lost, but now with Jax's help and his father's "gospel" they shall be found.

"The Past Is Never Dead. It's Not Even Past"[16]

It may just be that I'm not terribly religious, but, even though I get the allusions, I'm not entirely convinced that this Christian model of history is the best way to understand the club's struggles with the past. It's not just that Jax doesn't suffer a sacrificial death. That falls to Opie Winston—though I suppose one might regard Jax and Opie as dividing the messianic labors between them, with Opie dying for the club's sins and Jax leading the charge of the Second Coming, returning to judge the sinners and reign on behalf of the righteous.[17] But, all that aside, there's another philosophical model of progressive history that I think makes more sense of the series.

The German philosopher Georg Wilhelm Friedrich Hegel (1770–1831) argues that history follows a rational course of development that begins with civilization's earliest and crudest forms of thinking but culminates in modern science and philosophy. Thinking develops and matures through a process Hegel calls "dialectic."

What is a dialectical process? In simple terms, a dialectic is a back-and-forth movement, like a dialogue (a related word). One set of ideas goes head-to-head with another in a way that eventually overcomes the limitations of each and raises thinking, even the social order, or even the world itself to a higher and better condition. This process has often been described as one in which an initial "thesis" is set against an opposing "antithesis," with the opposition between the two provoking a process that "sublates" or "uplifts" them into a hybrid or unified "synthesis." For example, one might argue that the dialectical contest between unbridled free market capitalism, on the one hand, and totalitarian state socialism, on the other, has produced a superior hybrid in the form of regulated markets and the modern liberal welfare state. This dialectical hybrid preserves what's good and right in those originally one-sided positions, forging them into something higher.

As a leader of SAMCRO, Jax fits this model. He is the biological son of the romantic visionary J.T., but then becomes the stepson, loyal vice president, and protégé of the Machiavellian, power-hungry, and violent Clay. After unearthing *The Life and Death of Sam Crow*, Jax begins to internalize his biological father's legacy in opposition to the education he received from his stepfather.[18]

J.T.'s rooftop lessons occupy Jax for quite some time, as he works out his relationships with Wendy and Tara, acquires norms of compassion that result in him saving the life of the witness who had fingered Bobby, and contemplates his own future as well as the club's. But a Hegelian development does not progress along a straight line. Rather, it works its way back and forth between thesis and antithesis. Jax's development certainly follows suit.

Things swing dialectically back in Clay's direction when Jax travels to Ireland and discovers his father's paramour and love child. Angry that his biological father had fled his family and SAMCRO to bury himself in "Irish pussy," Jax repudiates him, accusing J.T. of being "weak"—a Clay-esque term of denunciation, for sure. When Jax confronts Piney at his cabin in the pines, however, the dialectical pendulum swings back in the other direction. Piney tells Jax, "And then you came up. You reminded me so much of John ... It felt like maybe our idea still had a chance" ("Family Recipe").

But a Hegelian idea (or person or MC) matures not simply as a repetition of the original, even of the Redwood Originals. And an antithesis to a thesis doesn't just appear out of thin air. An antithesis crystalizes because of problems internal to the original thesis; and the uplifting work of sublation culls as much from the antithesis as from the thesis. In other words, progress draws from both opposing parties in a dialectic. The contest or opposition happens, because the original thesis has room to grow. It has room to grow, since it's somehow deficient or suffers internal contradictions. Clay rose to power because of J.T.'s shortcomings, including perhaps his incoherent wish to live both as a biker-outlaw and as a back-to-the-garden hippie, as well as his lack of any realistic sense of finances. Jax gets this and responds tartly to Piney, "Well, I'm not my old man."

Jax isn't his old man, that's for sure. But he's wrong when, in his last and most important confrontation with Piney, he shouts, "I don't want to hear about history!" Perhaps Piney is giving the dialectical movement a shove, for he gently corrects Jax in a very Hegelian manner. Piney draws Jax away from identification with Clay by offering a more positive vision of J.T., one that can serve Jax's own personal development, and by highlighting how much of J.T. is still in Jax: "I won't tell you how much you just sounded like your old man. … Your father was the best man I ever knew. But before you let him die, you should find him and know that for yourself." Piney was wrong to think that the original idea could be simply restored, but he's dead right that before Jax can move on into the future, he's got to know the past, really know it, and in doing so know himself (like they said at Delphi: "γνῶθι σεαυτόν").

In the end, the new boss ain't the same as either of the old bosses. Jax the MC president is a Hegelian synthesis, not a mere replica of St. John Thomas Teller. He does share J.T.'s wish to take the club in a more peaceful and family friendly direction, out of gun- and drug-running. He also erupts with ferocious determination to protect his family and friends—dispatching Kohn and recovering Abel—something he likely learned from his "fierce mother," Gemma. But he's likewise acquired some crucially important traits from Clay. Like Clay, Jax can be frighteningly cold and cunning. Destroying beasts as ruthless, cruel, and lethal as Agent June Stahl and Damon Pope takes a lot more than the impetuous violence practiced by Happy or Tig. It takes more careful calculation and a better knack for reading one's opponents than Opie or Bobby could ever have mustered, too. I have serious doubts that the visionary romantic hippie J.T. Teller could have managed it.

I also doubt that J.T. would have been street savvy enough to execute the complex, pragmatic calculations necessary to stave off the ATF, the CIA, local law enforcement, small time drug dealers, the Mayans, well-funded white supremacists, international real estate barons, a Mexican drug cartel, the Real IRA, the Russian mob, Damon Pope, and—last but not least—Clay Morrow. Whew! Unlike Clay, Jax has a vision of the club motivated by ideals such as solidarity, peaceableness, and fairness, rather than just the base desires for wealth and power. He also has a moral compass to guide the club in pursuing those ideals. But unlike J.T., Jax is a power to be feared. Had Jax been at the helm back in the day, Clay's assassination attempt might have ended rather differently.

Pope discerned something of Clay in Jax when he read Jax's desire to keep Tig alive as a shrewd exercise in "turning pain into advantage," which, Pope goes on to explain, "turns players into kings" ("Laying Pipe"). But it was Pope's mortal error not also to discern the iron loyalty that Jax had drawn from J.T. Then he wouldn't have made the mistake of believing that Jax would turn Tig over for execution as if he were a poker chip. Jax has become stronger and better than both J.T. and Clay. His dual paternity has sublated, thrown upward, a synthesis that is truly Teller-Morrow—like the name of the club's garage—but also more than just an aggregate of the two.

The closing tableau of Season 5 is, of course, disturbing. At the end of Season 4, Tara and Jax recreated the portrait of Gemma and J.T. as the founders of the MC. The new *recorsi*, however, replaces Tara with Gemma, apparently sending the message that there's no escaping the sordid side of the club's history. The icy glare Gemma fires at Tara as she strides in to take the young mother's place reminds us that the series began with Gemma's attempt to dispose of Jax's first wife and also that in Gemma there remains one very important "antithesis" and father-killer still on the loose.

Having neutralized Clay, Jax will have to come to terms with his father-killing, wife-assailing, MC-matriarch mother. He will have to face the contradictions and deficiencies within himself that generate the massive gravitational force with which she has welded him to the club and maintained her position at its center of power. He will have to take from her what virtues he can and reject what vices he must if his and SAMCRO's dialectic progress is to advance yet further.[19]

Notes

1. Literally "son of Jack," where Jack is a nickname for John. And if you don't know what a "John Thomas" is, ask a Brit. I suppose in a way the moniker does make sense, since J.T. is the big phallus, the grand sire, of the show's decidedly phallocratic universe.
2. Apparently, as the episodes revolving around Juice's struggle with his past indicate, only whites—at least those designated "white" on official documents—may belong to the MC. When in Episode 10, Season 5, Jax meets with Bobby and Chibs to discuss Juice's fate and his fears about his father's race, Bobby remarks, "You gotta be kidding," and Jax proclaims, "Maybe it's time to change a few by-laws," to which Chibs affirms, "Amen."

3. RICO stands for the "Racketeer Influenced and Corrupt Organizations" Act of 1970, part of the US criminal code used to prosecute organized crime.

4. Confirming this, philosopher William Irwin, editor of the series in which this volume appears, has in fact had this dictum in the Greek tattooed on his right deltoid. See http://chronicle.com/blogs/tweed/and-still-more-scholarly-ink/20545 (accessed May 2, 2013).

5. Hesiod, *Works and Days*, 109–201; Ovid, *Metamorphoses*, 1.89–150.

6. The First 9 wear a special patch on their cut and include: John Teller (deceased), Clay Morrow, Piedmont "Piney" Winston (deceased), Keith McGee (deceased), Lenny "The Pimp" Janowitz (imprisoned in Stockton), Wally Grazer (deceased), Thomas "Uncle Tom" Whitney (deceased), Chico Vellenueva (deceased), and Otto "L'il Killer" Moran (deceased—not to be confused with "Big Otto" Delaney).

7. Giambattista Vico, *The New Science*, rev. trans., 3rd ed., Thomas Goddard Bergin and Max Harold Fisch (Ithaca: Cornell University Press, 1976): Book I, §1106.

8. Ibid., §241.

9. A contrasting figure to Clay's degeneracy is handsome, caring, strong, and strait-laced Deputy Chief David Hale, who earns everyone's (sometimes grudging) respect by sustaining the imaginative virtues and ideals of law and legal judgment (forms of rationality). He believes in justice as lawfulness, and holds little more than contempt for the instrumental, even utilitarian, compromises Chief Wayne Unser strikes between the law and the club. "Unser" in German means "our," and so the chief is literally "our" Wayne; or, in line with the theme of decline and decay, perhaps the cancer-ridden chief is better described literally not only as our waning Wayne, but simply our wane—our fading decline through our internal malignancy. By "instrumental" reason, by the way, I mean reasoning that's not grounded in moral principles, that doesn't recognize anything as good in itself beyond the satisfaction of desire, that acts merely in service to antecedent desires it does little if anything to shape or establish. By "utilitarian" here, I mean acting in ways simply for the purpose of increasing pleasure and minimizing pain.

10. It would be the subject of another essay, but the threats the MC faces seem to reflect the broader anxieties of white, small town America as it struggles with crime, international capital, overweening government, immigration, changes in racial demographics, and economic decline.

11. Vico, *New Science*: Conclusion, §1102.

12. Lincoln Potter's very name conjures up ideas of federal power ("Lincoln") and the destruction of community (Henry F. "Potter" from Frank Capra's 1946 holiday classic film *It's a Wonderful Life*).

13. There are hundreds of forms of Christianity, many with differing views of history, and so it will be impossible for my remarks here to be accurate to all of them.

14. Tig, of course, had killed Pope's own daughter, Veronica Pope, whose initials also designate her as Pope's VP. As an aside, I observe that the show's proclivity to kill women by fire in boxes beneath the ground (remember the women cooked when the Mayan's burned down the Son's assembly plant in Season 1?) suggests to me an unconscious misogyny.

15. "J" for Jesus and "X" for Christ, often symbolized with the Greek "I" or iota (the Greek not distinguishing "J" and "I") and "X" or Chi.

16. William Faulkner, *Requiem for a Nun* (New York: Random House, 1950), Act I, Scene 3.

17. Another reading along Christian lines is that J.T. was the savior of the lost Vietnam generation who died for America's sins. Jax, then, is Jesus come again to establish the New Jerusalem after dispatching the anti-Christ, Clay Morrow. Jax, then, is the Jesus of the Revelation, not the Gospels, which makes sense of all that Patmos stuff. I love, by the way, the social commentary implied by "Opie," the namesake of Mayberry's favorite son growing up to become an ass-kicking biker who marries a porn star and dies like one of Valhalla's warriors in a hopeless, racially inflected, prison death match. In some ways, too, Unser and Hale invert Andy and Barney, but Floyd the barber is ever-present.

18. For further discussion of Jax's and Clay's "Machiavellianism," see Chapter 6 by Timothy Dale and Joseph Foy.

19. For further discussion of virtues and vices within the world of SAMCRO, see Chapter 1 by Jason Eberl.

CHAPTER 18

Anarchism and Authenticity, or Why SAMCRO Shouldn't Fight History

Peter S. Fosl

The philosopher and essayist George Santayana (1863–1952) famously stated, "Those who cannot remember the past are condemned to repeat it."[1] Or, as Agent June Stahl once said, "We dig up the dirt. And then we go after the present" ("Better Half"). Stahl is interested in the past in order to establish a "history" of ongoing criminal conduct by SAMCRO that can be used to support a RICO prosecution. But others on *Sons of Anarchy*, Jax Teller in particular, are equally concerned with coming to terms with the past, seeing it as a source of self-knowledge that might help them break themselves and the club out of some unhealthy established cycles (no pun intended).

How we position ourselves in relation to history has a dramatic effect on who and what we are. Karl Marx (1818–1883) argued that we must advance the collective historical process in which we're immersed in order to realize ourselves and our society most fully. Our job is to help the work of world history press forward, instead of being ensnared by the past and perpetuating the same old oppressive institutions and practices. A later German thinker, Martin Heidegger (1889–1976), argued that our task is to take up a relationship to history that's distinctive to each of our individual selves. We must appropriate and live out our own histories "authentically." Let's see what sort of aid these thinkers might have to offer Jax and SAMCRO in their quest for self-knowledge.

Sons of Anarchy and Philosophy: Brains Before Bullets, First Edition.
Edited by George A. Dunn and Jason T. Eberl.
© 2013 John Wiley & Sons, Inc. Published 2013 by John Wiley & Sons, Inc.

"I'm Looking Forward to Working with You, Mr. Marks"

Or is it Mr. "Marx"?

Like other German "Left Hegelians," the socialist philosopher Karl Marx followed Georg Wilhelm Friedrich Hegel (1770–1831) in reading history dialectically—that is, as a conflict-driven process in which the limitations of some initial position provoke an opposing position and results in a back-and-forth movement between the two until a better position is achieved, preserving what's best in both of them.[2] For Marx, however, that dialectic is embedded in the material conditions and relationships of society in a way Hegel never considered, namely, in the struggle between economic classes. More specifically, for Marx what drives history is the clashing interests of those who control the means of production—the factories, fields, and other instruments through which the human world is created and sustained—and those who work them. For Marx, it's only through resolving this "class struggle" that human beings can overcome the historical wounding he calls "alienation" (in German, *Entfremdung*) and achieve our full potential.[3] Thinking about the challenges SAMCRO faces in terms of the class struggle is revealing.

Marx and Engels open the first chapter of their 1848 *Manifesto of the Communist Party* by announcing that, "the history of all hitherto existing society is the history of class struggles."[4] Certainly, the club's history is nothing if not a history of struggle. But is it *class* struggle? On the surface, no; at least not as a matter of worker struggle. Teller-Morrow Automotive Repair seems a standard, if not exactly normal, capitalist enterprise, typical of what Marxists call the *petit bourgeoisie*, the lowest and smallest capitalists, basically small business owners and small-scale farmers. And Teller-Morrow seems engaged in ordinary, everyday capitalist business practices.

Teller-Morrow employs and profits from the labor of non-club workers, skilled in the crafts of motorcycle and automotive repair. Teller-Morrow's employees, however, seem relatively insignificant background figures in the dramas and struggles that engage the club. They're generally sent away whenever club members need to discuss club business. In addition, in Season 4, the MC goes into the porn business, and in Season 5 Jax ups the ante of "exploitation"—the

Marxist term for extracting wealth from the labor of others—by partnering with Nero Padilla to run an escort service. (Nero's name itself, echoing the first-century Roman emperor, signals dominion, corruption, and decline.)

Along these lines, the conflicts among the various criminal organizations can be interpreted as conflicts among small businesses for market share. The Mayans' attack on SAMCRO's gun assembly facility in the pilot episode reads as an act of industrial sabotage against a competitor's factory. The Irish, the Russians, the Lin Triad, the Asian real estate investors, and the Lobos Sonora and Galindo Cartels are easily seen as forces of international capitalism, threatening to crush or consume local American businesses.

Viewed in this way, *Sons of Anarchy* becomes the story of white, American, middle-class, capitalist anxieties as the club struggles to come to terms with demographic changes (the decline of white supremacy, Hispanic immigration, the re-expansion of social diversity), as well as the impact of global capitalism. It's not only extremists like the Nords who tremble with these sorts of anxieties. Sure, alliances are often struck between the Caucasian-centric Sons and other ethnically or racially defined organizations, such as the Mayans, the One-Niners, and the Lin Triad, but the alliances are tenuous and fraught with explosive and murderous potential. Worry about racial conflict almost always hangs in the air. Just ask the Grim Bastards' T.O. Cross about how Chibs Telford did his cousin Randall Hightower, Opie Winston's killer, after Jax promised to spare him ("Crucifixed").

Sons of Anarcho-Syndicalism

But there's a more radical reading that can be made of the show and the MC. We can think of the club not as a small business, but as a would-be "anarchist-syndicalist commune." Anarcho-syndicalism is a kind of anarchism based in labor unions, where workers take control of the economy not through a top-down government bureaucracy but through revolutionary labor associations called "syndicates."[5] The club resembles just such a syndicate: it's hierarchical, but, unlike capitalist enterprises, it's a democratically governed hierarchy. Voting concerns not only who'll hold office but also the production and distribution of wealth.

Friedrich Engels (1820–1895), Marx's sometime collaborator, articulated what has become thought of as the classical Marxist view of
the state. According to Engels, the state is something of a necessary
evil. After a socialist revolution, the state must continue to operate for
as long as it takes to crush capitalism and create a communist (that is,
classless) society. But once communism is well established, things will
be run more anarchistically—without a state and without one class
subjugating and exploiting another.[6] The state is essentially an instrument of class struggle, so without class struggle it will no longer be
necessary. The state will therefore gradually "wither away," as both
the "anarchy" of capitalist markets and the centralized command
economy are replaced with socialist anarchism:

> State interference in social relations becomes, in one domain after
> another, superfluous, and then dies down of itself. The government of
> persons is replaced by the administration of things, and by the conduct
> of processes of production. The state is not "abolished." It withers
> away.[7]

Here we see a difference between Marxists and classical anarchists
such as the French Pierre-Joseph Proudhon (1809–1865) and the
Russian Peter Kropotkin (1842–1921), for whom the state should
immediately be abolished.[8] The difference came to divide anarchists
and Marxist-Leninists during the Soviet Revolution.[9]

If anarchism means anything, it means a life of maximal liberty. In
the view of Emma Goldman (1869–1940), the anarchist theorist
whose words made such an impression on young John Teller when he
encountered them written on a wall while hiking on the Nevada–
California border, anarchism promises freedom from the big three
instruments of oppression: the state, the church, and private property
(or capitalist-based economic relations).[10] More specifically, she
defined anarchism as: "The philosophy of a new social order based
on liberty unrestricted by man-made law; the theory that all forms of
government rest on violence, and are therefore wrong and harmful,
as well as unnecessary."[11] Anarchists aspire to being autonomous,
living only by laws they give to themselves. Anarchists don't bow to
the dictates of those who claim the authority of a deity or a higher
power. And, like Marxists, anarchists of Goldman's stripe call for the
democratic control of the economy on behalf of society as a whole,

rejecting both the coercive top-down government bureaucracies and the profit-driven capitalism that serve only the interests of the wealthy few.

The original Sons of Anarchy seem to have lived according to anarchist political ideals. We might think of the founding moment of SAMCRO as a choice in favor of the anarchistic rather than Marxist alternative to state power, with the First 9 immediately replacing their allegiance to the state with the formation of a voluntary democratic collective, rather than waiting for the state to "wither away." The affinity-based club[12] of ex-soldiers has also replaced the church with the MC, as signified by the room where they make their decisions being labeled the "chapel."[13]

SAMCRO seems anarchistic in its principal economic relations, too, with decisions about production, distribution, and labor made by members of the MC collectively. The club also exhibits another trait of anarchistic economic theory—mutual aid. Kropotkin pinned his hope for the viability of anarchism as a social system on what he believed was the ineluctable human tendency to help each other, which had been nurtured by evolution. The basis of society, he wrote:

> is a feeling infinitely wider than love or personal sympathy—an instinct that has been slowly developed among animals and men in the course of an extremely long evolution, and which has taught animals and men alike the force they can borrow from the practice of mutual aid and support, and the joys they can find in social life.[14]

We see examples of this mutual aid in the way the MC provides for members' material needs. Jax explains to Lyla Winston after Opie's death that the MC will take care of her and the kids ("Stolen Huffy").[15] Like Luann Delaney, Lyla won't be thrown to the wolves just because her old man is gone. Not only do members of the MC provide each other with mutual aid in the form of muscle, but they also share material wealth rather freely. The principle of distribution of the club's earnings is pretty vague, but it certainly doesn't resemble a standard capitalist "free" market. The club seems to live by the old socialist principle, "From each according to his or her ability, to each according to his or her need." In Tara, the MC even has its own socialized health-care service.

SAMCRO's Class Struggle

But as anarchists living in an oppressive society, the Sons can at best enjoy only a partial freedom. Are they oppressed or exploited workers, then? In relation to the Irish and the Galindo Cartel, yes. They assemble and transport weapons, mule drugs, and work as assassins, while these larger organizations get rich off them, and Damon Pope takes (or, rather, took) a share of their earnings. SAMCRO's history on this reading is *not* the history of one capitalist firm competing against other capitalists but of workers struggling to gain independence from their capitalist bosses—especially from international capitalists and crony capitalists working in league with the state—so they can take charge of their own lives.

Theirs is a struggle for economic independence, solidarity, and free-dom from exploitation by the powerful. Their struggle takes place on multiple levels. Opie struggles with how economic hardship forces Lyla to endure exploitation in the sexual marketplace, offering her body and her sexuality as products to be bought and sold. He would like to free her from a world where people are treated like things and carry a price tag like any other commodity. The club initially struggles against Jacob Hale's plan to build new luxury homes in Charming, a development that would change the character of the town, bring SAMCRO under more intense police scrutiny, and even perhaps imperil the future of the club. But harsh economic realities persuade Jax of the need to switch sides and come to Hale's assistance. At least we can say that Jax had the club's interest at heart when he climbed in bed with Hale. By contrast, when Clay sells out SAMCRO for cold cash by striking a deal with the Galindo Cartel *before* bringing it to a vote in chapel, it's a wholesale betrayal of the club's anarchist principles.

Not to defend Clay, but the struggle to remain true to anarchist principles and live as outlaws beyond the corrupting power of capitalism isn't easy. And it's by no means clear that the club's anar-cho-syndicalism will prevail. J.T. tried to establish a commune free of capitalism, religion, and the state but failed. Jax repeatedly tries to free the club, himself, and his family from the world's dialectical struggles, but so far he's failed too.

Throughout most of the series, SAMCRO has been forced to buckle under the claims of international capital (the Real IRA, the Russian

Mafia, the Lin Triad, and the Galindo Cartel), domestic capital (Pope, the LOAN, and the Cacuzza crime family), and the state (June Stahl, Lincoln Potter, the CIA, and the RICO investigation). The club's struggle has largely been defensive, like workers today who feverishly fight to hold on to what they have in the face of powerful global forces breaking unions and pushing down wages and benefits. History is a determined adversary, as Marx well understood when he wrote, "The tradition of all the dead generations weighs like a nightmare on the brain of the living."[16] The club fights its battles in a world that it did not create and on a playing field that is never level.

But a few things seem to have changed for the better as of the end of Season 5, as Jax manages brilliantly to hold the collective together. Exhibiting the mix of cunning and decency he acquired through the dialectical synthesis of his two fathers,[17] he deflects the external threat posed by both RICO and international capital by realigning the contracts between the Real IRA, the Galindo Cartel, and the Lin Triad. He dispatches religion, too, at least symbolically, by killing (the) Pope. While religion via (the) Pope is neutralized, a new partnership is forged with Mr. Marks (Marx). The RICO prosecution seems dead in the water and, as long as Otto holds his tongue (so to speak), it seems unlikely soon to return.

"Shuffle on Back to Mayberry"

Still, as Season 5 ends, it remains unclear whether Jax will move forward—and, if he does, whether it will be as the new Clay, the new J.T., or a synthesis of the two. The inherited (that is, *historical*) weakness of the Teller clan is a "heart defect," and Jax's cruel treatment of Wendy and Clay in the Season 5 finale seems to have exposed that defect in Jax. Perhaps what Jax needs is not to imitate either J.T. or Clay, but to move forward—and away from Gemma—into a renewed form of anarchism. But how? One place to look for an answer is in the philosophical concept of "authenticity," as developed in the work of another German philosopher, Martin Heidegger.[18]

There's no mistaking the fact that *Sons of Anarchy* draws a lot from Shakespeare's *Tragedy of Hamlet*. Like Hamlet, Jax is an heir apparent forced to reckon with a dead father who was murdered by his stepfather and mother. Jax is often called the "prince"—most notably by

Agent Stahl, who accurately grasps the club's inner dynamics. As fans of Shakespeare know, Prince Hamlet kills his stepfather; but Hamlet's mother (the Queen), along with Hamlet himself, becomes collateral damage of his quest for revenge. Jax, by contrast, takes the throne, but he doesn't kill Clay, and Queen Gemma remains on the scene and powerful. Jax even prevents another son (Opie) from killing Clay to avenge another father's death. Why? As ever, because of history. The Irish will deal only with Clay because of the "history" they have with him.[19] History can be punishing.

There may, however, be a better option than literal or figurative patricide open to Jax and the club as they come to terms with their history. But if history is inescapable and the socialist revolution is nowhere in sight, what other option remains for those who don't want to be crushed under the weight of the past? Heidegger argued that even if we can't escape history, we can at least *appropriate* it authentically into our present and on that basis *project* ourselves into the future of our choosing.

Heidegger understood that we are historical beings to our very core, which means that we project ourselves forward into the future, choosing our goals on the basis of the meanings and possibilities we discern in the present. These meanings and possibilities, however, have been given to us by our historical past—not just by our personal histories as individuals but also by the past of the communities to which we belong. Being an outlaw biker or a surgeon or a porn producer are all meaningful possibilities that are available only to people who are born at certain times and places. They are all possibilities that have been prepared by a long history that precedes us. Socrates (469–399 BCE) couldn't have been a biker. Whereas Marx spoke of the past as a "dead weight" that fetters and limits us, Heidegger better appreciated the fact that it is the meanings and possibilities inherited from past that make it possible for us to frame the projects and set the goals that give our lives significance here and now.

Heidegger's term for this relationship that we all have to our past, present, and future is "historicity" (*Geschichtlichkeit*). We work out who we really are and what our world truly is by working through the implications of our histories. From Heidegger's point of view, Clay is dead wrong when he tells Gemma after killing SAMBEL President Keith McGee, "Time don't mean shit" ("Turas"). Try telling that to the IRA, whose struggle against the English is rooted in wrongs that are centuries old—or to any of the Sons in Belfast for that matter![20] David Hale misses the big picture, too, when he demands that Unser cut off his history with SAMCRO, high-handedly admonishing the old-timer, "If you can't detach yourself from your history with these shitheads, well, then maybe you'd better shuffle on back to Mayberry" ("Capybara"). In a way, the entire show is a demonstration of the falsity of this statement. Nobody in America is going back to Mayberry.

We can't escape history, but, according to Heidegger, we have the choice to relate to it either authentically or inauthentically. In other words, we can live the way that we're expected to by the great teeming masses, doing what we're told or what's commonly done, caring about the same things as those around us, and never reflecting on the goals of life. This is what Heidegger calls *inauthenticity*, and it describes how most people go through life. Even Clay, despite his flouting the moral norms of society at every turn, is inauthentic in this sense, since his ultimate ambition—a comfortable retirement with a nice nest egg—is the standard issue American dream. The alternative is *authenticity*, in which we take a few steps back from our historical situation and realize that not all of the possibilities and meanings it affords us are necessarily best for us. Authenticity requires that each of us make a resolute effort to discern what best gives meaning and coherence to our own lives. When Jax's discovery of his father's manuscript launches him on a journey of reflection, in which he no longer can unquestioningly accept that everything done by the club is good, he's taking his first steps into what Heidegger would call authentic human existence.

For Heidegger, authentic existence doesn't require denying or fighting against history, but it does require facing the contingency of our existence, our mortality, our "being-toward-death," as Heidegger calls it. Facing the inevitability of death reminds us that our lifespans are finite and that each of us is responsible for what we make of our lives. Authenticity involves both a stark, honest confrontation with our finitude and a clear understanding of the possibilities our histories afford us, so that we can make our own choices concerning who we each shall be. Jax, of course, faces death in nearly every episode, but seldom as traumatically as when Pope required him to select someone to die in the ritualized death-match/execution that the drug kingpin had arranged. The inescapability of making that choice and Jax's decision to offer his own life rather than sacrifice one of his brothers—a decision that Opie ultimately prevented him from implementing—brought Jax face to face with death in a way that Heidegger would surely say had poised the new club president for an authentic engagement with his own and his club's history.

"We Got a Little History–Let's Talk About the Present"

Season 4 opens with Piney Winston telling Gemma, "Hey, history's dead, sweetheart. It's gotta stay that way, huh?" But even Piney couldn't abide by that maxim, for he's soon enlisting the past, in the form of Maureen Ashby's letters, to threaten Clay with the exposure of J.T.'s murder. That's no surprise, of course, because one of the most important facts about the past is that it doesn't stay in the past. We can't escape the past, which is why Heidegger says we must appropriate it authentically.

The club's blowtorch removed the ink from Kyle Hobart's back, but the physical and mental scars from that experience aren't going away. Still, the inescapability of the past has never prevented anyone from trying to escape from it. The *Sons of Anarchy* opens with Gemma's vain attempt to kill the past by persuading Wendy to overdose, a misguided effort to offer Jax and Abel a new beginning unburdened by history. A lot of the past does get buried over the course of this series (as Josh Kohn will tell you); but, as Gemma and the others must surely realize by the Season 5 finale, no one can really destroy or live beyond the claims of history. Gemma gives it to Jax straight when they discuss Tara's anger over his dalliance with the porn star, Ima: "The sting of that betrayal ain't gonna fade" ("With an X").

The most important dimension of the Sons of Anarchy's engagement with history isn't SAMCRO's participation in history's march toward the better society expected by Marx and the anarchists. Sure, this dimension of history is an element of the show, but what really stands out is the personal aspiration for authenticity on the part of characters like Jax, who must engage the past as they project themselves into the future. Heidegger argues that the task facing us all is to take up our lives authentically as historical individuals, not as part of some grand historical or cosmic drama. Authenticity is a matter of self-knowledge, so Jax's quest to understand himself and the obstacles and pitfalls he faces on account of the club's history must be part of that old philosophical task enshrined at Delphi—"Know thyself." Whether he will actually achieve real and enduring self-knowledge and authenticity remains to be seen. But so it is for all us sons and daughters of history.

Notes

1. George Santayana, *The Life of Reason*, Vol.1: "Reason in Common Sense," ed. Marianne S. Wokeck and Martin A. Coleman (Cambridge, MA: MIT Press, 2011), 172.
2. For background on Hegel, see my other chapter in this volume (Chapter 17).
3. People can be alienated from their labor (when they don't control it), from each other (when they are unable to develop the best kinds of social relations), and from themselves (when they can't fully realize their potential). See Marx's *The Holy Family* (1845) and *The German Ideology* (1846).
4. Karl Marx and Friedrich Engels, *Manifesto of the Communist Party* (Radford, VA: Wilder Publications, World Library Classics, 2007), 8.
5. The I.W.W. (Industrial Workers of the World) is probably the best-known anarcho-syndicalist organization in the United States. It was especially powerful among lumberjacks in the early twentieth-century. Popular leftist political theorist Noam Chomsky considers himself an anarcho-syndicalist (see Peter Jay's interview with Chomsky, "The Relevance of Anarcho-Syndicalism," *The Jay Review* (25 July 1976)). See also British anarcho-syndicalist Rudolf Rocker's 1938 pamphlet, "Anarcho-Syndicalism." The CNT (Confederación Nacional del Trabajo) was important in the Spanish Civil war of 1936–1939.
6. While "anarchism" has traditionally been a left-wing movement opposed to capitalism and economic relations based on private property (i.e. right-wing ideologies and practices), there are libertarians (who oppose the state but accept capitalism) who describe themselves as right-wing, property rights anarchists. The term "right-wing anarchists" is also sometimes applied to anti-modernist anarchists and to Trotskyist Marxists in opposition to Stalinists and other Marxists.
7. Friedrich Engels, *Anti-Dühring. Herr Eugen Dühring's Revolution in Science* (Moscow: Progress Publishers, 1947), 332–333.
8. Well known for the anarchist slogan "Property is theft!" and for defining anarchism as "order without power," Proudhon's most influential work has been *What Is Property?* (1840). For more on the philosophy of anarchism, see Chapter 7 by Bruno de Brito Serra.

9. For an anarchist critique of Lenin's statist practices, consult Emma Goldman, who like many other anarchists supported the Bolshevik Revolution. She was deported to Russia in 1919 as the revolution was in its infancy but quickly became disillusioned by the way Marxists were running it, in particular by their violent suppression of dissent, including the dissent of anarchists. See her volume, *My Two Years in Russia*, published as *My Disillusionment in Russia* (New York: Dover Publications, 2003).

10. Emma Goldman, "Anarchism: What It Really Stands For," in *Anarchism and Other Essays* (Rockville, MD: Serenity Publishers, 2007), 35–46. Jax recites J.T.'s quote from this essay in "Patch Over": "Anarchism … stands for the liberation of the human mind from the dominion of religion; the liberation of the human body from the dominion of property; liberation from shackles and restraint of government. It stands for social order based on the free grouping of individuals" (44). Jax's reading the quote, however, marks a kind of foreboding repetition of J.T.'s original reading, as he himself crosses the NV–CA border in that episode, riding with Bobby in flight from the ATF to hide club guns with the Devil's Tribe, and stumbling into a near-lethal shoot-out with the Mayans on the way—not exactly the kind of liberation J.T. had imagined.

11. Ibid., 37.

12. An "affinity group" being the preferred social unit for many anarchists, since it's an autonomous and voluntary association based on common interests and beliefs.

13. For further discussion of how the Sons have incorporated traditional religious symbolism into their club dynamics, see Chapter 11 by Kevin Corn.

14. Peter Kropotkin, *Mutual Aid: A Factor in Evolution* (Charleston, SC: Forgotten Books, 2012), xiii.

15. In similar ways, workers in the United States in the late 1800s created what became known as "beneficial societies" to provide mutual aid to each other in the form of medical care, funeral benefits, support in times of hardship, etc. One of the first important beneficial societies was founded by the Ancient Order of United Workmen in 1868. Labor unions and other non-profit associations today still offer some of these forms of mutual aid.

16. Karl Marx, *18th Burmaire of Louis Bonaparte* (Rockville, MD: Wildside Press, 2008), 15.

17. As discussed in my other chapter in this volume (see Chapter 17).

18. Heidegger's magnum opus, in which he develops the accounts of authenticity and historicity discussed in this chapter, is *Being and Time*,

trans. Joan Stambaugh, rev. Dennis J. Schmidt (Albany: State University of New York Press, 2010).

19. Later, of course, Jax's sparing of Clay follows from his deference, albeit in a strained way, to the collective's democratic decision, through Bobby's intercession, not to have Clay meet Mr. Mayhem. Had Jax been an impulsive monarchist like Hamlet, Clay would've been toast.

20. For a discussion of the struggle of the Real IRA against the British, see Chapter 8 by Philip Smolenski.

CHAPTER 19

Good Old Fashioned Mayhem

Greg Littmann

SAMCRO is a very modern criminal organization, taking advantage of drug and firearm prohibition to make money under cover of being a club for motorcycle enthusiasts. But despite the modern trappings—the Harleys, Glocks, and M4s—the values of the Sons and their old ladies are even more traditional than those of mainstream society. In fact, their view of life is strikingly close to the view found in the earliest Western literature we have: the bloody tales of warring Bronze Age warriors told by the ancient Greek poet Homer in his epics, the *Iliad* and the *Odyssey*. Perhaps that's only natural. Both the culture of the modern warriors of *Sons of Anarchy* and that of the warriors of 3000 years ago arise out of chaos. Both reflect a world where violence and death are simply facts of life and where the law is whatever the strongest crew says it is, but only for as long as its power lasts. The *Iliad* tells the story of the war in which a confederation of Greek kings attacks the city of Troy, while the *Odyssey* recounts how one veteran of that war, King Odysseus, made it back home against the odds.

The parallels between the culture depicted in *Sons of Anarchy* and the one depicted by Homer's epics make the show philosophically interesting, because moral philosophy in Greece began as a reaction against Homeric values. But despite the criticisms of philosophers, Homer's works were revered in the ancient world and the values he promoted persisted as a general view of what it is to live life well. In fact, Homeric values even remain a part of twenty-first-century Western morality, with

Sons of Anarchy and Philosophy: Brains Before Bullets, First Edition.
Edited by George A. Dunn and Jason T. Eberl.
© 2013 John Wiley & Sons, Inc. Published 2013 by John Wiley & Sons, Inc.

outlaws like the Sons being particularly pure in their commitment to them. We might call it a "warrior" morality, since the conquering warrior epitomizes its conception of a life well lived, whether that warrior defeats others on the battlefield or in the corporate boardroom.

"I Got This": The Way of the Warrior

What is a *warrior*? Jax Teller tells the club that Opie Winston, killed in a gladiatorial prison fight, "went out a warrior" ("Stolen Huffy"). Opie fights hard until he's beaten down and murdered with his own weapon. Though he knows that death is the only possible outcome, he marks himself as a warrior by volunteering for the combat and putting up a valiant fight.

Broadly speaking, all humans are in Opie's position. We're thrust into life without our consent and must struggle and fight to survive, all the while knowing that no matter how well we fight, in the end we will die. The most fundamental question we face isn't "How can I survive?" because we *won't* survive. Rather, it's "How should I live?" For Homer, the best response is Opie's. We can't win in the end, but we can show others how well we can fight.

Many modern "warriors" don't fight with weapons and armor, but compete instead for professional advancement in business or glory in sports or politics. Founded by Vietnam veterans and hardened by outlaw life, SAMCRO has a more traditional conception of the warrior as a man who's able to handle himself in literal life-and-death *combat*. Each member's cut displays the Grim Reaper, carrying a modified M16 rifle in place of the traditional scythe, announcing the wearer as a warrior and a killer. Those who've drawn blood for the club also wear the "Men of Mayhem" patch.[1]

A man who can't fight isn't going to be patched in. Chuckie Marstein is a loyal "friend of the club," but he's no tough guy and is often treated dismissively by the Sons—how often is Chuckie in the scene simply to be told to leave the room? The Sons honor a warrior like Piney Winston who's no longer able to fight—although he's not afraid to "weaponize" his oxygen tank—but only because he already proved himself in the early days of the club. Still, even those who've proven themselves aren't allowed to show signs of vulnerability. When Juice Ortiz tries to hang himself, he risks being patched out.

The Sons are exceptional fighters and facing danger with courage is often *thrilling* for them—bleeding from a head wound after a shoot-out, Happy declares, "I am rapturous!" ("To Thine Own Self"). This attitude is shared by Homer's heroes. One man is judged "better" than another if he kicks more ass in combat. Every major male character in the *Iliad* and *Odyssey* is an exceptional warrior—aside from those who are too old or too young and the slave who looks after Odysseus's pigs. In fact, the war with Troy depends almost entirely on a handful of noblemen with astonishing gods-given talents. Imagine a modern war in which each side has access to a handful of superheroes like the Avengers or the Justice League.

Just as the Sons bear the Reaper on their cuts, Homeric warriors often decorated their armor with violent images to make clear their status as killers. Odysseus relates the time he met the ghost of Heracles: "Terrible was the golden belt he wore as a baldric over his breast, depicting miraculous scenes—bears, wild boars and glaring lions, conflict and battle, bloodshed and the massacre of men."[2] To be thought a coward or weakling was a terrible shame. When the ghost of Achilles asks about his son, Neoptolemus, he doesn't enquire whether the young man is happy. All he wants to know is whether Neoptolemus grew up to be a great warrior like him, and Achilles is delighted to learn that his son has killed many men.[3] Old warriors who no longer fight are respected, provided they have proven themselves when younger. Just as the Sons are advised by Piney, the Greek heroes of the *Iliad* are advised by the old veteran warrior Nestor, king of Pylos. Homeric heroes also enjoy facing danger for its own sake. The Trojan hero Hector inspires his troops by reminding them that the joy of warfare lies in the choice between standing to fight and running away. We see this *joie de guerre* when Jax fights an IRA chief who questions his readiness to stand in for Clay Morrow as MC president and deal-maker with the Irish—both men show tremendous glee while exchanging blows ("Orca Shrugged").

Fighting Dirty: Brutality and Revenge

To SAMCRO, it's more important to win than to fight fairly. The Sons expect honesty from one another within the club, but when dealing with outsiders, gaining an advantage through lies and trickery is something to be proud of. As John Teller puts it, "Inside the club, there had to be truth. Our word was our honor. But outside, it was all about deception. Lies were our defense, our default" ("Old Bones"). When SAMCRO sets out to execute League of American Nationalists member A.J. Weston, they recruit a tattoo artist to cut him and then they ambush him in the bathroom when he goes to wash up ("Na Trioblóidí"). Likewise, when they want to eliminate enemies like June Stahl, Jimmy O'Phelan, and Damon Pope, they use ambush and surprise to their advantage. They call themselves "outlaws" because they recognize no rules beyond those of their group. Outsiders are fair game.

Likewise, the Homeric heroes measure success in life by victory, not by fighting fairly. Odysseus in particular is a master of deception, boasting, "I am ... known to all for my deceptive skills—my fame extends all the way to heaven."[4] After ten years of siege, the Greeks finally manage to get inside the city of Troy when Odysseus comes up with the idea of building a huge wooden horse that the Trojans mistake for a gift from the gods. Unaware that the horse is full of Greek soldiers, the Trojans bring it inside their walls. Odysseus defeats the Cyclops by tricking him into getting drunk, stabbing him the eye while he's asleep, and then hiding under a sheep to escape his cave. The Greeks also love to ambush unprepared enemies. On one foray, Odysseus and his fellow hero Diomedes creep up on a Trojan camp and slaughter them in their sleep. On another occasion, Odysseus slips into Troy disguised as a beggar—just as Jax disguises himself as a drunken bum to sneak up on some Mayans ("Pilot")— kills a lot of Trojans in a surprise attack, and then runs away before they can fight back.

SAMCRO's warriors don't merely fight, but often act with vengeful brutality. When the Sons capture a rapist, they castrate him and let him bleed to death ("Fun Town"). When they discover that disgraced ex-member Kyle Hobart has kept his Reaper tattoo, they burn it from his back with an acetylene torch ("Giving Back"). In "Balm," we learn that Chibs Telford was given his "Glasgow smile" scars by Jimmy O and, in "NS," Chibs can't resist returning the favor just before killing Jimmy.

The Sons view revenge as a moral duty. When Piney believes that the One-Niners were responsible for killing Opie's wife, he sees evening the score by killing Laroy Wayne as the only honorable course of action ("The Revelator"). And when Opie is murdered in jail, Jax recognizes an obligation to take vengeance and promises the officer responsible, "I'm going to find out who you are and where you live and then I'm going to kill you"—and he does! ("Laying Pipe"; "Small World"). Finally, when Clay puts a hit out on Tara Knowles and endangers the lives of Gemma Morrow's grandsons, the enraged grandmother announces, "He's gonna die by the hands of a son"—referring not only to a "Son" but Clay's own stepson, Jax ("Hands").

Homeric heroes must also be brutal and take revenge against their enemies. Agamemnon rallies the Greek troops by promising that every male Trojan will be slaughtered, both children and adults, and every female dragged off into slavery. When a Trojan warrior begs Achilles to spare his life on the grounds of youth, Achilles slashes his guts open with a sword without even bothering to answer: "The young fool, he'd no idea, thinking *Achilles* could be swayed! Here was a man not sweet at heart, not kind, no, he was raging, wild."[5] Later, Achilles assures another pleader that he'll never spare a Trojan's life under any circumstances.

The climax of the *Odyssey* is Odysseus's revenge spree against the young noblemen who've been squatting in his palace, eating his food, and wooing his wife while he's been away. He bars all exits and then he and his son slaughter the lot of them, including those desperately trying to escape, until he "stood among the corpses of the dead, spattered with blood and gore, like a lion when he comes from feeding on some farmer's bullock, with the blood dripping from his breast and jaws on either side, a fearsome spectacle."[6]

SAMCRO doesn't usually take revenge on the *family* of someone who wronged them.[7] For example, when they capture Weston to kill him for raping Gemma, they allow his son to live and spare him the sight of his father's slaying. Homeric heroes, on the other hand, accept that family is a legitimate target for revenge. When Agamemnon discovers that two captives are the sons of his enemy Antimachus, he cries, "Now pay for your father's outrage, blood for blood!"[8]

There are many ways in which the Homeric heroes outstrip the brutality of SAMCRO. When Melanthius, who tends Odysseus's goats, turns out to have been collaborating with Odysseus's enemies, it isn't enough to simply kill him. Instead, Odysseus ties Melanthius's arms behind his back and hangs him from the ceiling of a storeroom overnight. The next day, his men finish the job: "With a pitiless knife they sliced his nose and ears off; they ripped away his genitals as raw meat for the dogs, and in their fury they lopped off his hands and feet."⁹ Odysseus's idea of justice makes Clay castrating a child rapist look like an act of mercy! Note that none of this is for the purposes of extracting information. The Sons aren't above using torture to get at the truth, as they do to a rogue member of SAMBEL who betrayed the club to Jimmy O ("Firinne"). But the Sons don't normally use torture as a tool for vengeance as Homeric heroes do.

"God Wants Me to Be a Fierce Mother"

"The bond that holds this club together isn't blood or brotherhood. It's just fear and greed now," complains Jax soon after he takes over the presidency ("Sovereign"). But this isn't true. His own actions, and those of most Sons, reflect a deep loyalty to SAMCRO and the people within it. Loyalty to friends is essential to their conception of living life well.¹⁰ The Sons will happily betray outsiders, but someone like Clay who betrays his closest friends oversteps all bounds of decency, even the code of honor among outlaws. Jax, on the other hand, not only regularly risks his life for the Sons, but tries to protect them by directing them into safer business ventures. "I ain't afraid to get bloody," he tells Clay. "I'm just afraid all that blood is going to kill SAMCRO" ("Hell Followed"). Jax even takes on the mantle of president when what he really wants to do is leave the club, just to save SAMCRO from a disastrous future.

The other Sons are no less devoted to their brothers in the club. When Jax's son, Abel, is kidnapped, the Sons don't hesitate to fly to Ireland to track him down. When imprisoned in Stockton, Juice puts up with being deliberately injured so he can be sent to the infirmary in order to lure another prisoner into an ambush with promises of sex. Chibs refuses to sign papers for Agent Stahl that would incriminate SAMCRO, even though Stahl threatens to expose his actions to the Real IRA, which would mean the death of his wife and daughter. Half-Sack Epps loses his life when he rushes Cameron Hayes in a desperate attempt to protect Tara and Abel. When it comes to loyalty, Otto Delaney takes the prize. Up to the point when he finally turns on the club for failing to protect his wife, Luann, Otto gives up first his freedom, then his sight, and finally his life for the club.

Likewise, for Homer, you can't live a good life without good and loyal friends. Someone who lets their friends down is worthless. The closest relationships in Homer's works are between men who are friends, their bonds forged in the battles of the Trojan War, just as the friendships of the First 9 were forged in Vietnam. Many of these relationships are at *least* as close as family. King Alcinous notes, "A friend with an understanding heart can be as dear as a brother."[11] In the *Iliad*, Achilles takes this one step further. He cares so much for his friend Patroclus that, when he's killed in battle, Achilles laments that he'd have been hurt less by the death of his father or son.

In fact, the outcome of the Trojan War is decided by the strength of the friendship between Achilles and Patroclus. Before Patroclus's death, the Greek and Trojan armies were locked in a stalemate. Achilles, the mightiest of the Greek warriors, could have broken the stalemate at any time if he would have just come out of his tent and fought, instead of sulking over an insult to his honor. Nothing moves him until Patroclus is impaled with a spear by the great Trojan warrior Hector. Achilles finally returns to battle out of his need to avenge Patroclus by killing Hector, just as Jax needs to kill the prison officer to avenge Opie. When Achilles marks Hector for death, Achilles knows that he's fated to die soon after Hector. Yet Achilles chooses to kill Hector rather than live without avenging his friend.

Anarchy theoretically involves abandoning social institutions, but no civil disorder has ever been so complete that it's eliminated the oldest and most fundamental of all social institutions, the family. Not all members of SAMCRO have families and not all Sons with families live up to their responsibilities, but, for those who do, commitment to family often rivals their commitment to the club. Opie even backs out of SAMCRO's activities for a time to make his wife happy. Throughout the series, Jax's primary motivation has been to protect his family. He risks his life to save Tara when she's cornered by a stalker and even crosses an ocean to rescue his son Abel.

In Jax's mind, part of being successful in life is protecting his family and promoting their interests. Jax sees his father's failure to protect his family when he allowed himself to be killed as a moral failure. In "NS," Jax says, "I'd never turn on my club, or my family. I'm not my father." He later assures Tara, "I'm not my father. I'm not weak" ("Out"). Revenge is often motivated by loyalty to family.

Consider Piney's attempted shooting of Clay for murdering Donna, Opie's shooting of Clay for murdering Piney, and Jax's slowly brewing but inevitable revenge against Clay for murdering his father, John Teller.

As harsh as Gemma can be, her primary role is maternal nurturer. She provides emotional support and advice for Clay, Jax, and Tara, does her best to provide for the future of her deteriorating father, and dotes on her grandsons. She repeatedly states that her first loyalty is to her family, going so far as to say that she'd "be dead without my boys" ("J'ai Obtenu Cette"). Jax, on the other hand, is willing to give up Abel in order to provide him with a good life. In "Bainne," Jax decides to leave his son with a loving couple in Ireland to spare him a life of crime. To Gemma, this is unthinkable. As she explains to a group of horrified nuns at gunpoint, she'd rather that a child of her blood was chopped in two than raised by strangers.

The value of family was no less central to Homeric culture. Family was more valuable than wealth. King Menelaus of Sparta complains that all the treasure he collected in the Trojan War brings him no happiness, because of the deaths of so many friends in the fighting and because his brother was murdered while he was away. For Odysseus, family counts more than anything else. He tells King Alcinous, "a man's fatherland and his parents are what he holds sweetest, even though he has settled far away from his people in some rich home."[12] The feeling is mutual. Odysseus's wife weeps for him night and day back at the palace, while Odysseus's father misses him so much that he's given up living at the palace and has spent the past 20 years on his farm, sleeping in the dirt and doing without a bed, blankets, or cloak. For Homeric heroes, as for SAMCRO, duty to family is a common motive for revenge. In fact, Agamemnon's fate parallels John Teller's. It's revealed in the *Odyssey* that he returned from the Trojan War only to be killed by his wife and her lover, who then took over his kingdom of Mycenae. Agamemnon's son Orestes later grows up and slays his father's murderer.

Laws of the Outlaws

Despite calling themselves "Sons of Anarchy," the Sons don't *really* want to get rid of social institutions altogether. SAMCRO itself is a social institution that's central to the life of every Son. The "outlaws" are bound by a set of bylaws and take on a heavy burden of duty to the club and its members. But they never give up their right to question authority and they are active participants in club politics. While the office of president carries a lot of power in SAMCRO, the president is no dictator. Major policy changes are decided by a vote and every member is allowed to voice his opinion when SAMCRO meets in "chapel." This liberty extends as far as quitting the club. When Jax gets sick of Clay and decides to go nomad, SAMCRO votes to allow him to go. So while the Sons' conception of a good life might require living cooperatively in communities, it also requires a great deal of personal freedom.

Like the Sons, Homeric heroes were willing to cooperate as members of a society, but also believed that living well requires personal freedom. They were willing to support leaders, but insisted on having their voices heard. In the *Iliad*, Agamemnon is recognized as the most powerful king among the Greeks and other kings generally submit to his decisions. However, when important warriors disagree with him, they make it known without hesitation. Like Jax being allowed to go nomad, Achilles is permitted to quit the Trojan War. When Agamemnon insults his honor by taking one of his slave girls, Achilles gives him a piece of his mind, refuses to fight anymore, and goes back to his tent to sulk.

Yet a warrior's freedom to speak isn't complete. It depends on the degree to which he has proven himself. Jax is given leeway to criticize Clay that would never be allowed to a prospect like Half-Sack. Likewise, Achilles is permitted to accuse Agamemnon of greed, but no such grace is given to a scrawny little hunchback named Thersites, who dares to criticize Agamemnon on exactly the same grounds. Odysseus hits Thersites with a scepter right on his hump, hard enough to leave a bloody welt, points out that he isn't anybody of any consequence, and promises to kick Thersites's ass if he keeps talking.[13] Similarly, when "Filthy Phil" Russell and Eric Miles are first initiated as prospects, Jax reminds them of their position in the club in no uncertain terms: "Shut up! You don't say anything unless a member tells you to" ("The Push").

Of course, the Sons are part of broader communities than just SAMCRO. Gang territory in *Sons of Anarchy* is a patchwork of feuding independent states with no higher authority keeping them at peace, much like the autonomous city-states of Bronze Age Greece. As in Greece, alliances shift, though some organizations have stronger bonds of cooperation than others, as with the bond between SAMCRO and the Grim Bastards. Within its own territory, SAMCRO takes on the responsibility of protecting people and keeping order. As Clay points out, "people get jammed up in this town, they don't go to the cops. They come to us" ("Fun Town"). Like SAMCRO, Homeric heroes may act as killers, but their usual role is to keep the peace and protect the people in their territory. Odysseus, for all his bloodthirsty acts, is praised as a gentle and compassionate king, a "loving father"[14] to the people of Ithaca whom he ruled with "never an injustice to a single person in the land."[15] For those who've remained loyal to him, Odysseus's return is a cause of great celebration.

Do Fear the Reaper

These parallels between SAMCRO's and Homer's conceptions of a good life show us both what is commendable and condemnable about life in the MC. On the one hand, the strict bonds of loyalty to friends, family, and community are tighter than in most other social structures. On the other hand, ruthlessness, violence, and vengeance are equally strict cultural norms among these "mechanics and motor-cycle enthusiasts." Is there a way out of this brutal social system that doesn't require buying into the materialism and conventionalism of the restrictive society from which John Teller and the rest of the First 9 had dropped out? Teller had recognized that the Sons of Anarchy was a failure that needed to be transformed or abolished: "I found myself lost in my own club. I trusted few—feared most. Nomad offered escape and exile. I didn't know if leaving would cure or kill this thing we created" ("Balm").

Western moral philosophy began with Socrates (469–399 BCE), Plato (429–347 BCE), and Aristotle (384–322 BCE) as a reaction to the perceived failure of the Homeric value system. The question remains today whether a less honor-obsessed and more rationalist ethic should guide human moral decision making or whether it's better to follow the way of the warrior, viewing life as a contest for gain and glory, and caring nothing for the stranger or outsider.[16]

Notes

1. For further discussion of the symbolic significance of the "Reaper," see Chapter 10 by Charlene Elsby and Chapter 11 by Kevin Corn.
2. *Odyssey*, trans. E.V. Rieu (London: Penguin Classics, 2003), Book 11, lines 609–612.
3. *Odyssey*, Book 11, lines 491–492.
4. *Odyssey*, Book 9, lines 19–20.
5. *Iliad*, trans. Robert Fagles (London: Penguin Classics, 1990), Book 20, lines 526–529.
6. *Odyssey*, Book 22, lines 400–403.
7. Though the jailer's wife ended up as collateral damage ("Small World"); and they did force Mayan President Marcus Álvarez to give up his own son to be killed by Happy Lowman after his son botched an attempt on Clay's life ("Hell Followed").
8. *Iliad*, Book 2, line 165.
9. *Odyssey*, Book 22, lines 475–477.
10. For further discussion of the value of loyalty, see Chapter 3 by James Edwin Mahon.
11. *Odyssey*, Book 8, lines 584–585.
12. *Odyssey*, Book 9, lines 32–34.
13. *Iliad*, Book 2, line 288.
14. *Odyssey*, Book 5, line 12.
15. *Odyssey*, Book 4, lines 690–691.
16. This discussion is continued in my other chapter in this volume (Chapter 20).

CHAPTER 20

The Road Out of Mayhem

Greg Littmann

John Teller titled his manuscript *The Life and Death of Sam Crow: How the Sons of Anarchy Lost Their Way*. Horrified at what his club had become since its founding, he was looking for a way to get SAMCRO back on track before he was murdered by Clay Morrow. In J.T.'s original conception, the Sons of Anarchy were genuinely devoted to anarchy as a political principle. He quotes political philosopher Emma Goldman (1869–1940): "Anarchism stands for the liberation of the human mind from the domination of religion; the liberation of the human body from the coercion of property; liberation from the shackles and restraint of government. It stands for a social order based on the free grouping of individuals" ("Patch Over").[1] The life he imagined was not just one of freedom, but simplicity and peace— "a Harley commune, some real hippy shit," as his son Jax Teller describes it ("Pilot"). He also quotes Albert Einstein: "Any intelligent fool can make things bigger, more complex, and more violent. It takes a touch of genius—and a lot of courage—to move in the opposite direction" ("The Pull").[2]

Is it regrettable that the Sons strayed from Teller's original vision? Should they strive to go back to the simple, peaceful commune he had in mind? The alternative J.T. envisioned has ancient roots, as does the sort of community SAMCRO eventually became. In many ways, the values SAMCRO holds dear reflect those of the "warrior" ethic typified by the heroes of Homer's epics the *Iliad* and the *Odyssey*.[3] Such

Sons of Anarchy and Philosophy: Brains Before Bullets, First Edition.
Edited by George A. Dunn and Jason T. Eberl.
© 2013 John Wiley & Sons, Inc. Published 2013 by John Wiley & Sons, Inc.

values include what many of us would recognize as positive qualities, such as strong bonds of family, friendship, and community, but they also include possibly less desirable qualities, such as ruthlessness, brutality, and a drive for vengeance. Later Greek philosophers—Socrates (469–399 BCE), Plato (429–347 BCE), and Aristotle (384–322 BCE)— promoted alternatives to these warrior values, some of which can already be seen within the MC and may provide a way out of the troublesome life of mayhem that J.T. and Jax seek to leave behind. In addition, while "anarchism" as a political philosophy arose in the nineteenth century, the earliest of all the fathers of anarchy was the Greek philosopher Diogenes of Sinope (404–323 BCE). Like J.T., Diogenes was disgusted with the values of his day and searched for a better way for human beings to live. He left no writings of his own, but showed by example how he believed one should live.[4]

Father of Anarchy

John Teller wrote, "true freedom requires sacrifice and pain" ("Patch Over"). Diogenes, on the other hand, believed that life was meant to be easy. He claimed that a life in accordance with nature is delightful, but we've traded it for something difficult because of our greed for money and possessions. "Greed is the metropolis of all evils," he liked to say, five centuries before a New Testament writer made a similar observation (1 Tim 6:10). Life in accordance with nature is free, reasonable, and happy. There are, of course, some hardships to be endured, but having the right attitude makes hardships light.

Diogenes refused to get a job. Not only does work make life hard, it distracts us from devoting ourselves to more important things, like philosophizing. As long as we're beholden to others for money, we're not free. The employed work when the boss says, eat when the boss says, and sleep when the boss says.[5] The mere fact that Tig Trager works at Teller-Morrow Automotive Repair gives Clay the right to tell him what to do, which isn't enough anarchy for Diogenes. People who seek the patronage of the rich, as the white supremacist A.J. Weston seeks the backing of wealthy businessman Ethan Zobelle, aren't in any better position. Weston may not be getting a regular wage, but Zobelle still pulls his strings. Even running your own auto-repair shop or gun-running operation is too much work to allow you to be truly free. J.T. was echoing Diogenes's view of freedom and society when he wrote, "Most human beings only think they want freedom. In truth they yearn for the bondage of social order, rigid laws, materialism; the only freedom man really wants is the freedom to become comfortable" ("Patch Over").

It's all very well for Diogenes to tell us not to chase possessions, but don't we need *some* possessions in order to live a good life—a toothbrush and a pair of white sneakers at least? Besides, isn't there something valuable about riding a Harley, drinking a beer, blasting AWOLNATION's "Burn It Down" on your stereo, or otherwise enjoying your material possessions? Diogenes conceded that we need some very basic possessions, but he believed that we'd be happiest with very little. He lived in a barrel he had scavenged, owning only the clothes on his back, a wooden staff, and a leather bag. He walked barefoot, even in the snow. Seeing a child drinking out of his hand, Diogenes threw away his own cup. Seeing another child using a crust to scoop up lentils, Diogenes threw away his spoon. Whereas even a hard-bitten outfit like SAMCRO recognizes the importance of funeral rituals and gives full honors to Opie Winston and Half-Sack Epps after their deaths, Diogenes left instructions that his corpse be thrown to the wild beasts.

Like J.T., Diogenes believed that we must throw off the social conventions that bind us. Human beings are hemmed in by rules of our own creation that make life needlessly hard by forcing us to act against nature. Social conventions shouldn't merely be ignored, but should be deliberately violated in order to tear them down. Diogenes ate, slept, and conversed whenever and wherever it suited him. He claimed that it was morally permissible to eat the flesh of any animal, even human flesh—although he may not have approved of the violence, Diogenes wouldn't have been as disgusted as the rest of us by Tig tearing off a rival's ear with his teeth ("The Culling"). Family, the bedrock of society for Homer and SAMCRO alike, was to be abolished. There would be no marriage. Instead, men and women would be free to be promiscuous and children would be held in common by the community. Whereas female unfaithfulness was grounds for slaughter in the Homeric world and possibly even in the world of SAMCRO, Diogenes's scheme would permit a woman to live with any man she wished whenever she liked, in what Goldman would recognize as a "free grouping of individuals." In violation of civilized

Greek etiquette, Diogenes ate in the street, drank in wine shops, and, most famously, masturbated in public like Chuckie Marstein, expecting people to "accept that"! Diogenes's point was that masturbating is a natural activity that harms nobody, it being only social convention that says we shouldn't do it whenever and wherever we like—and as far as we know, he died with all his fingers intact.

"You Can't Sit in this Chair Without Being a Savage"

John Teller had no idea of why his vision of a "Harley commune" had gone astray. "I never made a conscious decision to have the club become one thing or another," he wrote. "It just happened before my eyes. Each savage event was a catalyst for the next. And by the time the violence reached epic proportion, I couldn't see it. Blood was every color" ("Hell Followed"). Both J.T. and Diogenes failed to realize that there's a problem with throwing away social institutions: new institutions tend to assert themselves. Even if we could reduce society to a true anarchy, it wouldn't last. A new order would be established the second a big guy like Clay takes advantage of the lawlessness to mug a small guy like Chuckie for his lunch. In states of anarchy, strong, violent men rise to the top, banding together with other strong, violent men for protection. In this environment, power goes to those with a proven talent for killing other people.[6]

Of course, J.T. thought SAMCRO's big mistake was dealing in illegal firearms. It wasn't simply the act of moving off the social grid that embroiled his club in so much violence. But regardless of whether SAMCRO is dealing in assault rifles or making legal porn at Cara Cara, the price of turning their backs on society is having to rely on themselves for defense against aggressors, rather than depending on the authorities. In that environment, power goes to the strongest and most violent, as order reasserts itself in basic and ancient patterns.

Without an authority that protects everyone, your safety depends on the likelihood that someone would take revenge if you're killed. Damon Pope, for example, alerts Jax to the terrible consequences his right-hand man August Marks will inflict on anyone stupid enough to kill him ("J'ai Obtenu Cette"). With no police, law courts, or prisons, punishing a killer falls on the victim's family and friends. It's up to Jax to avenge his father's death, because going to the cops is out of the question. But when it's up to us to take revenge for the ones we love, our bias makes our justice blind and cruel: "When we take action to avenge the ones we love, personal justice collides with social and divine justice. We become judge, jury, and God. With that choice comes daunting responsibility. Some men cave under that weight. Others abuse the momentum" ("Fun Town"). Where revenge is the only justice, failure to take revenge marks you as weak and invites others to push you around. As J.T. laments, reporting on how this lawless world had contributed to his own moral degeneration, "If I was wronged, by anyone, in or out of the club, I had to be compensated—money or blood. There was no turning the other cheek" ("Smite").

So perhaps anarchy isn't the way to go. But that doesn't mean that Teller and the rest of the First 9 were wrong to rebel against the materialistic values of the society they were born into. Nor does it mean that the only alternative to anarchy is to adopt the warrior ethic of Homer or SAMCRO. What if, instead of abandoning society, we reform it and make it better?

Plato Takes Abel Out of a Bad Environment

Like John Teller and Diogenes, the ancient Greek philosopher Plato was disgusted by the materialism and corruption of his society. His solution wasn't to give up on society, though, but to reform its underlying values. Rather than following the lead of Homeric heroes or SAMCRO and measuring how well we're doing by our wealth or the honor and respect we get from others, we should measure it by how wise and morally good we are. In this view, Plato was inspired by his mentor Socrates, who accused his fellow citizens of the city of Athens of caring only for wealth and flattery when they should be concerned about the health of their souls. Having a morally healthy soul is the only thing that really matters, but not because of reward in some future life beyond the grave. Rather, without a healthy soul, even worldly goods are worthless because one will lack the judgment to use them well. Plato wouldn't be surprised that the money and power coveted by someone like Clay turn toxic in his hands, not because they're inherently bad, but because Clay values them more than the state of his soul.

Of course, Homeric heroes and the Sons alike have a moral code that they enforce among themselves. But they are brutal and callous in their treatment of outsiders, since their moral concerns generally extend no further than their personal connections. Outsiders are just tools to be used. SAMCRO fobs off Russian gangsters with counterfeit money in return for Jimmy O, while the innocent people who may be shot by the firearms SAMCRO deals don't figure in their calculations at all. The MC even uses a charity motorcycle run as cover to transport illegal weapons ("Eureka"). The Sons recognize a duty to protect family, friends, and their local community, but they usually check their moral concerns at the borders of Charming.

This moral disconnect is most jarring to see in Gemma Morrow, who's often kind and can be a nurturing supporter to her family and friends. She sometimes even goes out of her way to help strangers, giving money to a beggar ("The Sleep of Babies") and stopping to help an apparent mother in distress ("Albification"). Yet she's a loyal supporter of an organization that contributes to suffering by distributing weapons that are sure to kill innocents. As kind as she is, Gemma is a moral monster who helps to prop up a harmful criminal organization. She feels bonds of duty, but almost exclusively to the extent of her social ties.

Plato rejected the Homeric values of personal loyalty and vengeance as guiding principles in favor of a system of justice that protects all citizens, regardless of their relationships. Just laws aim at the advantage of citizens in general, rather than the select few at the top of the social hierarchy. Unlike revenge, justice is guided by reason and not wild and destructive passions.

Whereas J.T. and Diogenes want society to become less organized, Plato wants it to become *more* organized. Whereas the First 9 installed a democratic process in the club's bylaws to protect individual freedom, Plato reminds us that democracy is rule by people with no expertise in ruling. Plato's *Republic* describes an imaginary ideal city-state.[7] The people would be divided into three classes: the working class, the warrior class, and the ruling class. The working class produces or maintains things—they farm, repair automobiles, perform surgery, and so on. The warriors protect the workers and the ruling class orders the city through laws. In the city-state described in the *Republic*, only those who have the highest aptitude for governing and who have no personal interests that would conflict with the common good (like wealth!) are permitted to rule. According to Plato, society runs most smoothly if everyone sticks to what he or she does best. For example, Tara Knowles's vocation, as both Gemma and her supervisor remind her, is to be a *healer*. Plato would judge that Tara serves her community best and is happiest in that role.

While Plato rejects the Homeric goal of becoming a great warrior in favor of attaining wisdom and virtue, he retains great respect for the skills of warriors and many of the values inculcated through warrior training. Nobody in Plato's *Republic* is born directly into the ruling class. Instead, the most promising and intelligent warriors are chosen at age 30 for additional training to qualify them to rule. The warriors are drilled to make them physically tough and fearless in the face of death. At the same time, however, a warrior must balance lethality with an ability to be gentle in order to serve as a protector of the city. Warriors have no value if they're not serving a good social purpose. Tig is an excellent example of what happens when a warrior is guided by his own passions rather than reason. A long-standing asset to SAMCRO, Tig becomes a liability when he takes justice into his own hands to inflict personal revenge, attempting to kill Laroy Wayne, leader of the One-Niners, whom he's been told were responsible for shooting Clay ("To Be, Act 1"). When he accidentally kills Damon Pope's daughter, his own daughter, and later Opie, suffer the consequences.

In line with Diogenes's proposals, the city-state of Plato's *Republic* abolishes the family among the warrior and ruling classes, as family loyalties could compete for the rulers' loyalty to the common good. People often care more about their families getting ahead than they do about being just to others. Gemma cares so much about Jax taking his seat as president of SAMCRO—with herself, rather than Tara, standing behind him—that she manipulates him and those around him to get him to the head of the table. In politics and business, favoritism toward family is a hallmark of corruption.

But if John Teller's vision is too anarchic, the city-state of Plato's *Republic* is too authoritarian. The desire for freedom is strong in humans. We like to make up our own mind about what we'll do, even if we end up doing things that aren't best for us—like smoking cigars, partying into the wee hours, or racing down the open road on Harleys. J.T. and the rest dropped out of a conformist society that was pressuring them to live life the way other people thought it should be lived, and they were right to reject such conformity. They were never going to find a meaningful existence pretending to be something they weren't just to satisfy the people around them.

Perhaps there's a middle way between the doomed anarchy of John Teller and Diogenes and the stifling authoritarianism of Plato's *Republic*. Perhaps it is possible to have a moral society that doesn't alienate us from things we care about, like personal freedom and family. Let's look to Plato's student Aristotle for another account of how we should live.

Aristotle versus the Outlaws

According to Aristotle, to live a good human life, you must be a good human being. But what does it mean to be a good human being? Aristotle points out that to say something is a "good X" is to say that it does the job of an X well. If we say that a particular Harley-Davidson motorcycle is a "good Harley," we mean that it does well what a Harley is supposed to do—it can do zero to 60 in 3.3, doesn't wobble when you ride, and doesn't break down every time it rains. Likewise, to be a "good human being" is to perform the function of a human being well.

Aristotle claims that you can tell what something's function is by seeing what it's best suited for. Imagine seeing a motorcycle for the first time. You notice that the seat is the perfect shape for sitting on, while the wheels serve well to move the vehicle. Once Clay gets on and starts to ride it around, you can see even more clearly just how well it works as a mode of transportation and you rightly conclude that that's its purpose. To Aristotle's mind, what goes for devices also goes for animals. You can tell by watching that the function of a fish is to swim and a bird to fly, rather than vice versa, because the fish excels at swimming and the bird at flying.

What human beings do well compared to every other animal is to *reason*. The Sons are proud of their ability to brawl, but compared to brawlers from other species, they're not so great. Half-Sack, Tig, or Jax may be able to take on any human challengers in a boxing match, but put a grizzly bear in the ring with them and they'll lose every time. On the other hand, if the competition involves the use of reasoning, even the least intellectual members of SAMCRO, like Tig and Happy, will be able to soundly defeat even the smartest bear. This is why Aristotle concludes that exercising reason is the function of a human being and that the best life for us involves exercising reason well—not only in drawing conclusions about what's true and false, but also in deliberating about how to act. In addition, a good person also experiences emotions in a rational way, neither overreacting nor underreacting to circumstances. Aristotle approves of men learning to fight, but, unlike Homer, he believes that a man's value lies not in how well he excels at killing, but in how well he's cultivated his intellectual and moral virtues, which involves the proper use of reason.[8]

Like Plato, Aristotle rejects the Homeric values of personal loyalty and vengeance as guiding social principles in favor of impartial justice. Just laws serve the common good, rather than simply benefiting the strong: "Governments which have a regard to the common interest are constituted in accordance with strict principles of justice," writes Aristotle, "and are therefore true forms; but those which regard only the interests of the rulers are all defective and perverted forms, for they are despotic, whereas a state is a community of freemen."[9] Aristotle also agrees with Plato that it is better to seek the good of your community than to be preoccupied solely with your private good: "For even if the end [happiness] is the same for a single man and for a state, that of the state seems at all events something greater and more complete both to attain and to preserve; for though it is worthwhile to attain the end merely for one man, it is finer and more godlike to attain it for a nation or for city-states."[10]

Aristotle believes that friendship is one of the most important things in life. In fact, he thinks that friendship is essential for our continuous moral development, but not just any friends will do. For starters, we don't need a large number of associates, just a small number of *close* friends—the number *must* be small, since it's impossible to know a lot of people well. A small, tightly knit group like SAMCRO is perfect. However, even if we spend a lot of time with a small circle of friends and know them well, they still might not be the right *kind* of friend.

Aristotle maintains that there are three possible foundations for friendship: pleasure, usefulness, and mutual goodness. The first kind of friendship is based on enjoying pleasurable things together—riding Harleys, drinking beers, firing off some AKs, or whatever else it is you like to do with others. This is the sort of friendship that most of the members of SAMCRO share. Friendship based on usefulness depends on what the friends can do for one another. We don't see Clay and Wayne Unser hanging out much just for the sheer pleasure of each other's company, but they do have a mutually beneficial relationship. It's helpful for Clay to have the local police chief as a friend, while Unser benefits from Clay protecting his trucks and keeping Charming safe from the Mayans and the Nords.

However, the highest form of friendship, according to Aristotle, is based on mutual admiration of each other's moral qualities: we love these friends not merely for the good times they show or the aid they render us, but most of all for their goodness and excellence. Of course, we're seldom drawn to people solely because of their virtue. The beginnings of most friendships are in shared pleasurable activities or mutual benefit. But, according to Aristotle, the deepest and most enduring friendships are the ones that also involve this sort of mutual admiration.

Such friendships yield the greatest inherent satisfaction, but they have other benefits as well. For one thing, associating with good people is liable to steer us in a good direction, while bad associates have just the opposite effect on our lives. If young, idealistic John Teller had stuck with what Jax describes as "hippy shit" and had never started to associate with the likes of Clay Morrow, he probably never would have spiraled into self-loathing and hopelessness. And if his clever son Jackson hadn't grown up among the Sons of Anarchy but among gentle hippies, he might now be the president of a small company selling his own brand of eco-friendly, soy-based products, instead of heading up a motorcycle gang running illegal guns, muling cocaine, and partnering with a "companionator."

How Many Miles to Utopia?

Where does all of this leave us? Certainly not with a precise set of directions about what to value and how to live. The sort of "self-help" that philosophers offer doesn't typically take the form of tidy little checklists. But looking at SAMCRO through the eyes of these three philosophers may help to shed light on where SAMCRO's value system went wrong and where our own value systems might likewise be flawed.

Diogenes, like John Teller, recognizes that attachment to material things and obedience to social convention imprison us and make us unhappy. It was greed that inaugurated SAMCRO's spiral into violent criminality. In ordinary society, most of us aren't launched on a career of violence by our inordinate love of money, but our need to work and our fear of violating social taboos may keep us from the things that really bring us joy.

Plato understands that we can't rid ourselves of society and must instead reorient our values so that personal success becomes measured not by the acquisition of money and power, but by wisdom and moral goodness. In order for society to function well, we must extend the scope of our moral concern beyond just friends and family and begin to care genuinely about what happens to strangers. The Sons—with the exception of Clay—are deeply loyal to their close personal associates, but they seem to have little concern for those outside their small circle. In this respect, they aren't much different from many of us in mainstream society. As a corrective, Plato urges us to seek justice for all citizens.

Aristotle agrees that we must stop measuring success in terms of power and money. We should turn instead to self-improvement. Like Plato, he recognizes that attachment to material things can distract us from what's truly important and that we must place justice over the interests of our friends and family. But Aristotle offers us a more realistic conception of how we might balance our social commitments and personal attachments, as well as the role that friends and family might play in our flourishing as human beings. We don't need to reject money or family or surrender all of our freedoms to the state. It wouldn't be good for us if we tried. But we need to recognize our duties beyond the circle of our friends, family, or motorcycle club. We have duties even to people who mean nothing to us personally.

Aristotle, Diogenes, and Plato all give us food for thought as we attempt to work out for ourselves how we should live. We may not sell guns to street gangs, or murder our business rivals, or even speed down the highway on a Harley shooting at people. All the same, if we find that we care more about defeating our rivals for status and money than we do about being good persons, or if we find that the only moral duties we recognize are toward people we personally care about, then we might have more in common with the Sons of Anarchy than we'd like to admit. So, in the spirit of self-reflection, the next time you put on your shirt to go to work, ask yourself if it would be more honest of you to wear a jacket with the Grim Reaper holding a bleeding M16 scythe.

Notes

1. Emma Goldman, "Anarchism" in *Anarchism and Other Essays* (New York: Create Space, 2012), 8. For more on the philosophy of anarchism, see Chapter 7 by Bruno de Brito Serra.
2. Like a lot of the most famous things allegedly said by Einstein, he actually never said this. Still, anything sounds profound if you attribute it to Einstein.
3. For discussion of the Homeric parallels with *SOA*, see my other chapter in this volume (Chapter 19).
4. The best source we have for the life of Diogenes of Sinope is a biography written by another ancient Greek, Diogenes Laertius, *Lives of Eminent Philosophers*, trans. R.D. Hicks (Cambridge, MA: Harvard University Press, 1979).
5. Diogenes's complaint here parallels the later critique of the industrial workplace by Karl Marx. For further discussion of Marx's views in comparison to the anarchic life of SAMCRO, see Chapter 18 by Peter Fosl.
6. For further discussion of this "state of nature" and how to avoid it, see Chapter 5 by George Dunn.
7. Plato, *Republic, in Plato: Complete Works*, ed. John M. Cooper (Indianapolis: Hackett Publishing Company, 1997).
8. For further discussion of Aristotle's concept of moral virtues and their cultivation, see Chapter 1 by Jason Eberl.
9. Aristotle, *Politics, in The Complete Works of Aristotle*, ed. J. Barnes (Princeton, NJ: Princeton University Press, 1984), Book 3, lines 1279a17–21.
10. Aristotle, *Nicomachean Ethics, in The Complete Works of Aristotle*, ed. J. Barnes (Princeton, NJ: Princeton University Press, 1984), Book 1, lines 1094b7–11.

Contributors
Philosophers of Mayhem

Leslie A. Aarons is Assistant Professor of Philosophy at City University of New York, LaGuardia Community College. She teaches and publishes in environmental ethics, public philosophy, feminist philosophy, and continental philosophy. She embraces her inner philosopher-vixen, and is quoted as saying that she puts her "sweet butt on the line every day to break down the 'boys club' mentality in philosophy!"

Minerva Ahumada is Assistant Professor of Philosophy at City University of New York, LaGuardia Community College. Her interests include ethics, meta-ethics, continental philosophy, Latin American philosophy, and the interstice between philosophy and literature. Thanks to *SOA*, she now cringes whenever she hears someone say, "I got this."

Massimiliano (Max) Cappuccio, a.k.a "Road King" among the bikers, rides a customized Harley-Davidson Sportster 1200 cc, which loyally follows him across three continents. Their road trips include two American coast-to-coasts and some long journeys through the Middle East and Europe. In his spare time he is Assistant Professor in Philosophy of Mind and Cognitive Science at the United Arab Emirates University (Emirate of Abu Dhabi), where he coordinates the interdisciplinary program in cognitive science. He is also a member of the Laboratory of Psycholinguistics, run in collaboration with New York

Sons of Anarchy and Philosophy: Brains Before Bullets, First Edition.
Edited by George A. Dunn and Jason T. Eberl.
© 2013 John Wiley & Sons, Inc. Published 2013 by John Wiley & Sons, Inc.

University Abu Dhabi, and a correspondent member of the Laboratory of Neurophilosophy of the State University of Milan. He's currently running a NRF–UAEU-sponsored research project on the unreflective nature of athletic skills to improve sport performances.

Kevin Corn teaches comparative religion in the Department of Philosophy and Religion at the University of Indianapolis. A contributor to *True Blood and Philosophy* (Wiley Blackwell, 2010), he is also the author of books and articles focused on the history of American religious movements and on religious violence. Kevin is obsessed with religion, violence, and the freedoms of the open road, though his Jewish mother's ghost torments him with warnings that all who mount motorcycles will surely die or at least put out an eye.

Timothy M. Dale is Assistant Professor of Political Science at the University of Wisconsin–La Crosse. He teaches political philosophy and his research interests include democratic theory, political messaging in popular culture, and the scholarship of teaching and learning. He is the co-editor (with Joseph Foy) of *Homer Simpson Marches on Washington: Dissent in American Popular Culture* (University Press of Kentucky, 2010) and *Homer Simpson Ponders Politics: Popular Culture as Political Theory* (University Press of Kentucky, 2013). He is also the co-author (with Steve DeLue) of *Political Thinking, Political Theory, and Civil Society* (Pearson, 2009). He enjoys setting up elaborate plot lines in his lectures that keep people guessing until the end of an episode.

Bruno de Brito Serra is currently completing his Ph.D. in Philosophy at Durham University. His research interests focus primarily on ancient philosophy, philosophy of education, political philosophy, and philosophy of mind. He is particularly interested in the relationship between rationality and emotion in politics, education for citizenship, the use of propaganda in democratic states, and modern theories of sovereignty. His favorite way to meet women is to leave his motorcycle on the street until some obnoxious guy sits on it, then punch him in the face and take off with his grateful girlfriend.

George A. Dunn lectures in philosophy and religion at the University of Indianapolis and the Ningbo Institute of Technology in Zhejiang

Province, China. He is a co-editor of *True Blood and Philosophy* (Wiley Blackwell, 2010) and of *Hunger Games and Philosophy* (Wiley Blackwell, 2012) and has contributed to similar books on *Iron Man*, *Mad Men*, *Battlestar Galactica*, *Terminator*, and other pop culture topics. Unlike Jax, George accepts Nietzsche's maxim that whatever doesn't kill us makes us stronger … except dolls … they're just creepy.

Jason T. Eberl is Associate Professor of Philosophy at Indiana University–Purdue University Indianapolis. He teaches and publishes in bioethics, medieval philosophy, and metaphysics. He's the editor of *Battlestar Galactica and Philosophy* (Wiley Blackwell, 2008), and co-editor (with Kevin Decker) of *Star Trek and Philosophy* (Open Court, 2008) and *Star Wars and Philosophy* (Open Court, 2005). He has also contributed to similar books on Stanley Kubrick, J.J. Abrams, *Harry Potter*, Metallica, *Terminator*, *The Hunger Games*, *The Big Lebowski*, and *Avatar*. He tattoos a smiley face on his body every time he catches a student plagiarizing a term paper.

Charlene Elsby is a Ph.D. candidate in Philosophy at McMaster University in Hamilton, Ontario. Her dissertation is entitled "Aristotle on Things That Don't Exist" and she also works on metaphysics, philosophy of mind, and philosophy of language. She has contributed chapters to *The Philosophy of J.J. Abrams* (University Press of Kentucky, forthcoming) and *Futurama and Philosophy* (Open Court, forthcoming).

Peter S. Fosl is Professor of Philosophy and chair of both the philosophy and the PPE (philosophy, politics, and economics) programs at Transylvania University in Lexington, Kentucky, a state where outlaws find themselves at home. He's the editor of *The Big Lebowski and Philosophy* (Wiley Blackwell, 2012) and co-author (with Julian Baggini) of *The Philosopher's Toolkit* (Wiley Blackwell, 2010). He has also contributed to books on Metallica, *Terminator*, *Heroes*, and *Lost*. His scholarship addresses issues of skepticism in the history of philosophy, especially the work of David Hume. Frequently, you can find him hiking, in mind if not always in body, somewhere near the Nevada border, musing upon philosophical quotations on cave walls. His website can be found at www.PeterFosl.us (accessed April 9, 2013).

Joseph J. Foy is Associate Professor and Associate Campus Dean at the University of Wisconsin–Waukesha. He's the editor of *Homer Simpson Goes to Washington: American Politics through Popular Culture* (University Press of Kentucky, 2008) and *SpongeBob SquarePants and Philosophy* (Open Court, 2011). He's also the co-editor (with Timothy Dale) of *Homer Simpson Marches on Washington: Dissent through American Popular Culture* (University Press of Kentucky, 2010) and *Homer Simpson Ponders Politics: Popular Culture as Political Theory* (University Press of Kentucky, 2013). Although he dedicated his life to studying politics, it took a lesson from Deputy Chief Hale before he finally learned to recognize the "greater devil" when he saw it; on that day, he moved into university administration.

Randall M. Jensen is Professor of Philosophy at Northwestern College in Orange City, Iowa. His philosophical interests include ethics, ancient Greek philosophy, and philosophy of religion. He's contributed chapters to similar books in this series, on *South Park*, *24*, *Battlestar Galactica*, *The Office*, *Batman*, *The Hobbit*, and *Superman*. So far he's managed to resist the temptation to bring a gavel to classes or committee meetings.

Tim Jung is Adjunct Professor of Philosophy at City University of New York, LaGuardia Community College. His interests include metapsychology, continental philosophy, and moral sentimentalism. He's the author of "Freudian Arrested Development" in *Arrested Development and Philosophy* (Wiley Blackwell, 2011). Upon laying eyes on her, he knew that he would have to fight Tig for the hand of Venus Van Dam.

Leigh C. Kolb is an instructor at East Central College in Union, Missouri, where she teaches composition, journalism, women's literature, and African-American literature. She frequently writes about film and television through a feminist and anti-racist lens, and has spoken about using the rhetoric of social change in the composition classroom. She's more suited to being a nomad than an old lady.

Alex Leveringhaus is a post-doctoral research fellow in the Oxford Institute for Ethics, Law, and Armed Conflict (ELAC) at the University of Oxford. A political philosopher by training, he's interested in just war theory. He researches and publishes on the ethics of military humanitarian intervention, as well as the ethical and legal implications of new military technologies. An academic by day, he dons a "Reaper" at night and rides the streets of Oxford as the notorious VP of SAMOX (Sons of Anarchy Motorcycle Club Oxford). He'd like to emphasize that he's merely a "motorcycle enthusiast."

Greg Littmann is a rogue philosopher who smuggles philosophy out of academia and onto the streets where it belongs. He is Associate Professor of Philosophy at Southern Illinois University Edwardsville, where he teaches metaphysics, epistemology, and critical thinking. He has published in metaphysics and the philosophy of logic and has contributed to volumes on *The Big Bang Theory*, Black Sabbath, *Boardwalk Empire*, *Breaking Bad*, *The Daily Show*, *Doctor Who*, *Game of Thrones*, and *The Walking Dead*. The life of a philosophical outlaw is full of danger and adventure, with motorcycle chases and blazing gunfights a daily occurrence, but some people are just born to be wild.

James Edwin Mahon is Professor of Philosophy and Adjunct Professor of Law at Washington and Lee University. His primary research interests are in moral philosophy and early modern philosophy. He has written on philosophy and popular culture for *The Girl with the Dragon Tattoo and Philosophy*, *The Culture and Philosophy of Ridley Scott*, *The Philosophy of Ang Lee*, *Psych and Philosophy*, and *The Good Wife and Philosophy*. He is from the Republic of Ireland, where the IRA is not a retirement account.

Philip Smolenski is a Ph.D. student at Queen's University at Kingston. His main interest concerns the work of John Rawls' political philosophy, as well as philosophical issues surrounding terrorism and stateless communities. He has contributed an essay on *Fringe* to *The Philosophy of J.J. Abrams* (University Press of Kentucky, forthcoming). When he's not fighting for the cause, he enjoys a pint of Guinness and rides along the coast with his old lady.

Andrea Zanin is a South African-born freelance writer/editor currently based in London. She's a *cum laude* English honors graduate from the University of Johannesburg with expertise in discourse analysis, and has serious designs on a master's (who wouldn't want to be called "Professor," right?). Author of pop-culture blog Rantchick.com, Andrea reckons herself a current voice and literary anarchist; she takes great pleasure in using her rage against the machine to bash "the establishment" (in all its forms) in the face with a metaphoric skateboard.

List of Episodes
The Life (and Death?) of Sam Crow

Season 1

	First aired
Pilot	Sept. 3, 2008
Seeds	Sept. 10, 2008
Fun Town	Sept. 17, 2008
Patch Over	Sept. 24, 2008
Giving Back	Oct. 1, 2008
AK-51	Oct. 8, 2008
Old Bones	Oct. 15, 2008
The Pull	Oct. 22, 2008
Hell Followed	Oct. 29, 2008
Better Half	Nov. 5, 2008
Capybara	Nov. 12, 2008
The Sleep of Babies	Nov. 19, 2008
The Revelator	Nov. 26, 2008

Season 2

	First aired
Albification	Sept. 8, 2009
Small Tears	Sept. 15, 2009

Sons of Anarchy and Philosophy: Brains Before Bullets, First Edition.
Edited by George A. Dunn and Jason T. Eberl.
© 2013 John Wiley & Sons, Inc. Published 2013 by John Wiley & Sons, Inc.

Fix	Sept. 22, 2009
Eureka	Sept. 29, 2009
Smite	Oct. 6, 2009
Falx Cerebri	Oct. 13, 2009
Gilead	Oct. 20, 2009
Potlatch	Oct. 27, 2009
Fa Guan	Nov. 3, 2009
Balm	Nov. 10, 2009
Service	Nov. 17, 2009
The Culling	Nov. 24, 2009
Na Trioblóidí	Dec. 1, 2009

Season 3

	First aired
SO	Sept. 7, 2010
Oiled	Sept. 14, 2010
Caregiver	Sept. 21, 2010
Home	Sept. 28, 2010
Turning and Turning	Oct. 5, 2010
The Push	Oct. 12, 2010
Widening Gyre	Oct. 19, 2010
Lochan Mor	Oct. 26, 2010
Turas	Nov. 2, 2010
Firinne	Nov. 9, 2010
Bainne	Nov. 16, 2010
June Wedding	Nov. 23, 2010
NS	Nov. 30, 2010

Season 4

	First aired
Out	Sept. 6, 2011
Booster	Sept. 13, 2011
Dorylus	Sept. 20, 2011
Una Venta	Sept. 27, 2011
Brick	Oct. 4, 2011

With an X	Oct. 11, 2011
Fruit for the Crows	Oct. 18, 2011
Family Recipe	Oct. 25, 2011
Kiss	Nov. 1, 2011
Hands	Nov. 8, 2011
Call of Duty	Nov. 15, 2011
Burnt and Purged Away	Nov. 22, 2011
To Be, Act 1	Nov. 29, 2011
To Be, Act 2	Dec. 6, 2011

Season 5

	First aired
Sovereign	Sept. 11, 2012
Authority Vested	Sept. 18, 2012
Laying Pipe	Sept. 25, 2012
Stolen Huffy	Oct. 2, 2012
Orca Shrugged	Oct. 9, 2012
Small World	Oct. 16, 2012
Toad's Wild Ride	Oct. 23, 2012
Ablation	Oct. 30, 2012
Andare Pescare	Nov. 6, 2012
Crucifixed	Nov. 13, 2012
To Thine Own Self	Nov. 20, 2012
Darthy	Nov. 27, 2012
J'ai Obtenu Cette	Dec. 4, 2012

Index

Sons of Anarchy and Philosophy: Brains Before Bullets, First Edition.
Edited by George A. Dunn and Jason T. Eberl.
© 2013 John Wiley & Sons, Inc. Published 2013 by John Wiley & Sons, Inc.

Winston, Lyla, 6, 13, 134, 180–181, 205, 206
Winston, Piermont "Piney," 13, 20, 21, 58, 63, 70, 76, 78, 79, 125, 129, 160, 169, 177, 190, 194, 196–197, 199n6, 210, 215, 216, 217, 221
"With an X," 59, 181, 210
World War II, 89

Xunzi, 56

Zen and the Art of Motorcycle Maintenance, 140, 145, 148
Zobelle, Ethan, 6, 9, 11, 17, 21, 61, 62, 67, 98, 121, 164n7, 193, 226
Zobelle, Polly, 179